KILL TEAM

SKIRMISH COMBAT IN THE
41ST MILLENNIUM

CONTENTS

PRODUCED BY GAMES WORKSHOP IN NOTTINGHAM

With thanks to the Mournival and the Infinity Circuit for their additional playtesting services

Warhammer 40,000: Kill Team Core Manual © Copyright Games Workshop Limited 2018. Warhammer 40,000: Kill Team Core Manual, Warhammer 40,000: Kill Team, GW, Games Workshop, Space Marine, 40K, Warhammer, Warhammer 40,000, the 'Aquila' Double-headed Eagle logo, and all associated logos, illustrations, images, names, creatures, races, vehicles, locations, weapons, characters, and the distinctive likenesses thereof, are either ® or TM, and/or © Games Workshop Limited, variably registered around the world. All Rights Reserved.

Games Workshop Ltd, Willow Rd, Lenton, Nottingham, NG7 2WS

games-workshop.com

INTRODUCTION

Warhammer 40,000: Kill Team is a fast-paced tabletop miniatures game that pits teams of elite specialists, ragtag zealots and hard-bitten veterans against one another in vicious battles to the death. Draw your blades, check your ammo, mutter a quick prayer to your gods and get ready to join the fight!

SQUAD VERSUS SQUAD

Games of Kill Team revolve around vital conflicts between small but powerful bands of warriors rather than huge armies. They are an opportunity to tell cinematic tabletop stories in which every single combatant counts, and every model you command develops their own personality and history.

Can the enemy's leader be eliminated before he can reach – and activate – the doomsday weapon? Can your scouting force sever the enemy's lines of communication and get clear before they are caught? Will the freshly deployed squad of elite specialists be taken down by the battle-hardened band of veterans, and will the eagle-eyed sniper take down his tenth kill in a row? These and countless other narratives await to be uncovered!

In this book, you will find all the background information and tabletop rules required to dive headlong into the world of Kill Team. The following pages are replete with examples of the sorts of kill teams that might be assembled. You will see some of the apocalyptic war zones through which such warbands fight, and how their desperate fire fights and vicious

battles can be every bit as impactful upon the fates of worlds as can the onslaught of massed regiments or super-heavy engines of war.

Reading on, you will find a wealth of narrative information and random tables for many of the major Warhammer 40,000 factions. Intended to provide collectors with a wide range of exciting inspiration, these tables present various types of kill team that each faction might field, the sorts of missions they might be sent upon, as well as the strange personality quirks that their warriors and leaders might possess. These sections are designed to be toolkits from which players can draw as little or much as they like – one collector may roll up every aspect of their kill team and choose to play in character upon the tabletop in order to get a truly narrative experience, while another may simply use these tables as idea-fuel for conversions or kill team designs.

Poisonous mists drift amongst the predatory foliage of an alien jungle as the Drukhari of the Slicing Noose kill team clash in savage battle with the Necrons known as the Exalted Scythe.

Finally, this book provides a full suite of rules for playing a wide variety of skirmish-level Kill Team battles.

Alongside the rules to create your kill teams, you will also find an array of custom scenarios perfectly suited to squad-on-squad battles to the death. There are also sets of Kill Team tactics to evoke everything from a sniper's killer headshot to an unhinged knifeman's rampage, and even a full campaign system during which your kill teams can advance their skills, gain new warriors and wargear, and conquer swathes of different territories in the war to take control of a sprawling Imperial hive city. By combining these mechanics with narrative inspiration from the background tables, your gaming group can enjoy a truly unique and personal hobby experience that will generate war stories you'll talk about for years to come!

KILL TEAMS

Creating a kill team can be as simple as purchasing a single box of Citadel Miniatures, assembling and painting them to a standard you're happy with, and getting ready to play. On the other hand, some hobbyists derive great satisfaction from melding multiple troop types into a single, cohesive warband. They model, convert and paint up every individual figure to have its own aesthetic, personality and equipment to bring to battle. Many players enjoy the narrative element of this sort of project, drawing inspiration from their favourite codex or Black Library novel, from esoteric aspects of the Warhammer 40,000 universe, or even from Warhammer 40,000 computer games. There is a real thrill in painstakingly recreating a favourite band of warriors from a book or game and seeing them come to life on the tabletop. In either case, the tables of background traits, team missions, pre-generated names and more found later in this book will go a long way towards helping even a first-time hobbyist create a unique character and backstory for their kill team.

In Kill Team battles, every warrior in your warband is a vital link in the chain. Even the lowliest Grot or Astra Militarum Conscript can fire the shot that makes the difference between glorious victory and ignominious defeat. However, certain figures amongst the ranks of every kill team deserve a special mention. These are the team's leader and its specialists.

Kill team Leaders direct their warriors in the field. Whether they are tyrannical monsters or disciplined line officers, hard-bitten survivors or zealous demagogues, these individuals are the exemplars of their respective kill teams, and in many ways form the embodiment of the player upon the battlefield. Many kill team Leaders have access to powerful weapons and specialised wargear that allow them to cut a path of ruin through an enemy warband, and it is their leadership, force of will and authority that keeps the kill team fighting when the odds are against them.

Specialists, meanwhile, are warriors who excel in a single area, typically armed with the sort of weaponry that allows them to make the most of their skills. Sharp-shooting snipers whose powerful firearms can take an enemy's head off from across the battlefield; masterful bladesmen whose thrumming power swords have tasted the blood of a hundred foes; madcap demolitions experts with belts full of explosives and a crazed gleam in their eye; all of these and many more embody the specialists that can be added to a kill team in order to give it powerful, battle-winning abilities.

KILL TEAM TOKENS

The Kill Team Starter Set box and the Kill Team Faction Starter Set boxes each come with a set of tokens for use in your games of Kill Team.

You do not need these tokens to play Kill Team, but if you have a set you'll find the tokens shown on the right to be a very useful way of keeping track of which of your warriors have done what in each battle round. The core rules explain when each token is used, and what significance it has.

You'll also find the objective markers included in each set of tokens useful in your games of Kill Team, where they can represent areas or items of vital importance to your mission.

Move token

Charge token

Fall Back token

Advance token

Objective markers

Ready token

Shoot token

Shaken tokens

SHADOW WAR

'One blade, driven into the correct heart, at the right moment, will save or slay a world as surely as the firepower of entire armies.'

- *Warmaster Hokaeto,*
Supreme Imperial Commander,
Desmaxian Crusade

SQUAD WARFARE

A single squad of warriors, well equipped and well trained, can tip the balance of a war. Whether daring assassins, hawk-eyed scouts or grizzled veterans out for revenge, these warriors can alter the destiny of entire planets through their efforts.

DARK IMPERIUM

The Warhammer 40,000 setting is a sprawling and horrific dystopia where all is war. For ten millennia, battle has raged from one end of the galaxy to the other, fought across countless strange worlds, between myriad factions and races. Though planets without number have burned in the name of victory or vengeance, still there is no end in sight to the killing. If anything, the galaxy grows darker by the day.

Scattered across the stars, the Imperium of Mankind fights wars beyond count. The Space Marines, the Astra Militarum, the Adeptus Mechanicus and more battle furiously for the survival of their species, offering praise to the Emperor – or his Machine Cult equivalent, the Omnissiah – for every victory. The Imperium is the single largest empire in the galaxy and its military might is colossal, yet it is assailed from without and within; only faith, hatred and a never-ending butcher's bill of martyred soldiery keeps Humanity from being overrun.

Even as the Emperor's servants fight to preserve the Imperium, so the worshippers of the Chaos Gods pour all their hatred, fury and obsession into tearing it down. Ten thousand years ago, the terrible schism known as the Horus Heresy split the Emperor's realm, fully half of the mighty Space Marine Legions pledging their souls to the Dark Gods of Chaos in return for power, glory or revenge. Though they were defeated at the siege of the Emperor's Palace on Terra, the Traitor Legions have never given up their Long War against the Imperium that made them – if anything, they fight with more bitterness and cruelty now than they ever did in the dim and distant past. The Heretic Astartes are dark mirrors of the Emperor's noble Space Marines, their ranks twisted by mutation and riddled with corruption. Such forces as the diseased Death Guard and sorcerous Thousand Sons lead their attack, while hidden cults scramble to do their masters' bidding, desperate for the promise of fleeting power.

Though it is the war between the Imperium and the forces of Chaos that sets the stars aflame, these are far from the only warring factions in this dark galaxy. Alien hordes of every stripe surge into battle, looking to expand their empires or crush their hated foes. From beneath the surface of ancient worlds, the android Necrons rise up to butcher the living and reclaim their demesnes of old. From the webway – the strange labyrinth dimension that lies between realspace and the warp – come the enigmatic Aeldari, hosts and raiding parties of Asuryani, Drukhari and Harlequins spreading death and mayhem for reasons only they comprehend. Barbaric hordes of Orks and ravenous Tyranid swarms scour entire worlds of life. Genestealer Cults stage vicious uprisings. The T'au Empire annexes one world after another.

For ten thousand years, the galactic war has waxed and waned. Yet in the closing years of the 41st Millennium the mayhem and bloodshed has grown worse after the Great Rift – a roiling mass of warp storms like a great wound in reality – split the galaxy in two. One half has been plunged into darkness, while the other still clings to the radiance of the Emperor's light. The fight for survival and domination spirals towards outright madness, and worlds shudder to the tread of endless invading armies.

Yet not every conflict is apocalyptic in scale, and it is not always the largest army that carries the day. Sometimes, amidst the screaming madness and billowing flames of the wider war, victory or defeat lies in the hands of a small band of heroes or villains, hell bent upon achieving their mission at any cost.

BEHIND ENEMY LINES

The battles fought by kill teams take many forms. Sometimes a vital enemy commander, demagogue priest or dangerous witch must be slain by a sniper's bullet or glinting blade from the shadows. Alternatively, a vital strategic asset may need to be eliminated, be it an enemy command centre, the generator for a bank of void shields, the control matrix for an orbital defence battery or a foul shrine to the Dark Gods.

Other battles may see a band of embattled scouts attempting to reach friendly lines, bearing vital strategic information that must reach their masters at any cost. Perhaps the enemy's communications or supply routes need to be cut off before a major offensive can begin. Some kill teams are deployed to scout the foe's strength prior to battle, to locate and eliminate enemy patrols, or simply to wreak as much havoc upon the foe's infrastructure as they can, blowing up targets of opportunity wherever the chance presents itself.

Other kill teams may fight wholly different kinds of battles. A small band of warriors may find themselves the only line of defence between teeming hordes of evacuees and a rapidly approaching murder squad. Two opposed squad leaders may develop a bitter rivalry that can only be settled by a blade-to-blade clash in no man's land. A handful of heroes may set out on a holy crusade that only they can complete, or a band of roguish opportunists may descend upon a war-ravaged world to loot whatever they can.

> '*Forward scouts report heavy resistance. Infantry elements bogged down amidst the Imperatus manufactorum complex. Colonel Diert's outflanking armour driven back by enemy super-heavy engines along the Kalterwash. Strategos predicts insufficient time to mass a suitable offensive before xenos super-weapon is triggered. Recommend deployment of Archangel Team by Valkyrie drop-insertion. Emperor protect us, my lords, they are now our only hope.*'
>
> *- Last strategic missive before official sanction of Operation Aquila Rising*

In all instances, battles between kill teams tend towards close-quarters firefights through tangled terrain. They are desperate and bloody affairs that see deeds of incredible heroism and breathtaking savagery enacted on a close and personal scale.

Warriors sprint headlong from one patch of cover to the next, leaning out to spray fire at half-seen enemies amongst the ruins and the undergrowth. Blade-wielding killers lope through the shadows, slipping into the ideal position from which to launch their attack.

Grinning heavy-weapons troopers heft their massive firearms and let fly, their hails of firepower rendering them every bit as lethal as a mainline battle-tank would be in a larger-scale conflict. Hand-picked special forces advance methodically, laying down ferocious covering fire as their comrades push towards their objectives.

Grenadiers chuckle maniacally to themselves as they prime bandoleers of explosives before hurling them into the enemy's midst to raise thunderous detonations. Grim field surgeons dash from one fallen comrade to the next, pumping stimulants into wounded bodies and offering mercy to those too injured to press on. All the while, guns thunder and steel clashes with hungry ferocity, both sides fighting with everything they have.

Every battle between rival kill teams tells a tale of heroism and adventure, desperation and cruelty. Every shot, every blade-stroke and hurled grenade counts, every moment of sudden inspiration or low cowardice can mean the difference between victory and defeat. With the fates of armies, war zones and worlds at stake, battle becomes ever more desperate, for only one side can prevail.

A Galaxy Vast and Dark…

It is the 41st Millennium, and the human race stands upon a precipice. Ruled by the immortal Emperor from his Golden Throne on Terra, the Imperium of Mankind stretches out to the very fringes of the galaxy. The Imperium is assailed from within and without by the alien, the mutant and the heretic. For all its might, this empire is crumbling: its worlds are scattered and often isolated; its vast martial strength is fettered by bloated bureaucracy; its people are controlled through ignorance, fear and superstition. Only the guiding light of the Emperor holds the Imperium together, the psychic beacon of the Astronomican guiding Mankind's ships through the darkness of the void.

Those ships travel through the warp, the hellish dimension of raw psychic energy that lurks beneath the skin of realspace. By plunging into the tides of the warp, spacecraft can travel vast distances in a fraction of the time they might otherwise take. Moreover, it is by manipulating the energies of the warp that the psychic mutants known as Astropaths can communicate across the vast gulfs between Imperial worlds. Yet the warp is not a sterile plane; by its very nature, warp energy is pernicious and mutative, while its depths are inhabited by myriad predatory abominations that Mankind has come to know as Daemons.

The warp has always posed a terrible threat, its energies spilling into the galaxy in ferocious storms, its denizens seeking to subvert and conquer realspace. Yet in the closing years of the 41st Millennium a storm like no other has torn its way across the stars. Known as the Great Rift, this catastrophic phenomenon has split the Imperium almost in two, leaving countless worlds cut off from the Astronomican. So has the war for survival become more desperate than ever before.

HEROES ALL

Every kill team is different, but all have certain features in common. Each is directed by a determined leader. Each also contains a handful of skilled specialists whose martial abilities make them vital assets in the field, supporting the remainder of the kill team's soldiers and leading them to victory.

Kill teams are assembled for a vast variety of different missions, many of which simply could not be completed by a larger and less specialised force. Some are assassins or saboteurs, using stealth or rapid-deployment technologies to strike without warning at targets far behind enemy lines. Where a larger force would quickly be detected by sentries or be forced into engagements with defending forces, a kill team can slip quietly into position, silence any who might stand in their way, and then strike the killing blow. Many an apostate cardinal or xenos war-leader has discovered too late that their inner sanctum was far less safe than they believed as doors have blown in, guards have been gunned down and the kill team's warriors have put their target to the sword. Countless shield generators, doomsday weapons and summoning circles have been blown sky-high by demolitions charges planted by elite operatives.

Other kill teams are protectors rather than destroyers. Their mission may be to escort a vital dignitary through the blazing hell of no man's land, or to provide skilled sentries for a hidden arco-laboratory or church of the faith. It may be to watch over a crucial hidden passage

A kill team of Tempestus Scions advances on their objective, hot-shot lasguns blazing.

through a fortress' otherwise impenetrable defences, to hunt enemy infiltrators amidst ruined manufactorums, or to stand as a final line of defence before the command sanctum from within which an entire war front is being controlled. Whatever the case, the hand-picked warriors of the kill team must ensure that their duty is discharged no matter the odds they face.

Other kill teams receive even more esoteric assignments: the ritualised slaughter of specific targets in order to summon daemonic entities, lacing an enemy army's rations with mutagenic gene-poisons, or painting a quarry with psycho-receptive resonators in preparation for a catastrophic psychic bombardment. The list is endless, with every mission being more vital, dangerous and challenging than the last.

In some cases, a team is assembled intentionally to fulfil a specific mission or achieve a particular goal. They may include an ideal spread of combatants for the task at hand, and carry precisely the correct equipment and munitions to eliminate their targets. Deathwatch kill teams, squads of combat-optimised Skitarii and perfectly balanced Asuryani assassination bands are good examples of these sorts of forces.

On other occasions, kill teams may be formed in the field. A hard-bitten squad of Astra Militarum Veterans might band together to survive an especially savage war zone; a group of Adeptus Astartes warriors might find themselves joining forces to combat an onrushing horde of enemies; a handful of murderous Night Lords might coordinate their efforts in order to spread terror and death through an Imperial command complex.

Many kill teams are drawn wholesale from amongst the ranks of a larger army in the field, and assigned a specific mission that they must complete before returning to their comrades. Whether it be a mob of Ork Kommandos sent to blow up the enemy's ammunition dumps, a combat squad of Ultramarines assigned as an honour guard to the shrine of an Imperial Saint, or a band of Kabalite Warriors charged with upholding the reputation of their Archon through feats of arms, such groups have the advantage of having fought as one in many conflicts. Though they may lack the diversity of specialists available to a more mixed kill team, their warrior bond and clearly defined way of making war stand such kill teams in good stead when the fighting intensifies.

THE BEST OF THE BEST

Regardless of a kill team's origins and composition, it will always be directed in battle by an especially charismatic, cunning or domineering individual. Some of these leaders enact their will through the respect of their warriors or the rank invested in them by their military station. Others, such as the Boss Nobz that rule over Ork mobs, take charge by dint of being the biggest and toughest, able to clobber any of the ladz who do not follow their orders to the letter. Still others ply the lash of fear, or command absolute obedience through mind control or sacred religious station. Whichever holds true, a kill team's leader is both its brain and its heart, the strategic mastermind who ensures that their warriors fight in the optimum fashion and hold their ground when the odds are against them.

Specialists are the other asset common to every kill team. Though they can take many forms – from master assassin to berserk killer, volatile pyromaniac to wily trapper – these skilled individuals bring vital equipment and talents to the battlefield. While every warrior within a kill team matters, and all can win victory with their comrades through sufficient faith and fortune, it is the specialists who most often land the killing blow.

The longer a kill team fights together, and the more missions that they successfully complete, the more deadly a military force they become. Warriors initially thrown together by fate, or the orders of distant superiors, learn to fight seamlessly alongside one another. They become adept at anticipating each other's actions, and build bonds of loyalty that see them fight harder than ever when they do so side-by-side.

Many teams develop private combat languages, be they subtle inflections, hand signals or encoded vox-clicks, that allow them to communicate stealthily and efficiently when fighting behind enemy lines. Such kill teams are united by victories and defeats shared, by hardships faced and comrades lost; many will affect ad hoc markings or honour badges in remembrance of their greatest – or darkest – hours. While they may become insular and hostile towards outsiders, or difficult for their superior officers to handle, long-serving kill teams also build well-deserved reputations as elite military assets, best deployed when no one else can get the job done.

KILL TEAM AGRIPPIUS

During the war for Tholdax, the Imperial advance stalled amidst the war-torn streets of Hive Ganymede. Though they outnumbered the traitor forces three-to-one, the Astra Militarum could not contend with the incredible tactical acumen of the heretics' leader, a champion of the Alpha Legion known as the Serpent's Shadow. This devious figure was marked for death, the job falling to a hand-picked band of Ultramarines battle-brothers known as Kill Team Agrippius.

The team's leader, Sergeant Agrippius, was renowned for his steely will and ability to push his brothers on to deeds that seemed remarkable, even for post-human Space Marines. This effect was all the more pronounced considering the exceptional skill of the specialist warriors within the squad's ranks. Brother Crassus was the team's demolitions expert, who used his timed krak-charges to cripple the unmarked APC in which the Alpha Legion target travelled. To Brother Ignatio, the squad's marksman, fell the job of gunning down the target's bodyguards, a task which he fulfilled admirably as he made shot after pinpoint shot through the eyepieces of their helms as they disembarked. Finally, the coup de grâce was landed by Brother Taurian, who blew the stranded APC – and the target inside – sky-high with his reverently maintained missile launcher.

As kill teams gain experience, so too do their leaders and their specialists reach ever higher levels of personal skill. Commanders that at first were daunted by their role become bellowing firebrands or shrewd strategists whose authority over their warriors is absolute. Snipers become increasingly accurate until they can thread a shot through the smallest gap and fell their victim every time. Close-combat specialists become more dangerous with each battle they survive, some transforming into sublimely skilled and elegant killers, while others degenerate into scarred berserkers that cut notches into their gore-stained weapons for each enemy slain. Explosives experts become artists of destruction, zealots find the fires of their faith burning ever higher, heavy weapons troopers become engines of slaughter and field-medics become adept at swiftly and calmly restoring even catastrophically wounded warriors to fighting efficiency.

So do kill teams grow into legendary bands of warriors, heroes or villains about whom tales are told and legends spun. The rivalries between such squads are fierce indeed, and the ferocious battles they engage in are amongst the most dynamic and close-fought conflicts of the 41st Millennium.

THEATRES OF WAR

The galaxy is vast, and in this dark age there is precious little of its immense span that does not echo to the sound of gunfire and burn with the fires of war. Yet even amongst this whirling maelstrom, certain war zones have a reputation for their size and ferocity.

From storm-tossed ocean planets and hellish jungle-covered death worlds to ruined cityscapes, fortified strongholds and even the claustrophobic corridors of derelict spacecraft, kill teams go into action across myriad different battlefields. Each brings its own variety of conditions, challenges and opportunities for a cunning commander and their skilled followers to exploit. Each also plays host to dangers untold.

The supreme commanders of the 41st Millennium have incredible military forces at their disposal. Entire fleets of deep-space battleships clash above war-torn worlds, disgorging wave upon wave of invading warriors in cavernous landing craft. Brigades of heavily armoured fighting vehicles clash across cratered plains. Vast hordes of infantry meet in desperate battle, while fighter craft and wings of bombers duel overhead.

Yet there are many scenarios in which the precise application of a small but highly trained force can garner far greater success than the sledgehammer deployment of massed armies. Many missions must be accomplished in secrecy, while for other conflicts the element of surprise is as valuable a weapon as any amount of heavy artillery. On Prassima V, a kill team of Alpha Legionnaires used the shrine world's long-defunct network of holy water aqueducts to bypass thousands of zealot militia and strike directly at Cardinal Munce. Emerging into the cardinal's spire-top gardens, the traitors ambushed the squad of White Consuls Space Marines charged with guarding Munce's life. The loyalists fought hard but, out of position and taken by surprise in their inner sanctum, they were slain. Munce was left dangling upside down amidst his own entrails from the crook of the statue of Saint Katherine, while the Alpha Legionnaires' escape was covered by explosive booby traps that they left in their wake to be triggered by frantic militiamen. The same kill team struck a further three times, fanning the flames of panic and anger until Prassima V was consumed by a vicious internecine holy war.

Sometimes, a commander must wield kill teams and massed forces in concert, the one paving the way to victory for the other. On Stenoth, during the Wars of Admonishment, the Imperial advance was stymied by a preposterously immense Ork fortress known as Gork's Gut. A city-sized edifice that – at its highest points – broke the upper atmosphere, Gork's Gut was wreathed in kustom force fields and defended by millions of Orks.

The first two Imperial offensives were crushing failures, the Emperor's armies flung back by the sheer weight of firepower and the ablative, scrap-metal resilience of the fortress' structure. Before the third wave went in, several kill teams of Blood Angels Primaris Space Marines deployed onto the structure's topmost towers, swiftly vanishing into its enormity on targeted missions. Though the Blood Angels faced stern opposition from mobs of Ork Nobz and greenskin Kommandos, they succeeded in knocking out the fortress' shield generators, demolishing its main gate from within, and assassinating – at steep cost in lives – the Orks' warlord. When the final Imperial attack was launched, it surged to victory thanks to the kill teams' efforts.

Thousands more war zones have seen drastic changes in fortune after a kill team struck a crushing blow, while in others the very nature of the terrain or the conditions makes the deployment of kill teams far more effective than sending in armies. The tangled arboreal world of Lucifere II, for example, is all but unnavigable for anything larger than infantry on foot. Yet it is here that Gunnery Sergeant 'Stonetooth' Harker and his notorious Catachan Devils hunted down and exterminated a slew of Tyranid vanguard broods, any of which could have called down a full-scale Tyranid invasion upon the life-rich world.

The cramped tunnelplexes of Elboryth are another war zone where kill teams prove particularly effective. Here, raiding bands of Drukhari, Adepta Sororitas and Necrons do constant battle as they attempt to wrest control of the planet's buried catacombs – and the riches that lie within – from each other.

While all-out war ravages the forge world of Ryza, smaller but no less deadly conflicts rage daily through the rear lines of both the Adeptus Mechanicus and the Orks. On one hand, raiding parties of Skitarii seek to sabotage greenskin war engines and assassinate their

Operating well ahead of the main T'au battle line, a team of Pathfinders marks out Imperial supply caches for devastating bombing runs by Sun Shark aircraft.

leaders. On the other, Ork Kommandos strike at crucial production sites and steal prototype weaponry for their Meks to cannibalise. Thus do the kill teams of both races aid their war efforts.

Many Imperial worlds boast sprawling hive cities or industrial macroplexes that stretch over continents, and that rapidly devolve into labyrinthine hellscapes once war consumes them. Kill teams excel in such conditions; they can move quickly through the ruined streets, flitting between bombed-out buildings, warriors covering each other as they move from one outcropping of twisted wreckage to the next. Snipers and heavy weapon specialists clamber up to vantage points amidst the looming skeletons of burned-out manufactorums and refinery plants. Combat experts dash from one smouldering crater to the next, rapidly closing on their foes even as courageous warriors scramble through rusting pipes and leap between teetering ruins to outflank the enemy's position.

Jungle worlds are host to many types of environments amongst which kill teams often do battle. Where bladed throttlevines and fang trees cluster close amidst sheer-sided ravines, where craggy mountain slopes or festering marshes are densely carpeted by carnivorous plant-life, kill teams demonstrate worth far beyond their numbers. Where battle tanks or massed infantry would flounder and fail, a kill team can slip on towards their objectives. Ambushes, booby traps and bladework rule such battlefields, with warriors forced to cut their way through hostile – and sometimes sentient – undergrowth before coming suddenly face-to-face with the foe.

Even upon the most sweeping and apocalyptic of battle-fronts, kill teams find many uses. Where Imperial trenchworks or heretical fortifications stretch to the horizon in all directions, where super-heavy war engines hurl munitions at one another from miles apart and massed attack waves clash in the blood and horror of no man's land, a subtle and well-placed blade may achieve what thousands of screaming warriors cannot. Command bunkers vanish in sudden fireballs as kill team charges detonate. Ammunition shipments or messenger drones vanish without trace, leaving entire regiments paralysed. Artillery strikes are called in with shocking accuracy by unseen spotters. Whole armies strike from unexpected quarters thanks to summoning rituals or teleportation rites performed by infiltrating elements.

RULES

'In a battle such as this, there is no help to be had, no support incoming or reinforcements to be called upon. Lay your plans carefully and consider every move, lest it prove your last.'

- Blood Angels Scout Sergeant Rafaen, during the battle for Hades Hive

CORE RULES

Kill Team puts each player in command of a force of hand-picked fighters tasked with a vital mission. The core rules on these pages contain everything you need to know in order to use your Citadel Miniatures to wage covert war against one or more opponents for control of the battlefields of the 41st Millennium.

TOOLS OF WAR

In order to play a game of Kill Team, you will need your Citadel Miniatures, a tape measure, a playing surface (which could simply be a table), and some dice. You may also find it helpful to have tokens that you can use to show when your models have acted – these are available in a number of Kill Team products.

Distances in Kill Team are measured in inches (") between the closest points of the bases of the models you're measuring to and from. An object (such as a model) is said to be within a certain range (e.g. 6") of something if the distance to that thing is that range or less. So, for example, a model is within 6" of another model as long as it is 6" or less from that model. If a model does not have a base, measure to and from the closest point of that model instead. You can measure distances whenever you wish.

Most games of Kill Team are played on an area of 30" by 22", which is the size of the gameboard included in the boxed game. You can play games of Kill Team on a playing surface of any size, though if it is any smaller than 24" by 24" you may find it feels a bit cramped!

Kill Team uses six-sided dice, sometimes abbreviated to D6. Some rules refer to 2D6, 3D6 and so on – in such cases, roll that many D6s and add the results together. If a rule requires you to roll a D3, roll a D6 and halve the result. When halving any dice roll, round fractions up before applying modifiers (if any) to the result. All modifiers are cumulative. Some rules refer to an 'unmodified roll' – this means the result shown by the dice, before any modifiers are applied.

If a rule requires a dice roll of, for example, 3 or more, this is often abbreviated to 3+.

As billowing smoke rolls through the war-torn streets of Hive Magnius Delta, Skitarii and Genestealer Cults kill teams engage in a savage firefight to seize control of vital supplies.

FIGHTING A BATTLE

Once you have your tools of war, you'll need to choose a mission to play. There is a mission included in these core rules – Covert War (pg 41) – but there are others in this book and available in other Kill Team products, and you can even make up your missions. The mission you play may have a bearing on which Citadel Miniatures you use or how you set up the battlefield. For more information about the different kinds of missions and choosing one to play, see page 48.

KILL TEAMS, ENEMY MODELS AND PLAYERS

The models that a player brings to a game of Kill Team are collectively known as that player's kill team. There are rules for choosing which models are included in your kill team – these are found on page 62. These rules may be influenced by the mission you have chosen to play. All models in the same kill team are referred to as 'friendly models', while all other models are referred to as 'enemy models'. All other players are referred to as 'opponents' or 'enemy players'.

A player is said to be 'controlling' the models in their kill team, and may be referred to as the 'controlling player' in the rules that follow.

RANDOM DETERMINATION

Some rules or abilities will ask you to randomly determine something, usually a model from a kill team. You may do this in a variety of ways, but the simplest is to assign a number to each and roll a number of D6 (or D10 – that is, ten-sided dice), re-rolling any results not assigned to an eligible model. For example, if you need to randomly select a model from a kill team of 5, you would assign each model a number from 1 to 5 and roll a D6, re-rolling any results of 6. If the group you're randomising is larger than 10, simply split the group into 2 or more smaller groups (of no more than 10), randomly determine one of those groups and then randomly determine the result within that group.

WARHAMMER 40,000

In Warhammer 40,000, mighty armies clash across spectacular tabletop battlefields. Where Kill Team focuses on individual squads, the *Warhammer 40,000* rulebook gives you all the rules you need to fight battles between entire battalions of warriors, war engines and heroes.

Each codex provides you with the background and rules for one of the many factions in Warhammer 40,000. With this information, you can make your kill team the foundation of an army!

DATASHEETS AND WEAPONS

The characteristics of models are described on datasheets, which you will need in order to use them in battle. This book includes all the datasheets you need to play Kill Team, and the details of the weapons used on the battlefield. Here we explain the information found on datasheets and in weapon profiles.

1. Model Name

Here you'll find the name of the model.

2. Profiles

These contain the following characteristics that tell you how mighty models (and their variants) are:

Move (M): This is the speed at which a model moves across the battlefield.

Weapon Skill (WS): This tells you a model's skill at hand-to-hand fighting. If a model has a Weapon Skill of '-' it is unable to fight in melee and cannot make close combat attacks at all.

Ballistic Skill (BS): This shows how accurate a model is when shooting with ranged weapons. If a model has a Ballistic Skill of '-' it has no proficiency with ranged weapons and cannot make shooting attacks at all.

Strength (S): This indicates how strong a model is and how likely it is to inflict damage in hand-to-hand combat.

Toughness (T): This reflects the model's resilience against physical harm.

Wounds (W): Wounds show how much damage a model can sustain before it succumbs to its injuries.

Attacks (A): This tells you how many times a model can strike blows in hand-to-hand combat.

Leadership (Ld): This reveals how courageous, determined or self-controlled a model is.

Save (Sv): This indicates the protection a model's armour gives.

Maximum Number (Max): This number tells you how many of this model you can include in a kill team.

3. Description

This tells you what the model is armed with. All weapons have a profile described later in the same section of the book as the datasheet. Some datasheets have variant models with their own profiles, and where this is the case they will be described here.

4. Wargear Options

Some models have the option to exchange the wargear listed in their description for other options. Where that is the case, the options will be listed here.

5. Abilities

Many models have exciting special abilities that are not covered by the core rules: these will be described here.

6. Specialists

You can choose for some of the models in your kill team to be specialists (pg 66). This section of a datasheet tells you what kind of specialist each model can be.

7. Keywords

All datasheets have a list of keywords, sometimes separated into Faction keywords and other keywords. The former can be used as a guide to help decide which models to include in your kill team, but otherwise both sets of keywords are functionally the same. Sometimes a rule will say that it applies to models that have a specific keyword. For example, a rule might say that it applies to 'all ADEPTUS ASTARTES models'. This means it would only apply to models that have the Adeptus Astartes keyword on their datasheet.

MODIFYING CHARACTERISTICS

You may encounter abilities and rules that modify a characteristic. All modifiers are cumulative, though you should apply any multiplication or division to the characteristic (rounding fractions up) before applying any addition or subtraction.

You may also encounter a characteristic that is a random value instead of a number. For example, a Move characteristic might be 2D6", or an Attacks value might be D6. Roll to determine this value each time the model uses that characteristic (e.g. when it moves or makes attacks). Note that, regardless of the source, characteristics of '-' can never be modified, and the Strength, Toughness and Leadership characteristics of a model can never be modified below 1.

Weapons

The weapons that the models in Kill Team use are described using a set of characteristics as follows:

Range: How far the weapon can shoot. Weapons with a Range of 'Melee' can only be used in hand-to-hand combat. All other weapons are referred to as ranged weapons.

Type: These are all explained under the Shooting and Fight phases of the core rules.

Strength (S): How likely the weapon is to inflict damage. If a weapon's Strength lists 'User', it is equal to the wielder's current Strength. If a weapon lists a modifier such as '+1' or 'x2', you should modify the user's current Strength characteristic as shown to determine the weapon's Strength. For example, if a weapon's Strength was 'x2', and the user had a Strength characteristic of 6, that weapon has Strength 12.

Armour Penetration (AP): How good it is at getting through armour.

Damage (D): The amount of damage inflicted by a successful hit.

Abilities: Some weapons have additional abilities that change how they are used or what happens when they are used. Where this is the case, it will be described here.

All of a model's weapons are described later in this book, in the appendix for that model's Faction.

POINTS AND FORCE

Each model and each piece of wargear has a points cost, as listed in each Faction's section later in the book. These points costs are used when choosing a Battle-forged kill team (pg 62), and the total points costs of all the models and wargear in your kill team is known as its 'Force'. A kill team's Force gives a value to a kill team that represents its strength, and is used when players are choosing kill teams of equal (or particular) strengths.

AURA ABILITIES

Some models have abilities that affect certain models within a given range. Unless the ability in question says otherwise, a model with a rule like this is always within range of the effect. For example, an Acolyte Hybrid with a cult icon gains the Cult Icon ability, which allows re-rolls on hit rolls of 1 for friendly models within 6". As the Acolyte Hybrid is always within 6" of itself, it benefits from this ability as well.

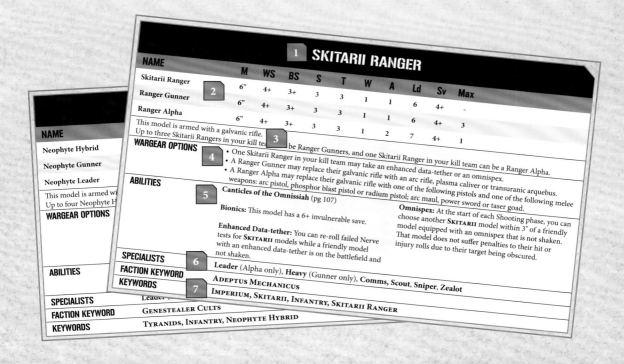

1 · SKITARII RANGER

NAME	M	WS	BS	S	T	W	A	Ld	Sv	Max
Skitarii Ranger	6"	4+	3+	3	3	1	1	6	4+	-
Ranger Gunner	6"	4+	3+	3	3	1	1	6	4+	3
Ranger Alpha	6"	4+	3+	3	3	1	2	7	4+	1

This model is armed with a galvanic rifle.

WARGEAR OPTIONS
- Up to three Skitarii Rangers in your kill team [can] be Ranger Gunners, and one Skitarii Ranger in your kill team can be a Ranger Alpha.
- A Ranger Gunner in your kill team may take an enhanced data-tether or an omnispex.
- A Ranger Gunner may replace their galvanic rifle with an arc rifle, plasma caliver or transuranic arquebus.
- A Ranger Alpha may replace their galvanic rifle with one of the following pistols and one of the following melee weapons: arc pistol, phosphor blast pistol or radium pistol; arc maul, power sword or taser goad.

ABILITIES

Canticles of the Omnissiah (pg 107)

Bionics: This model has a 6+ invulnerable save.

Enhanced Data-tether: You can re-roll failed Nerve tests for SKITARII models while a friendly model with an enhanced data-tether is on the battlefield and not shaken.

Omnispex: At the start of each Shooting phase, you can choose another SKITARII model within 3" of a friendly model equipped with an omnispex that is not shaken. That model does not suffer penalties to their hit or injury rolls due to their target being obscured.

SPECIALISTS — Leader (Alpha only), Heavy (Gunner only), Comms, Scout, Sniper, Zealot

FACTION KEYWORD — ADEPTUS MECHANICUS

KEYWORDS — IMPERIUM, SKITARII, INFANTRY, SKITARII RANGER

NAME										
Neophyte Hybrid										
Neophyte Gunner										
Neophyte Leader										

This model is armed wi[th]
Up to four Neophyte H[...]

WARGEAR OPTIONS

ABILITIES

SPECIALISTS

FACTION KEYWORD — GENESTEALER CULTS

KEYWORDS — TYRANIDS, INFANTRY, NEOPHYTE HYBRID

THE BATTLE ROUND

Each Kill Team mission is played in a series of battle rounds. During each battle round, all players act in an order determined in the Initiative phase. Each battle round consists of a series of phases, which must be resolved in order.

The phases are as follows:

1. Initiative phase
The players roll off to determine who will act first in each phase.

2. Movement phase
Players move any models that are capable of doing so, and may charge their enemies.

3. Psychic phase
Psykers can use powerful mental abilities.

4. Shooting phase
Models may shoot at enemy models.

5. Fight phase
Models pile in and attack with melee weapons.

6. Morale phase
Players test to see if their kill team is broken and if their models keep their nerve.

Once these phases have been played, the battle round has been completed and the next one begins, and so on, until the battle is concluded.

1. INITIATIVE PHASE

Victory in war can be decided in a split second, a moment in which one side gains the upper hand.

In the Initiative phase, the players each roll 2D6. The players' results determine who has the first turn in each phase in this battle round, with the highest scorer taking the first turn, the next highest taking the second turn and so on. The player with the first turn is referred to as the player with the initiative. Any players who roll the same result should roll their dice again to determine which of them has a turn before the other(s). Once the player order has been established, the Initiative phase ends and the Movement phase begins.

ROLL-OFFS

Some rules instruct players to roll off. To do so, each player rolls a D6 (or 2D6 if there are more than two players), and whoever scores highest wins the roll-off. In the case of a tie, those players re-roll their dice – if the second and subsequent rolls are also tied, keep on rolling until a winner is determined; this is the only time players can re-roll a re-roll.

SEQUENCING

You'll occasionally find that two or more rules are to be resolved at the same time – normally 'at the start of the Movement phase' or 'before the battle begins'. When this happens, the player who has the initiative chooses the order. If these things occur before or after the game, or before the player with the initiative for the battle round is decided, the players roll off and the winner decides in what order the rules are resolved.

RE-ROLLS

Some rules allow you to re-roll a dice roll, which means you get to roll some or all of the dice again. If a rule allows you to re-roll a result that was made by adding several dice together (2D6, 3D6 etc.) then, unless otherwise stated, you must roll all of those dice again. You can never re-roll a dice more than once, and re-rolls happen before modifiers (if any) are applied.

AT THE BEGINNING OF THE PHASE...

Some rules or abilities refer to the beginning or end of a phase. Rules or abilities used at the beginning of the phase are used before any player's turn in that phase. Rules or abilities used at the end of the phase are used after all players' turns in that phase.

2. MOVEMENT PHASE

Warriors move carefully towards their objective, advance quickly across the battlefield, or charge their enemies even as their comrades prepare to unleash covering fire.

In the Movement phase, each player will take it in turn to move all of the models in their kill team that they wish to move, following the order determined in the Initiative phase. Once a player has moved all of the models they want to, the next player does the same, and so on until all players have moved all of the models they wish to move. Once all players have done so, the Movement phase ends and the Psychic phase begins.

When it is your turn, pick a model from your kill team and move it. You can then pick another model from your kill team to move, until you have moved as many of the models in your kill team as you wish. No model can be moved more than once in each Movement phase – if you have Kill Team tokens, place a token next to each model you move as a reminder.

MOVING

You can change the position of a model on the battlefield by making a move with the model. Models can be moved in the Movement phase and the Fight phase, and some abilities may allow a model to make a move in other phases too.

Whenever you move a model, it can be moved in any direction or combination of directions, but cannot be moved across other models or their bases, nor can it cross the edge of the battlefield. You can pivot the model at the end of the move so that it is facing in any direction. The distance a model moves is measured using the part of the model's base that moves furthest from its starting position (including any pivots). If the model has no base, measure the move using whichever part of the model moves furthest from its starting position. A model that only pivots is still considered to have moved. A model must end its move on a surface it can stand on (though see Wobbly Model Syndrome on page 25).

MOVING OVER TERRAIN

Unless stated otherwise, a model can be moved over a piece of terrain but not through it (so models cannot move through a wall or a wreck, but can climb up or over them). A model can be moved vertically in order to climb or cross a piece of terrain, counting the vertical distance up and/or down as part of its move.

FLY

If the datasheet for a model says it can **FLY** (i.e. it has the **FLY** keyword), it can move across models and terrain – other than impassable terrain (see page 42) – as if they were not there, though it must end its move on a surface it can stand on, other than another model or another model's base. Do not measure vertical distance when moving a model that can **FLY**.

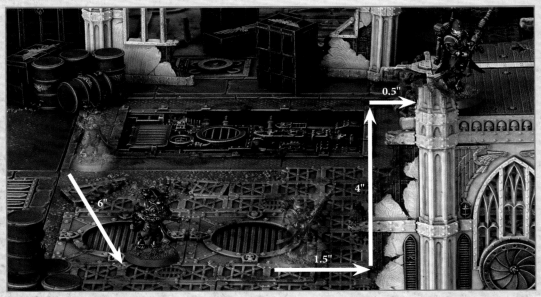

The Skitarii Ranger and Vanguard each have a Move characteristic of 6". Their player moves the Ranger 6" across the battlefield, and the Vanguard 1.5" towards the wall, 4" up the wall, and 0.5" across the top of the ruin to its final position.

Normal Move

Most moves made in the Movement phase are called normal moves. A model making a normal move can move a distance equal to or less than its Move characteristic.

Enemy Models

When you make a normal move (or Advance, see right) with a model, it may not be moved within 1" of any enemy models. When you pick a model to move, if it is within 1" of any enemy models, it cannot make a normal move (or Advance).

Falling Back

When you pick a model to move, if that model started the Movement phase within 1" of an enemy model, it cannot make a normal move. Instead, it can either remain stationary or Fall Back. A model cannot Fall Back if an enemy model finished a charge move within 1" of it in the same phase. If you choose to Fall Back, the model can move a distance equal to or less than its Move characteristic, but must end its move more than 1" away from all enemy models. If a model Falls Back, it cannot Advance, charge, React (see opposite) or be Readied (see right) in that phase. A model that Falls Back also cannot shoot later that battle round unless it can **Fly**. If you have Kill Team tokens, place a Fall Back token next to the model as a reminder.

Advancing

When you pick a model to move, instead of making a normal move with that model you can declare that it will Advance, unless it is within 1" of an enemy model. If you do so, make an Advance roll by rolling a D6. Add the result to the model's Move characteristic for that Movement phase. You can then move that model a distance equal to or less than its Move characteristic. A model that Advances cannot charge, React or shoot later that battle round. If you have Kill Team tokens, place an Advance token next to the model as a reminder.

Readying

When you pick a model to move, instead of making a normal move (including pivoting the model) you can Ready them, unless they are within 1" of an enemy model. A model that is Readied in the Movement phase has an advantage in the subsequent Shooting phase, as described on page 28. If you have Kill Team tokens, place a Ready token next to the model as a reminder. If the model moves for any reason, it is no longer Readied – remove this token.

The Skitarii player chooses to Fall Back with the Skitarii Vanguard. They move the model so it is more than 1" from the Neophyte Hybrid. The Skitarii player Advances with the Vanguard Alpha. They roll a 4, so – adding this result to the Vanguard Alpha's Move characteristic of 6" – may move it up to 10".

The Genestealer Cults player declares that the Neophyte Hybrid will charge both Skitarii Vanguard. The Skitarii player chooses for one of their Vanguard to Retreat as a Reaction to the charge, and moves their model 3" away. They then declare that their other Vanguard will fire Overwatch, and resolve that attack before the charge move is made.

CHARGING

When you pick a model to move, if it is not within 1" of an enemy model and is within 12" of an enemy model, instead of making a normal move you can declare that it will attempt to charge. Follow the charge sequence below.

> ### CHARGE SEQUENCE
> 1. **Choose target(s)**
> 2. **Enemy Reacts**
> 3. **Roll 2D6 and make charge move**

1. Choose Target(s)

Choose one or more enemy models within 12" of the charging model as the target(s) of the charge.

2. React

After you have declared a charge, any opponents take it in turn to make Reactions with any models from their kill teams that are allowed to do so, if they wish to do so, in the order determined in the Initiative phase. Once one opponent has resolved all of their models' Reactions, the next player can do so, and so on.

A model can React if it is the target of a charging model and it is more than 1" from an enemy model. A model can either fire Overwatch or Retreat when it Reacts. If, at any point, the charging model is slain, no further Reactions can be made for this charge sequence.

Overwatch

Overwatch is a special type of shooting attack that is described on page 31. A target model can potentially fire Overwatch several times in a battle round.

Retreat

A target model cannot Retreat if it has already made a move of any kind (or attempted to charge) in this phase. A model can Retreat if it has already fired Overwatch in this phase. When a model Retreats, it can be moved up to 3" by the controlling player. This move must end with the model further away from the charging model, and more than 1" from any other enemy models. A model that Retreats cannot React later in the battle round, and cannot shoot later in the battle round (unless it can **FLY**). If you have Kill Team tokens, place a Fall Back token next to the model as a reminder.

3. Make Charge Move

After all Reactions have been resolved, make a charge roll by rolling 2D6. The charging model can move up to this number of inches – this is their charge distance this turn. To make a successful charge roll, the model must finish its move within 1" of at least one of the target models. A model that does so is said to have charged, and the enemy models that are within 1" of it at the end of its move are said to have been charged. It cannot move within 1" of an enemy model that was not a target of its charge.

If the model cannot finish its move while following these restrictions, the charge fails and the model is not said to have charged – however, the model can move up to its charge distance, as long as that move takes it as close as possible to at least one of the targets of its charge, and not within 1" of any enemy models. A model can only make one charge attempt in each Movement phase, and once it has done so it cannot shoot later in the battle round. If you have Kill Team tokens, place a Charge token next to the model as a reminder.

The charge roll of 8 gives the Neophyte Hybrid a charge distance of 8". It is able to move to within 1" of one of its targets with this distance, so the Neophyte Hybrid is moved to within 1" of that model. If the player had not rolled high enough for the Neophyte Hybrid to reach any of its targets, the charge would have failed.

The Most Important Rule

In a game as detailed and wide-ranging as Kill Team, there may be times when you are not sure exactly how to resolve a situation that has come up during play. When this happens, have a quick chat with your opponent(s) and apply the solution that makes the most sense to you (or seems the most fun!). If no single solution presents itself, you and your opponent(s) should roll off, and whoever rolls highest gets to choose what happens. Then you can get on with the game!

Wobbly Model Syndrome

Sometimes you may find that a particular piece of terrain makes it hard to put a model exactly where you want. If you delicately balance it in place, it is very likely to fall as soon as somebody nudges the table, leaving your model damaged or even broken. In cases like this, we find it is perfectly acceptable to leave the model in a safer position, as long as all players have agreed and know its 'actual' location. If, later on, an opponent is considering shooting the model, you will have to hold it back in the proper place so they can check if it is visible.

Reinforcements

Some models have the ability to be set up on the battlefield mid-battle round, sometimes by using teleporters, grav-chutes or other, more esoteric means. Typically, this happens at the end of the Movement phase, but it can also happen during other phases. Models that are set up in this manner cannot move further, Advance or charge during the battle round they arrive, though they can otherwise act normally (use psychic powers, shoot, etc.) for the rest of the battle round. Models that arrive as reinforcements count as having made a normal move for all rules purposes, such as shooting Heavy weapons (pg 29). Any model that has not arrived on the battlefield by the end of the battle counts as having been taken out of action (pg 32).

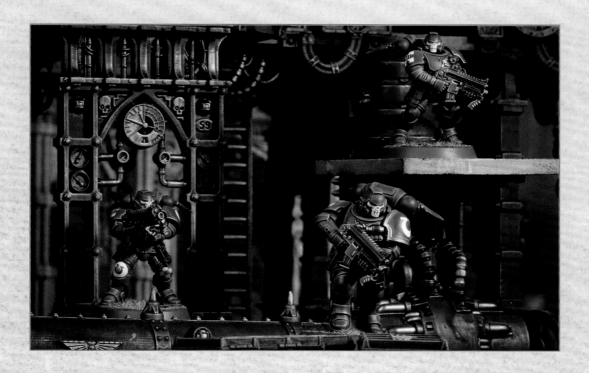

3. PSYCHIC PHASE

Warrior mystics and sorcerers wield the strange power of the warp to aid their allies and destroy their foes. Harnessing this force is not without risk, however, and with the smallest mistake, there can be horrendous consequences.

Some models are noted as being a **PSYKER** on their datasheet. Psykers can manifest their otherworldly abilities and attempt to deny enemy sorceries. In the Psychic phase, players take it in turn to choose a single psyker from their kill team with which to attempt to manifest one or more psychic powers, in the order determined in the Initiative phase. Each player can only choose a single psyker in each battle round, and once all players with any psykers have done so (or have decided not to), the Psychic phase ends and the Shooting phase begins. Each attempt to manifest a psychic power uses the following sequence.

PSYCHIC SEQUENCE

1. Choose power
2. Take Psychic test
3. Enemy takes Deny the Witch test
4. Resolve psychic power

1. Choose Power

First, declare the power that the psyker you have chosen will attempt to manifest. The powers a psyker knows, and the number of powers they can attempt to manifest or deny in each Psychic phase, are detailed on their datasheet. A psyker cannot attempt to manifest the same psychic power more than once in a battle round.

Psychic Powers

Unless stated otherwise, all psykers know the *Psybolt* psychic power, detailed below. Some know other powers instead of, or in addition to, *Psybolt* – the model's datasheets and other supplementary rules you are using will make it clear which powers each psyker knows. If a psyker generates their powers before the battle, do so immediately before any players begin to deploy their kill team.

Psybolt

Psybolt has a warp charge value of 5. If manifested, the closest enemy model within 18" of and visible to the psyker suffers 1 mortal wound (pg 33). If the result of the Psychic test was 11+, the target suffers D3 mortal wounds instead.

2. Take Psychic Test

You can attempt to manifest a psychic power with a psyker from your kill team by taking a Psychic test. To do so, roll 2D6. If the total is equal to or greater than that power's warp charge value, the power is successfully manifested.

Perils of the Warp

If you roll a double 1 or a double 6 when taking a Psychic test, the psyker immediately suffers Perils of the Warp. The psyker suffers D3 mortal wounds (pg 33). If the psyker is taken out of action (pg 32) by Perils of the Warp, the power they were attempting to manifest automatically fails and each model within 3" immediately suffers D3 mortal wounds.

'The warp. It is known by many names: the sea of souls, the empyrean, the immaterium… It is a realm of boundless energy that can both empower and destroy. It is the domain of Daemons, the predatory entities that serve the dreaded Chaos Gods, and that will greedily devour the soul of any living thing should they be given the chance.

It is from the warp that those with psychic abilities draw their power, to hurl crackling arcs of lethal energies at their enemies, to shield their comrades from harm, or to scry the skeins of the future. Such witchery may be undone using the very same forces that gave rise to it, or, more rarely, the source of a psychic null field.

Yet all must beware when the veil is pierced, for the minds of psykers burn like beacons in the warp. The deeper they draw from the well, the greater and more terrible are the malign entities that may be attracted to their mind-spoor.

At such times must the whispers of Daemons be resisted with the greatest fervour! All it takes is a single moment of weakness to invite damnation and death upon all.'

- Extract from Grimenghael's Treatise on the Perils of the Immaterium

3. Deny the Witch Tests

If there are any enemy psykers within 24" of a psyker that has manifested a psychic power, the controlling player can choose one of those models to take a Deny the Witch test to resist the psychic power. The number of times a psyker can make a Deny the Witch attempt in each battle round is specified on their datasheet. Only one model can take a Deny the Witch test for each psychic power that is manifested, regardless of the number of models that could make an attempt or the number of times each is allowed to try and Deny the Witch in each battle round.

If more than one player has an eligible model to take a Deny the Witch test, players take it in turn to choose a model from their kill team to take a Deny the Witch test with, or pass, in the order determined in the Initiative phase. If a player passes, it is the next player's turn to choose, and so on until a player chooses a model to take a Deny the Witch test or all players with eligible models have passed.

To take a Deny the Witch test, roll 2D6. If the total is greater than the result of the Psychic test that manifested the power, it has been successfully resisted and its effects are negated.

4. Resolve Psychic Power

So long as the Psychic test was successful, the psyker was not taken out of action as a result of Perils of the Warp, and the attempt was not successfully resisted by a Deny the Witch test, then the controlling player may resolve the effect of the psychic power, which will be described in the power itself.

If the psyker can attempt to manifest more than one psychic power in each battle round, the controlling player may then attempt to manifest another psychic power with them, following the same sequence, until they cannot make any more attempts or do not wish to make any further attempts.

4. SHOOTING PHASE

Gun muzzles flare, shots ring out, and grenades crack as sentries are eliminated; lone operatives are picked off, or multiple combatants are mown down in sudden crossfires.

In the Shooting phase, players take it in turn to choose a model from their kill team to shoot with. The Shooting phase is split into two sections: in the first section Readied models shoot, and in the second section other models shoot. No model can be chosen to shoot more than once in a Shooting phase – if you have Kill Team tokens, place a Shoot token next to each model which shoots as a reminder.

READY, FIRE!

Readied models shoot before all other models. Players take it in turn to choose a Readied model from their kill team to shoot with (following the sequence below), or pass, in the order determined in the Initiative phase. If a player passes, it is the next player's turn to choose. Once all players have done so, they do so again in the same order, until all players pass in succession. When all of the players pass in succession, the Ready, Fire! section of the Shooting phase is over.

FIRE AT WILL

Once the Ready, Fire! section of the Shooting phase is over, players take it in turn to choose a model from their kill team to shoot with, or pass, in the order determined in the Initiative phase. If a player passes, it is the next player's turn to choose. Once all players have done so, they do so again in the same order, until all players pass in succession. When all of the players pass in succession, the Shooting phase is over and the Fight phase begins.

Each shooting attack uses the following sequence:

SHOOTING SEQUENCE

1. **Choose model to shoot with**
2. **Choose ranged weapon and targets**
3. **Resolve attacks**
   - **Make hit roll**
   - **Make wound roll**
   - **Enemy makes saving throw**
   - **Inflict damage**
4. **Choose another ranged weapon and targets**

1. Choose Model to Shoot With

When it is your turn, choose a model from your kill team to shoot with. You may not choose a model that has made a charge attempt, Advanced, Fallen Back (unless it can **FLY**) or Retreated this battle round, or a model that is within 1" of an enemy model. Unless otherwise stated, the model attacks with all of the ranged weapons it is armed with, one after the other.

2. Choose Ranged Weapon and Targets

Having chosen a shooting model, you must pick the ranged weapon it will use and the target model (or models, see opposite) for the attacks. The weapons a model has are listed on its datasheet.

Range and Visibility

In order for a shooting model to target an enemy model, the enemy model must be within the Range of the weapon being used (as listed on its profile) and be visible to the shooting model. If unsure, stoop down and get a look from behind the shooting model to see if any part of the target is visible from any part of the shooting model. Models cannot target enemy models that are within 1" of friendly models – the risk of hitting your own troops is too great.

Number of Attacks

Each time a model shoots a ranged weapon, it will make a number of attacks. You roll one dice for each attack being made. The number of attacks a model can make with a weapon, and therefore the number of dice you can roll, is found on the weapon's profile, along with the weapon's type. A weapon's type can impact the number of attacks it can make (see opposite).

FAST DICE ROLLING

The rules for resolving attacks (pg 30-32) have been written assuming you will make them one at a time. However, it is possible to speed up your battles by rolling the dice for similar attacks together. In order to make several attacks at once, all of the attacks must have the same Ballistic Skill (if it's a shooting attack) or the same Weapon Skill (if it's a close combat attack) and be subject to the same modifiers. They must also have the same Strength, Armour Penetration and Damage characteristics, and they must be directed at the same model. If this is the case, make all of the hit rolls at the same time, then all of the wound rolls. Your opponent can then make the saving throws one at a time and suffer damage each time as appropriate.

Targets

If a weapon makes more than one attack, you can choose for the shooting model to make all of them against the same target, or to split them. If you choose to split its attacks, you must split them between an initial target model, chosen as described above, and any number of enemy models within 2" of that target that are also eligible targets. After determining the number of shots made (if necessary, see right), declare how you will split the shooting model's shots before making any hit rolls, and resolve all the shots against one target before moving on to the next.

For example, a Skitarii Vanguard is firing his radium carbine (an Assault 3 weapon, which means it fires three shots). He has two eligible targets, and they are within 2" of one another, so the controlling player decides that the Skitarii Vanguard will split his attacks. The player will make two attacks against one of the targets, and one attack against the other.

Weapon Types

There are five types of ranged weapon: Assault, Heavy, Rapid Fire, Grenade and Pistol. A model shooting one of these weapons can make a number of attacks equal to the number written on its profile after its type. For example, a model firing an 'Assault 1' weapon can make 1 attack with that weapon; a model firing a 'Heavy 3' weapon can make 3 attacks, etc.

Some weapons make a random number of attacks – D3 or D6, for example. Once a player has rolled to determine how many shots a weapon of this kind makes, they can choose a target or targets as normal.

Each type of ranged weapon also has an additional rule that, depending upon the situation, might affect the accuracy of the weapon or when it can be fired. These are as follows:

ASSAULT

Assault weapons fire so rapidly or indiscriminately that they can be shot from the hip as warriors dash forwards into combat.

You can choose to shoot with a model with an Assault weapon in the Shooting phase (or React with that model to fire Overwatch) even if it Advanced earlier in that battle round. If it does so, it can only fire Assault weapons, and you must subtract 1 from any hit rolls made when firing that weapon this battle round.

HEAVY

Heavy weapons are the biggest and deadliest guns on the battlefield, but require reloading, careful set-up or bracing to fire at full effect.

If a model with a Heavy weapon moved in the preceding Movement phase, you must subtract 1 from any hit rolls made when firing that weapon this battle round.

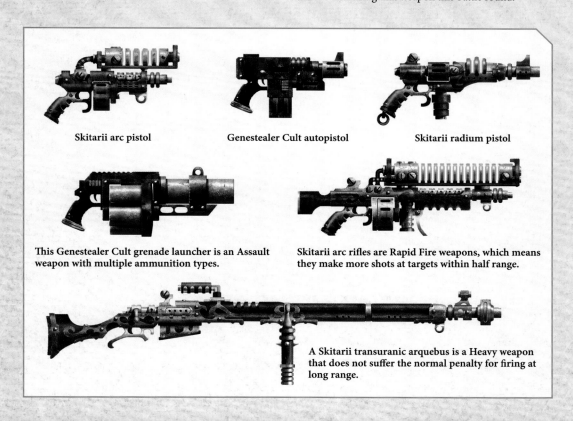

Skitarii arc pistol

Genestealer Cult autopistol

Skitarii radium pistol

This Genestealer Cult grenade launcher is an Assault weapon with multiple ammunition types.

Skitarii arc rifles are Rapid Fire weapons, which means they make more shots at targets within half range.

A Skitarii transuranic arquebus is a Heavy weapon that does not suffer the normal penalty for firing at long range.

RAPID FIRE
Rapid Fire weapons are capable of single aimed shots at long range and controlled bursts at close quarters.

A model firing a Rapid Fire weapon doubles the number of attacks it makes if all of its targets are within half the weapon's Range characteristic.

GRENADE
Grenades are handheld explosive devices that a warrior throws at the enemy while their squad mates provide covering fire.

A model in your kill team armed with a Grenade weapon may fire it in Overwatch or in the Shooting phase. If they do so, they cannot fire any other weapons that phase, and no other model in your kill team can fire a Grenade weapon that phase.

PISTOL
Pistols are carried one-handed and can even be used in a melee to shoot at point-blank range.

You can choose to shoot with a model with a Pistol weapon even if there are enemy models within 1", but it must target the closest enemy model (you can choose which if two or more are equidistant) and can only shoot with its Pistol weapon(s). In such circumstances, the model can shoot its Pistol even if other friendly models are within 1" of the same enemy model. It cannot fire a Pistol if it was charged in this battle round.

Each time a model armed with both a Pistol and another type of ranged weapon (e.g. a Pistol and a Rapid Fire weapon) is chosen to shoot, it can either shoot with its Pistol(s) or with all of its other weapons. Choose which it will fire (Pistols or non-Pistols) before making hit rolls.

3. Resolve Attacks
Attacks can be made one at a time, or, in some cases, you can roll for multiple attacks together. The following sequence is used to make attacks one at a time:

1. **Hit Roll:** To see if an attack hits the target, roll a D6 and apply the following cumulative modifiers:

HIT ROLL MODIFIERS	
Target model is at long range (see opposite)	-1
Target model is obscured (see right)	-1
Each flesh wound on the attacking model (pg 32)	-1
Attacking model's kill team is broken (pg 36)	-1

If the result is equal to or greater than the attacking model's Ballistic Skill characteristic, then it scores a hit with the weapon it is using. If not, the attack fails and the attack sequence ends. An unmodified hit roll of 1 always fails, and an unmodified hit roll of 6 always hits.

Obscured
Other models (even friendly models) and terrain may hide a target from view. If the target of an attack is even partially obscured from the best point of view of the firing model (that is, the point of view from a part of the firing model that gives the clearest line of sight), then it is said to be obscured.

When checking to see if a target is obscured, consider the main body of the firing and target models – do not include a model's base or parts that are 'sticking out' like aerials or weapons, but do include all limbs and a model's head. If there is still doubt, we recommend the players agree about what constitutes the main body of a model before the battle begins.

This model is completely visible and so is not considered to be obscured.

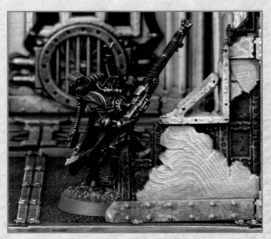

This model's leg is hidden behind the wall; it is therefore considered to be obscured. In addition, it is standing within 1" of the ruin that obscures it – this means it will be more difficult to injure (pg 32).

Long Range

A target is at long range if it is more than half the weapon's Range characteristic away from the attacking model. Grenade weapons are not affected by this rule.

For example, a boltgun has a Range of 24". Any target that is more than 12" away from a model attacking with a boltgun is at long range.

2. Wound Roll: If an attack scores a hit, you will then need to roll another dice to see if the attack wounds the target. The roll required is determined by comparing the attacking weapon's Strength characteristic with the target's Toughness characteristic, as shown on the following table:

WOUND ROLL	
ATTACK'S STRENGTH VS TARGET'S TOUGHNESS	**D6 ROLL REQUIRED**
Is the Strength **TWICE (or more than twice)** the Toughness?	2+
Is the Strength **GREATER** than the Toughness?	3+
Is the Strength **EQUAL** to the Toughness?	4+
Is the Strength **LOWER** than the Toughness?	5+
Is the Strength **HALF (or less than half)** the Toughness?	6+

If the roll is equal to or greater than the required number, the attack succeeds and the attack sequence continues. If the roll is less than the required number, the attack fails and the attack sequence ends. An unmodified wound roll of 1 always fails and an unmodified wound roll of 6 is always successful.

3. Saving Throw: The player controlling the target model then makes a saving throw by rolling a D6 and modifying the roll by the Armour Penetration characteristic of the attacking weapon. For example, if the attacking weapon has an Armour Penetration of -1, then 1 is subtracted from the saving throw. If the result is equal to, or greater than, the Save characteristic of the target model, then the damage is prevented and the attack sequence ends. If the result is less than the model's Save characteristic, then the saving throw fails and the model suffers damage. An unmodified saving throw of 1 always fails.

4. Inflict Damage: The damage inflicted is equal to the Damage characteristic of the weapon used in the attack. A model loses one wound for each point of damage it suffers. If a model's wounds are reduced to 0, any further attacks directed against this model by the attacking weapon are not resolved, and then the player controlling the attacking model makes an Injury roll for the target model (see overleaf).

Overwatch

Overwatch is a special type of shooting attack, made by a model that is the target of a charge and resolved in the Movement phase. It uses all the normal rules for shooting (e.g. the target must be in range and visible when they declare the charge), except that any attacks made must target the model attempting to charge, and a 6 is always required for a successful hit roll, irrespective of the firing model's Ballistic Skill or any modifiers.

Injury Roll

When a model's wounds are reduced to 0, the controlling player (unless stated otherwise, e.g. Inflict Damage on page 31) makes an Injury roll for that model. To make an Injury roll, the player rolls a D6 and applies the following modifiers, depending on how the damage was caused:

PSYCHIC POWER/SHOOTING ATTACK INJURY ROLL MODIFIERS	
Injured model is obscured from the psyker/shooting model, and within 1" of a model or piece of terrain that is between the two models	-1
Each flesh wound on the injured model	+1

CLOSE COMBAT ATTACK INJURY ROLL MODIFIER	
Each flesh wound on the injured model	+1

They then look up the result on the following table:

D6	RESULT
3 or less	Flesh wound
4+	Out of action

Flesh Wound

A model that suffers a flesh wound is restored to 1 wound remaining. A model with one or more flesh wounds suffers penalties to hit (pg 30) and is more likely to be taken out of action (see above). Mark one of the empty Flesh Wound boxes on that model's datacard (pg 63). If a model suffers a flesh wound and all of the Flesh Wound boxes on their datacard are marked, it is taken out of action instead (see right). In the Morale phase each player takes Nerve tests for each of their models that has one or more flesh wounds (pg 36).

Out of Action

A model that is taken out of action is seriously injured or may even be slain – either way it will play no further part in the battle. Remove that model from the battlefield.

Damage Characteristic

If a model loses its last wound to an attack that has a Damage characteristic of more than 1, the player whose model made the attack rolls a number of dice equal to that characteristic when making the Injury roll, rather than just one, and applies the highest result (after modifiers). If the attack has a Damage characteristic that is a random value (e.g. D3, D6), use the value rolled when inflicting damage.

For example, if a model with 3 wounds remaining fails its saving throw against a weapon with a Damage characteristic of 3, it will be reduced to 0 wounds and the player controlling the attacking model will roll three dice for the Injury roll, applying the highest result.

If a model loses its last wound when there are attacks or mortal wounds (see opposite) still allocated to it, these are not resolved.

4. Choose Another Ranged Weapon and Targets

If the attacking model has any other ranged weapons that it can fire, and you wish it to do so, return to step 2 of the shooting sequence (pg 28). Otherwise, the shooting sequence ends.

Invulnerable Saves

Some models possess abilities or wargear, such as supernatural reflexes or force fields, that grant them an invulnerable save. Each time you are required to make a save roll for a model with an invulnerable save, you can choose to use either its normal Save characteristic or its invulnerable save, but not both. If you use a model's invulnerable save, it is never modified by a weapon's Armour Penetration value. If a model has more than one invulnerable save, it can only use one of them – choose which it will use.

Mortal Wounds

Some attacks inflict mortal wounds – these are so powerful that no armour or force field can withstand their fury. Each mortal wound inflicts one point of damage on the target model. Do not make a wound roll or saving throw (including invulnerable saves) against a mortal wound – just inflict damage to the model as described on page 31. If a mortal wound reduces a model to 0 wounds, any further mortal wounds directed against this model by this attack are not resolved and the player whose model caused the mortal wound makes an Injury roll for that model (see opposite).

5. FIGHT PHASE

Warriors are silenced with a knife to the back, or cut down as their positions are overrun.

In the Fight phase, players take it in turn to choose a model from their kill team to fight with. The Fight phase is split into two sections: in the first section charging models fight, and in the second section other models fight. No model can be chosen to fight more than once in a Fight phase.

HAMMER OF WRATH

Models that charged in this battle round fight before all other models. Players take it in turn to choose a model that charged from their kill team to fight with (see below), or pass, in the order determined in the Initiative phase. If a player passes, it is the next player's turn to choose. A player cannot choose to pass if they have a model that charged that can fight. Once all players have chosen a model from their kill team or passed, they do so again in the same order, until all players pass in succession. When they do so, the Hammer of Wrath section of the Fight phase is over.

FIGHT FOR YOUR LIVES

Once the Hammer of Wrath section of the Fight phase is over, players take it in turn to choose a model from their kill team to fight with, or pass, in the order determined in the Initiative phase. If a player passes, it is the next player's turn to choose. A player cannot choose to pass if they have a model that can fight. Once all players have chosen a model from their kill team or passed, they do so again in the same order, until all players pass in succession. When they do so, the Fight phase is over and the Morale phase begins.

Models that can Fight

Any model that charged or was charged in this battle round, or that is within 1" of an enemy model, can be chosen to fight in the Fight phase.

Each time a model fights, use the following sequence:

FIGHT SEQUENCE

1. **Pile in up to 3"**
2. **Choose targets**
3. **Choose melee weapon**
4. **Resolve close combat attacks**
   - **Make hit roll**
   - **Make wound roll**
   - **Enemy makes saving throw**
   - **Inflict damage**
5. **Consolidate up to 3"**

1. Pile In

You may move the model up to 3" – the model must end the move closer to the nearest enemy model.

2. Choose Targets

First, you must pick the target model, or models, for the attacks. To target an enemy model, the attacking model must be within 1" of that model, and the enemy model must be visible to the attacking model. Models that charged this battle round can only target enemy models that they charged or that charged them earlier in the battle round. If there are no valid targets, this fight sequence ends.

If a model can make more than one close combat attack (see below), it can split them between eligible target models as you wish. Declare how you will split the model's close combat attacks before any dice are rolled, and resolve all attacks against one target before moving on to the next.

Number of Attacks

The number of close combat attacks a model makes against its target is determined by its Attacks characteristic. You roll one dice for each close combat attack being made. For example, if a model has an Attacks characteristic of 2, it can make 2 close combat attacks and you can therefore roll 2 dice.

3. Choose Melee Weapon

Each time a model makes a close combat attack, it uses a melee weapon – the weapons a model is armed with are listed on its datasheet. In addition to the melee weapons listed on their datasheets, all models are also assumed to be able to fight with a close combat weapon, which has the following profile:

WEAPON	RANGE	TYPE	S	AP	D
Close combat weapon	Melee	Melee	User	0	1

If a model has more than one melee weapon, choose which it will use before rolling the dice. If a model has more than one melee weapon and can make several close combat attacks, it can split its attacks between these weapons however you wish – declare how you will divide the attacks before any dice are rolled.

4. Resolve Close Combat Attacks

Close combat attacks can be made one at a time, or in some cases you can roll the dice for a number of attacks together. The attack sequence for making close combat attacks is identical to that used for shooting attacks (pg 30) except you use the model's Weapon Skill characteristic instead of its Ballistic Skill to make hit rolls, and apply the following cumulative modifiers to your hit rolls:

HIT ROLL MODIFIERS	
There is intervening terrain (see right)	-1
Each flesh wound on the attacking model	-1
Attacking model's kill team is broken (pg 36)	-1

5. Consolidate

You may move the model up to 3" – the model must end the move closer to the nearest enemy model.

Intervening Terrain

There is said to be intervening terrain between an attacking model and its target if there is any terrain between the models that makes it impossible for the models to be placed in contact with each other.

All of these models would suffer a -1 hit penalty in the Fight phase because their targets are behind intervening terrain. Either player could, however, use a model's pile-in move to get around the intervening terrain if they wished.

6. MORALE PHASE

The bravest heart may quail when the horrors of battle take their toll, but some fighters will rally even in the greatest adversity.

In the Morale phase, players take it in turn to play through the following sequence, in the order determined in the Initiative phase:

> ## MORALE SEQUENCE
> 1. Check if your kill team is broken
> 2. Remove Shaken tokens
> 3. Take Nerve tests

Once the first player has played through this sequence, the next player does so, and so on until all players have done so. Once they have done so, the Morale phase and the battle round are over. The players remove any tokens from their models (other than Shaken tokens, see right), and then the next battle round begins.

1. Check If Your Kill Team Is Broken

If all models in a kill team currently have flesh wounds, are shaken or are out of action, it is broken. Otherwise, if more than half of the models in your kill team currently have flesh wounds, are shaken or are out of action, it may be broken. Roll 2D6 – if the total is greater than the highest Leadership characteristic of any of the models in the kill team (other than those that are shaken or out of action), the kill team is broken. Once a kill team is broken, it stays broken for the rest of the game.

Models in a broken kill team need to take Nerve tests in each Morale phase. In addition, they suffer hit penalties as described in the Shooting and Fight phases, and there are additional penalties for broken kill teams in some missions.

2. Remove Shaken tokens

If you have any shaken models, they are now no longer shaken. Remove the Shaken token from each of these models.

3. Take Nerve Tests

You must take a Nerve test for each of your models that has a flesh wound, and for your other models if your kill team is broken. To take a Nerve test for a model, roll a D6 and apply the following cumulative modifiers:

NERVE TEST MODIFIERS	
Each other friendly model that is shaken or is out of action	+1
Each other friendly model (other than shaken models) within 2" of the model	-1

If the result of the Nerve test exceeds the model's Leadership characteristic, the test is failed. The model is shaken, and cannot do anything until it is no longer shaken: place a Shaken token next to it. Otherwise, the test is passed. The test is always passed on an unmodified roll of 1.

EXAMPLE BATTLE ROUND

These pages take you through an example battle round in a mission played by two players, Adam and Beth, showing you the sequence of the phases and the decisions and actions each player might make.

1. INITIATIVE PHASE

In the Initiative phase, the Adeptus Mechanicus player (Adam) and the Genestealer Cults player (Beth) roll off. Adam wins, rolling higher than Beth, so he has the initiative for this battle round.

2. MOVEMENT PHASE

In the Movement phase, Adam moves his kill team first, as he has the initiative. He makes a normal move with one of his Rangers (1), looking for a good clear view of the battlefield. His other Ranger (2) already has a good view, so he Readies that model instead. Finally, Adam Advances with his Vanguard (3) – he rolls a dice, scoring 1, and adds that to the Vanguard's Move characteristic for this phase, meaning it can move 7" (Adam hopes to use its Assault weapon in the Shooting phase).

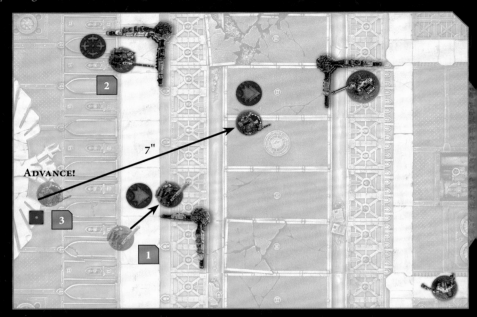

3. SHOOTING PHASE

Both players have a Readied model. These will shoot before any other models do so, but Adam gets to act with his Readied model first as he has the initiative. His Readied Ranger cannot target the Neophyte Leader, as the Neophyte Leader is within 1" of another friendly model. Instead, the Ranger shoots at the Neophyte Heavy. Adam checks what his Ranger can see, and sees that the Neophyte Heavy is obscured – he will have to subtract 1 from its hit rolls. He rolls two dice, and with his Ranger's BS of 3+ he needs to roll 4 or more for a hit (because of the modifier). He scores a hit! He then checks the weapon's Strength – 4 – against his target's Toughness – 3. This means he needs to roll 3+ for a successful wound. He rolls a 2, so Adam fails to wound his target and the attack sequence ends.

4. FIGHT PHASE

It's now the Fight phase. Although Adam has the initiative, Beth has a model that charged (and Adam doesn't), so she gets to choose that model to act first in this phase. First she piles in with her model, moving it closer to her target. Her Leader has an Attacks characteristic of 2, so she rolls 2 dice, looking for rolls of 4+ to hit. Both of her attacks miss.

It's now time for models that didn't charge to fight, and there's only one – the Ranger who was charged. Adam cannot pile in with this model – it's already as close as it can get to its target – so he simply attacks, rolling 1 dice and hoping for a 4+. He succeeds, and goes on to roll a 5 – more than enough to wound his target. Beth then makes a saving throw for her Leader, needing a 5+, and rolls a 3. Her Neophyte Leader is Injured, and Adam makes an Injury roll. Luckily for Beth, he only rolls a 1, and her Leader simply suffers a flesh wound, which she notes on its datacard.

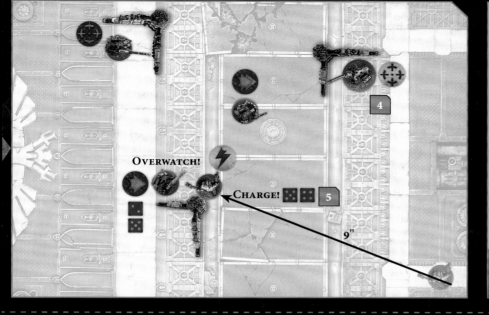

It is now Beth's turn to move her models. Her Neophyte Heavy (4) is well placed, so she Readies it. Then she chooses her Neophyte Leader (5) and declares a charge against the Ranger who moved! Adam gets a chance to React: the Ranger cannot Retreat, as it has already moved, so he declares it will fire Overwatch instead. He rolls 2 dice for its galvanic rifle – a Rapid Fire 1 weapon – as the target is within half range of the weapon. He's looking for rolls of 6 to hit, as is always the case when firing Overwatch. Both of his shots miss!

Then the Neophyte Leader charges. Beth rolls 2 dice and adds them together, getting 9 – this is how far she can move the Leader (enough to reach its target), and she does so, bringing it to within 1" of its target.

There are no psykers on the battlefield, so the players skip the Psychic phase and move on to the Shooting phase.

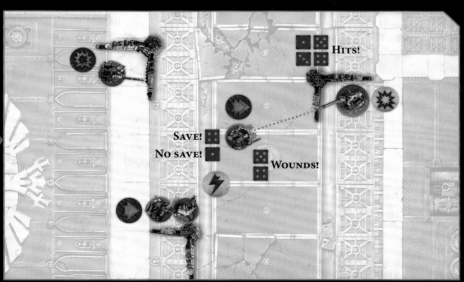

It's now Beth's turn to shoot with a Readied model – her Neophyte Heavy. The Vanguard is a prime target – it's in the open, and Beth won't have any penalties to her hit rolls. She rolls 4 dice for the Heavy's seismic cannon, and scores 2 hits. The Strength of the weapon is the same as the target's Toughness – 3 – so Beth needs to roll 4+ to wound her target. She does, and with both hits! Adam then rolls his model's saving throws, hoping for some good luck. The weapon has no AP, so Adam is looking for rolls of 4+. He rolls one 4, so that shot does no damage, but he also rolls a 1 – that one goes through! His Vanguard loses a wound, which takes it to 0 wounds. Beth then makes an Injury roll for the Vanguard. With a roll of 3, the Vanguard suffers a flesh wound – Adam makes a note of this on its datacard.

5. MORALE PHASE

There are no other models that can Fight, so with that phase over it's time for the Morale phase. Beginning with Adam, the two players check if their kill teams are broken (they do not need to test, as neither player has more than half of their models with flesh wounds, shaken or out of action) and then take Nerve tests for their models with flesh wounds (Adam rolls for his Vanguard and gets a 4 – it's not shaken, and Beth rolls for her Neophyte Leader, getting a 1 – it's also not shaken).

It's then the end of this battle round and time for the next one.

FIGHTING A BATTLE

In games of Kill Team, your hand-picked fighters will be tasked with a specific objective, whether this is to infiltrate enemy territory, sabotage critical resources or disrupt supply lines.

THE MISSION

Before you can fight a battle in a game of Kill Team, you must select a mission. The core rules include the Covert War mission (see opposite) which is ideal to get the action started quickly. Others can be found elsewhere in this book, in other books, or you could play a mission of your own creation. If you and your opponent(s) cannot agree on which mission to play, the players should roll off, and whoever wins decides on the mission. Alternatively, if you are playing a campaign, the campaign rules (pg 202-205) explain how to determine which mission you will play.

THE KILL TEAMS

Once you have chosen which mission to play, you must choose your kill team. For the Covert War mission you can include any miniatures from your collection, but the full rules for choosing a kill team can be found on page 62. The mission you are playing may include additional rules that change how you choose your kill team.

THE BATTLEFIELD

In the far future, battles are fought across an infinite variety of strange and alien planets where no land is left untouched by the blight of war. Crystal moons, derelict space hulks and nightmarish Daemon worlds are just a few of the fantastical landscapes that can be recreated whenever you play a game of Kill Team.

Once you have chosen your mission and your kill teams, you must set up the battlefield. A battlefield can be any surface upon which the models can stand – a dining table, for example, or the floor. We typically assume a battlefield is 30" by 22" – the same size as a Kill Team gameboard – though some missions will state other dimensions. The battlefield should always be large enough to accommodate all your models – if it is not, simply increase the size of the battlefield. If you are playing a game with three or four players you may wish

to increase the size of the battlefield to accommodate the extra models. This can be achieved by placing two Kill Team gameboards side by side, or by simply using a larger playing area.

Unless the mission you are playing instructs you otherwise, you should then create an exciting battlefield using any terrain features from your collection that you wish. The best games of Kill Team are played on battlefields that include a variety of terrain: some of it that can hide models from view, some of it that can be scaled to give models a better view of the battlefield, and some of it that provides a bit of cover for models dashing across otherwise open ground. In general, more is better, and we recommend having at least one, or preferably two, terrain features that can provide shelter for a handful of models or more in each 12" by 12" area (or each quarter of a 30" by 22" area).

Don't worry if your battlefield doesn't match these requirements, but keep in mind that playing on very small or very large battlefields, or ones that are either a barren wasteland or filled to overflowing with terrain features, may give an advantage to one side or the other.

Killzones & Expansions

If you are battling in a specific killzone (see page 44), or if you are using a particular expansion, there might be additional rules pertaining to setting up the battlefield, and special rules that alter how some terrain interacts with your warriors. Bear these in mind when creating your battlefield.

SCOUTING PHASE

Once you have set up the battlefield, some missions will tell you to play the Scouting phase. This phase is described in detail on page 49, but we suggest that you don't include this phase until after your first few games.

DEPLOYMENT

Once you have set up the battlefield (and, if relevant, played the Scouting phase), it is time to set up your kill teams. Each mission will explain how to do this. Once the kill teams are set up as described in the mission (and after anything else that the mission specifies happens before the battle begins), begin the first battle round.

OPEN PLAY MISSION
COVERT WAR

The time has come to prove your worth as the leader of a covert kill team. All that stands between you and success is another kill team determined to thwart you.

THE KILL TEAMS

To play this mission, each player must first choose a kill team from the miniatures in their collection. Any models can be included in the kill team. We recommend using 10 or fewer models in each kill team in this mission.

THE BATTLEFIELD

Create the battlefield and set up terrain. Then, the players each roll 2D6, re-rolling any tied scores. The highest scorer has the greatest strategic advantage in this mission, the next highest gets the second greatest advantage and so on.

The players then must take it in turn, in the order of greatest to least strategic advantage, to place a single objective marker to represent sites of tactical or strategic import. Each objective marker must be placed at least 8" away from any other objective marker and 6" from any battlefield edge. A player controls an objective marker if there are more models from their kill team within 2" of it than there are enemy models. Models that are shaken do not count. Whenever you measure to or from an objective marker, always measure to the centre of the marker.

The player with the greatest advantage then rolls on the primary objectives table to the right to determine which is used during the mission.

SCOUTING PHASE

If all players agree to do so, resolve the Scouting phase, as described on page 49.

DEPLOYMENT

The player with least advantage divides the battlefield into as many equal-sized portions as there are players (so for a two-player game, they would divide it in half). The players then take it in turn, in the order of greatest to least advantage, to decide which portion is their own deployment zone.

The players then take it in turn to deploy one model from their kill team, starting with the player with least strategic advantage. Models must be set up wholly within their own deployment zone, more than 6" from any enemy deployment zone. Once all players have set up one model, they do so again in the same order, and so on. If a player runs out of models to set up, skip them. Once the players have set up all their models, deployment ends and the first battle round begins.

BATTLE LENGTH

The battle lasts for five battle rounds.

VICTORY CONDITIONS

At the end of the battle, the player who has the most victory points wins a major victory. If more than one player is tied for the most victory points at the end of the battle, the player amongst them who had the least strategic advantage wins a minor victory.

PRIMARY OBJECTIVES TABLE	
D3	**VICTORY CONDITION**
1	**Secure the Battlefield:** At the end of the battle, each objective marker is worth 2 victory points to the player who controls it.
2	**Retrieve the Cache:** At the start of the first battle round, but before the Initiatve phase begins, randomly select one objective marker; remove the other objective marker(s) from the battlefield. At the end of the battle, the remaining objective marker is worth 6 victory points to the player who controls it.
3	**Infiltrate:** At the end of the battle, each objective marker in an opponent's deployment zone is worth 2 victory points to the player who controls it. (A player can control an objective marker in their own deployment zone, but will score no victory points for doing so.)

ADVANCED RULES

This section includes a variety of rules which add further detail and complexity to the game. They are not necessary in order to play, so they have been gathered together here for players to use if they wish. We recommend that new players ignore this section to start with, until they are familiar with the core rules.

TERRAIN

You've already encountered some rules for terrain – a model shooting at a target that is obscured (which will often be by terrain) finds it harder to hit their target and may find it harder to take them out of action. This section introduces further rules for terrain, covering how your models move through different kinds of terrain and what effect the terrain has on them. Some of these rules override the core rules for movement, so make sure you have agreed with your opponent(s) whether or not you are using these rules before beginning your game.

Types of Terrain

Terrain is described as open ground, difficult terrain, dangerous terrain or impassable terrain. Each has a different impact on your models, as described on this page. The rules for some terrain features tell you which kind of terrain they are. For all other terrain, before the game begins but once terrain has been set up, you should agree with your opponent(s) what is considered to be open ground, what is difficult or dangerous terrain, and what is impassable.

Some types of terrain slow a model's movement. Where this is the case, it applies to all of that model's movement, whichever phase it occurs in. Where a model moves a random distance (for example, when charging), the value is determined normally and then affected as described below.

Open Ground

Open ground is terrain that is relatively flat and free of obstacles and hazards.

The battlefield surface, the floors of buildings and ruins, platforms, connecting walkways, doors, hatches and ladders are all considered to be open ground. Some windows may also be considered to be open ground for some smaller models – make sure you have discussed this with your opponent(s) before the game. Models can move across open ground without penalty.

Difficult Terrain

Difficult terrain is terrain where models might lose their footing, or have to scramble over obstacles.

Difficult terrain includes steep or treacherous slopes, dense stands of foliage, pools of non-hazardous liquid, and any surface where models might lose their footing – on ice or a spoil heap, for example. Models move over difficult terrain at half their normal rate, so 1" of movement across difficult terrain counts as 2". For example, to cross a stagnant pool 1½" wide would take 3" of movement. Similarly, if moving over a frozen lake, a model with a Move characteristic of 6" would only be able to move 3" rather than 6". This penalty applies to all moves. Models that can **FLY** ignore this penalty.

Dangerous Terrain

Dangerous terrain is terrain which is hazardous, and which might harm a model that moves through it.

Dangerous terrain includes tar pits, deep or noxious pools, and areas of sentient and predatory vegetation. Models move over dangerous terrain at half their normal rate in the same way as with difficult terrain, but as soon as they would move into dangerous terrain, or begin their move if they are already in dangerous terrain (unless they remain stationary), the controlling player takes a dangerous terrain test by rolling a D6. On a 1, that model suffers 1 mortal wound. Models that can **FLY** ignore the movement penalty, as with difficult terrain, but if they begin or end their move in dangerous terrain (unless they remain stationary), the controlling player takes a dangerous terrain test for that model.

Impassable Terrain

Impassable terrain is terrain that models cannot enter or move over for any reason – it might be instantly lethal to any who would enter, or simply a large, solid obstacle.

Models cannot move into impassable terrain.

Climbing

Models can climb or traverse barriers of 1" or higher, and when they do so you measure the distance as you would normally for the kind of terrain they are moving through. A model that climbs cannot end its movement while climbing – it must be standing on a surface at the end of its movement. If it does not have sufficient movement to climb to a suitable surface, it cannot climb. A model can traverse an overhang while climbing, as long as it protrudes less than 1" from the surface the model is climbing.

Models that can **FLY** ignore these rules – they can move vertically without measuring the distance moved.

Barriers, Gaps and Leaping

Walls, pipes, barricades and other low obstacles form barriers that a model can either go around or leap over. A model can leap onto a barrier less than 1½" high without having to include the vertical distance when determining how far they have moved. In addition, a model can leap over a barrier less than 1½" high and no more than 1½" deep without having to include the vertical distance when determining how far they have moved.

As the pipe is less than 1½" tall or 1½" deep, the Ranger can leap over it without counting the vertical movement.

A model can also leap over a gap between two pieces of terrain (e.g. from one walkway to another), as long as the gap is less than 2" across, the model has sufficient movement to reach the other side of the gap (so that their base is entirely on the other side of the gap), and the model ends its move less than 1" higher than before it leapt. Note that if the model ends its move 6" or more lower than before it leapt, you will need to use the rules for jumping down (see below). When a model leaps, you do not have to include the vertical distance moved when determining how far the model has moved.

As the gap between the ruins is less than 2", the Neophyte Hybrid can leap from one to the other.

Models that can **FLY** ignore these rules – they can move over barriers and gaps without penalty.

Falling

Many terrain features have exposed edges, dangerous precipices, or precarious walkways. Before the game you should agree with your opponent(s) which terrain features it is possible for a model to fall from. Almost all buildings and ruins with more than one level are good examples of this.

Falling Tests

If a model is on such a terrain feature and within 1" of the edge when they are hit by an attack (or if something other than an attack causes them to lose a wound), they may be knocked off the edge. After all the attacks from the attacking model have been resolved against that model (or the wound has been lost and the Injury roll made if necessary), the player who controls that model takes a Falling test by rolling a D6. On a 2+, the test is passed and the model does not fall. On a 1, the test is failed and the model is knocked off the edge. Move the model over the edge by the shortest route possible, then straight down until they hit a lower level.

The Neophyte Hybrid fails their Falling test, so they are moved over the edge by the shortest route, then down.

Falling Damage

Roll a D6 for every full 3" the model has fallen. For each roll of 5+ they suffer 1 mortal wound. If the falling model would be placed on top of another model, make another roll as described above for the model underneath, using the same number of dice as for the falling model. The controlling player of the falling model makes any Injury rolls that result from a fall. After resolving any Injury rolls, the falling model is placed as close as possible to the point where they would have landed. This can bring them within 1" of an enemy model.

Jumping Down

A model standing somewhere it could fall from can choose to jump down from one level to another. When they do so, use the normal falling rules but roll one fewer dice than you normally would. For example, if a model jumps down 5" you do not have to roll a dice for them; if they jump down 6", however, you would roll 1 dice for them. A model jumping down cannot choose to fall on top of another model, and cannot jump down within 1" of an enemy model, unless they are making a charge move and that model was a target of the charge.

KILLZONES

It is a vast galaxy, and wars are fought across all kinds of battlefields. From shattered city streets to sprawling refineries and shell-pocked plains, kill teams must contend not only with their foes, but also the environments in which they operate.

When you have chosen a mission for your game of Kill Team, you may decide that it is fought in a particular killzone. This book includes rules for one killzone – the Sector Imperialis – but rules for other killzones are available in other Kill Team products. Each killzone has its own rules that govern how your models interact with the battlefield and terrain, and these rules are used in addition to the rules for terrain on pages 42-43.

In many cases the killzone you fight in will be determined by the gameboards and terrain in your collection, or by the mission you are playing. However, where you have a choice of killzones and the players cannot agree, the players should roll off. Whoever wins decides which killzone the battle is fought in.

KILLZONE: SECTOR IMPERIALIS

Shattered streets and ruins stretch for miles in all directions. Kill teams must pick their way through the blasted remains of the lives of whatever luckless civilians dwelt here as they hunt for their objective.

If you are playing a mission in a Sector Imperialis, one player rolls a D6 once the battlefield has been set up but before kill teams are set up, and consults the environment table to the right to determine what additional rule is used for this mission. In addition, if you are playing a mission in a Sector Imperialis, players can use any Sector Imperialis Tactics they have (these can be found in other Kill Team products).

ENVIRONMENT TABLE

D6	RESULT
1	**Deserted Habs:** No additional rule.
2	**Abandoned Munitions:** One extra model in each kill team can shoot with a Grenade weapon they are armed with in each battle round.
3	**Smoke in the Air:** All players must subtract 1 from their hit rolls in the Shooting phase.
4	**Traps:** The upper floors of ruins are dangerous terrain.
5	**Tunnels:** If a model from your kill team begins your turn in the Movement phase within 1" of a manhole and more than 1" from any enemy models, and they are not shaken, they can enter the tunnels. When they do so, remove them from the battlefield. At the end of your turn in the Movement phase of the next battle round, you can place that model within 1" of any manhole that is within 24" of the manhole they used to enter the tunnels, and more than 1" from any enemy models. They are considered to have made a normal move. While they are not on the battlefield, they are considered to be out of action for the purposes of Nerve tests and checking whether your kill team is broken. If they are not on the battlefield at the end of the battle, they are considered to be out of action.
6	**Hidden Cache:** In a campaign game (see page 204), the player who wins the mission gains 1 Materiel. Otherwise, there is no additional rule.

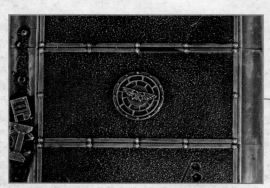

On a battlefield with tunnels (see the Environment table, above) these manholes allow models to move underneath the battlefield.

On a battlefield with traps (see the Environment table, opposite) the Skitarii here would be in dangerous terrain, while the Neophyte Hybrid wouldn't be.

45

MISSIONS

'Damnation man, this is a critical
moment! Brute force simply won't
be enough! Send word to Sergeant
Marius. His Blood Angels will get
the Governor out alive.'

*- General Kasmund Dar-Galot,
during the last days of the
Aximal Secession*

COUNTLESS BATTLES

In a galaxy at war there are no limits to the kinds of missions your kill teams will undertake, and no end to the dangers they face. Kill Team gives you the freedom to play the games you want, how you want, as described here.

DIFFERENT WAYS TO PLAY

Kill Team is a game that pits groups of diehards against one another, but beyond that core premise there is huge variety in the games you can play and the stories you can tell. The different ways of playing are described here under three headings – open play, narrative play and matched play.

Open Play

Open play is the least restrictive type of gaming because it can be as simple or as complex as you like. All you need to play an open play game are your painted miniatures, their datasheets, the Kill Team core rules, a mission, a set of dice, a tape measure and a flat surface on which to play. Then, just set up your models and begin the battle! A simple mission to get you started is included on page 41, and there are some additional ideas and missions on pages 50-51. You can add extra dimensions to your open play games by incorporating any of the rules or guidelines that appear in this and other Kill Team products, or invent missions and rules of your own.

Matched Play

Matched play games allow for kill teams to be tested against each other under conditions that give no particular advantage to either side, to see which kill team is strongest and which commander is canniest. Kill teams in matched play games are chosen following a set of rules that mean players can be sure that their forces will have a fair fight. Key to these rules are the points values that are given to each model and piece of wargear in matched play. You can find these values at the end of each Faction section in this book.

Matched play is ideal for competitive play as it provides clear guidelines on the size and strength of the kill teams taking part, as well as ensuring that all battles are as fair as they can be.

Narrative Play

Narrative play games are all about telling stories in the grim darkness of the far future. This can be as simple as devising a reason for two kill teams to battle each other, such as a deep-seated rivalry or a vital objective that must be secured. Creating a setting like this turns Kill Team into more than a competitive game, as each battle is woven into the ongoing story of the war-torn galaxy.

There are endless ways to build a story into your games. Kill teams might be modified to better reflect the plot, specific terrain might play a part in recreating the landscape and 'house rules' might be invented to represent the consequences of victory and defeat. There are a number of missions available in this book that represent some of the most common archetypes for these stories (pg 52-55). By linking together the narrative battles you fight, you can turn a story into a saga in which your kill team are the protagonists. The campaign rules in this book (pg 202-205) help you create such a tale.

No Wrong Way to Play

Each mission in this book tells you what type of play it is designed for. However, there's nothing stopping you from taking elements from a mission meant for matched play and using it for a narrative play game, or taking one of the narrative play missions and basing an open play game on the core idea of that mission. It's up to you!

SCOUTING PHASE

This section introduces the Scouting phase – a phase that takes place before the battle and represents the kill teams' efforts before they engage in direct conflict.

TACTICS

Some of the missions that follow in this section include Tactics that one or more players gain access to during that mission. For more information about Tactics and how to use them, see pages 64-65.

OBJECTIVE MARKERS

Many missions include objective markers. Each objective marker should be around 1" across. When a mission includes objective markers it will tell you how to set them up, but if you are unable to place an objective marker as described by the mission (e.g. because there is terrain in the way), you can instead place it as close as possible to its correct position. Whenever you measure to or from an objective marker, unless stated otherwise measure to the centre of the marker, and when measuring to another objective marker or the edge of the battlefield, only measure the horizontal distance. A player controls an objective marker if there are more models from their kill team within 2" of it than there are enemy models. Models that are shaken do not count.

SCOUTING PHASE

Operatives creep into position, eliminating sentries, disarming or laying traps and relaying information about the distribution of enemy forces. Their success or otherwise will determine who has the upper hand should it come to a contest of arms.

Once you have chosen a mission and your kill teams, and set up the battlefield, but before you set up your kill teams, you play the Scouting phase. This phase is used to determine the success of each kill team's planning, preparing and manoeuvring before the battle, and may have an impact on how the kill teams are set up, how the terrain affects the battle, and so on.

In the Scouting phase, each player secretly chooses one of the following strategies by hiding a D6 behind their hand with the relevant number showing on the top face of the dice.

1. Scout Out Enemy Forces
2. Plant Traps
3. Disarm Traps
4. Scout Out Terrain
5. Take Forward Positions
6. Eliminate Sentries

Once all players have done so, they reveal their choices simultaneously, with the effects described below.

Once they have done this, the Scouting phase is over and the players continue with deployment.

1. Scout Out Enemy Forces

If you choose this strategy, you can set aside up to 20 per cent of the models in your kill team (rounding up) during deployment. For example, if you have 5 models in your kill team, you can set aside 1 model, if you have 3 models in your kill team, you can set aside 1 model, and if you have 20 models in your kill team, you can set aside 4 models. Once all kill teams have been set up, you can then set these models up, following the rules for deployment in the mission you are playing. If more than one player chooses this, you must roll off. Whichever player wins gains the benefit of this strategy. The other player(s) gain no benefit.

2. Plant Traps

If you choose this strategy you can booby-trap up to D3 pieces of terrain, other than impassable terrain, that are no bigger than 8" in height, length or width. Before any models are set up, you must choose which pieces of terrain your kill team has booby-trapped, and note those down clearly on a piece of paper. If an enemy model moves within 1" of one of these terrain pieces, or begins their move within 1" of one (unless they remain stationary), they trigger the booby trap: reveal

to your opponent(s) that the terrain is booby-trapped, and roll a D6 for the enemy model. On a 1, they suffer 1 mortal wound. Models that can **FLY** do not trigger the booby trap unless they begin or end their move within 1" of a booby-trapped terrain piece (and do not remain stationary). After the model's move is complete, enemy models treat that piece of terrain, and all open ground within 1" of it, as dangerous terrain. It is no longer booby-trapped.

3. Disarm Traps

If you choose this strategy, choose an enemy player who chose the Plant Traps strategy. That player's strategy has no effect. If there is no such player, your strategy has no effect.

4. Scout Out Terrain

If you choose this strategy, choose up to D3 pieces of difficult or dangerous terrain (each piece of terrain can be no bigger than 8" in height, length or width). Your models can move through this terrain without penalty in this mission. In addition, if a friendly model suffers a mortal wound from this terrain, roll a D6. On a 5+, that mortal wound is ignored.

5. Take Forward Positions

If you choose this strategy, once all kill teams have been set up but before the first battle round begins, up to 20 per cent of the models in your kill team (rounding up) can make a normal move as if it were your turn in the Movement phase. If more than one player chooses this strategy, those players must roll off. Whichever player wins gains the benefit of this strategy. The other player(s) gain no benefit.

6. Eliminate Sentries

If you choose this strategy, once all kill teams have been set up but before the first battle round begins, up to 20% of the models in your kill team (rounding up) can make a shooting attack as if it were your turn in the Shooting phase. When they do so, they must target a model that has made a normal move as a result of the Take Forward Positions strategy. If more than one player chooses this strategy, those players must roll 2D6 to establish an Initiative order as if it were the Initiative phase, and then take it in turn to resolve any attacks as if it were the Shooting phase, in the order just established. If no player chose the Take Forward Positions strategy, this strategy has no effect.

BEHIND ENEMY LINES

Kill team operations take place under any number of unusual circumstances. On these pages you will find three examples of open play missions for playing games of Kill Team. You will also find a few ideas below to spark your imagination for other exciting open play games of Kill Team.

- Surrounded by a numerically superior foe, an elite force must break out or drive off the enemy.

- A ragtag band of survivors from various units come together in no man's land to try to get back to their own lines.

- A routine patrol is ambushed in dense terrain when returning with essential intelligence. They must escape to bring this information to their commander.

- A small band of planetary defenders must hold a vital communications array until reinforcements can arrive from orbit.

- Command wants to use a fleet of bombers to annihilate the enemy headquarters, but there is only one viable route to the target, covered by anti-air defences. These guns must be destroyed.

- A sorcerer is conducting a fell ritual. An army will not be able to get past his forces, but if a small team can defeat his elite guards they can stop the sorcerer before he completes his work.

- A spy has been wounded while trying to escape your camp and must be hunted down before he can get back to his comrades.

- A key artefact was buried in a ruined city when it fell. Your team must retrieve this artefact before the enemy can find it.

- A traitor has gone over to the enemy! Find and eliminate him before he can give up his secrets.

- The enemy has seeded this area with explosives. You must disarm them all before the rest of the army can move through.

OPEN PLAY MISSION
AERIAL STRIKE

Sometimes the only way to get troops into a critical fortified position is from above, dropping from the sky on grav-chutes or by other means to sabotage vital enemy equipment.

THE KILL TEAMS

This is a mission for two players. Choose which player will be the attacker and which will be the defender (roll off if you can't agree – the winner decides). Each player chooses a kill team (see page 62).

THE BATTLEFIELD

Create the battlefield and set up terrain. The defender then places 3 objective markers anywhere on the battlefield. Each objective marker must be at least 6" from other objective markers.

SCOUTING PHASE

Do not use the rules for the Scouting phase in this mission.

DEPLOYMENT

The defender sets up their models, anywhere on the battlefield. Divide the battlefield into four even quarters and number them 1-4. The attacker then rolls a D6 for each of their models. On a 1-4, that model is set up in the quarter corresponding to the number rolled. On a 5-6, the attacker may pick which quarter the model is set up in. The attacker's models must be set up more than 4" from any of the defender's models.

BATTLE LENGTH

The battle automatically ends at the end of battle round 5.

VICTORY CONDITIONS

If any of the attacker's models are within 1" of an objective marker at the end of a battle round, they may attempt to destroy it. Roll a D6 for each of those models. On a 5+, that objective is destroyed: remove it from the battlefield. At the end of the battle, each objective marker is worth 2 victory points to the attacker if it has been destroyed or 2 victory points to the defender if it is still on the battlefield. Each player also scores 1 victory point for each enemy specialist that is out of action at the end of the battle. The player with the most victory points is the winner. If the players have the same number of victory points, the defender wins.

OPEN PLAY MISSION
SEARCH AND RESCUE

When a key operative is lost behind enemy lines, the rest of their unit must retrace their steps and locate their missing comrade before the enemy does.

THE KILL TEAMS

This is a mission for two players. Choose which player will be the rescuer and which will be the defender (roll off if you can't agree – the winner decides). Each player chooses a kill team (see page 62).

THE BATTLEFIELD

Create the battlefield and set up terrain. The defender places 5 objective markers anywhere on the battlefield. Each objective marker must be at least 4" from other objective markers and the edge of the battlefield. They then divide the battlefield into even halves.

SCOUTING PHASE

Resolve the Scouting phase as described on page 49.

DEPLOYMENT

The rescuer picks a battlefield half to be their deployment zone and sets up a model anywhere in that deployment zone, more than 8" from the enemy deployment zone. Players then alternate setting up models in this way. If one player finishes deploying first, the other player may continue to set up models until all members of both kill teams are set up.

BATTLE LENGTH

The battle ends at the end of battle round 5.

VICTORY CONDITIONS

At the end of the Movement phase, roll a D6 in turn for each objective marker within 1" of any of your models and more than 1" from any enemy models (if both players can do so, take it in turn following the order determined in the Initiative phase). On a 6, immediately remove all the other markers from the battlefield, including any yet to be rolled for. From this point onwards, do not make any further rolls for objectives. At the end of the battle, whichever player has the most models within 2" of the remaining objective marker is the winner. If neither player has more models within 2" of the objective marker than their opponent, or if all of the objective markers are still on the battlefield, the rescuer wins.

OPEN PLAY MISSION
LINES OF BATTLE

Sometimes it is up to a single unit to try to hold a flank and stop the enemy from breaking through to their defenceless support and supply trains. If they fail, the war is almost certainly lost!

THE KILL TEAMS

This is a mission for two players. Choose which player will be the attacker and which will be the defender (roll off if you can't agree – the winner decides). Each player chooses a kill team (see page 62).

THE BATTLEFIELD

Create the battlefield and set up terrain. The defender then picks one battlefield edge to be the line they must hold.

SCOUTING PHASE

Resolve the Scouting phase as described on page 49.

DEPLOYMENT

The defender sets up their kill team anywhere within 6" of the battlefield edge they must hold. The attacker then sets up their kill team anywhere within 6" of the opposite battlefield edge.

BATTLE LENGTH

At the end of battle round 4, the attacker rolls a D6. The battle continues on a 3+, otherwise the battle ends. At the end of battle round 5, the attacker again rolls a D6. This time the battle continues on a 4+, otherwise the battle ends. The battle automatically ends at the end of battle round 6.

VICTORY CONDITIONS

The attacker can move their models off the defender's battlefield edge, if that model's move is sufficient to take it wholly over the edge of the battlefield. A model that does so has broken through – it is not out of action, but takes no further part in the mission. At the end of the battle, the attacker scores 1 victory point for each model that has broken through, while the defender scores 1 victory point for each of the attacker's models that has not broken through. The player with the most victory points is the winner. If the players have the same number of victory points, the defender wins.

NARRATIVE PLAY MISSION
DISRUPT SUPPLY LINES

The success or failure of an army depends on how well it is supplied, and kill teams play a vital part in both sabotaging and safeguarding supply lines. When high command receives intelligence that a supply line is in danger, they will quickly despatch a kill team to intercept and eliminate the saboteurs.

THE KILL TEAMS

This is a mission for two players. Choose which player will be the attacker and which will be the defender (roll off if you can't agree – the winner decides). Each player chooses a Faction keyword, and the players reveal their choices at the same time. Then each player chooses a Battle-forged kill team (see page 62) that only includes models with the Faction keyword they chose.

THE BATTLEFIELD

Create the battlefield and set up terrain. An example of how you might do this is shown below. The players roll off, and the player that wins chooses which of the short edges of the battlefield their deployment zone is touching. The defender then places three objective markers in their territory. Each objective marker must be at least 6" from other objective markers and the edge of the battlefield.

SCOUTING PHASE

Resolve the Scouting phase as described on page 49.

DEPLOYMENT

The players roll off, and then alternate setting up models, starting with the player who lost the roll-off. A player's models must be set up wholly within their deployment zone. If a player runs out of models to set up, skip them. Continue setting up models until both players have set up their kill teams. Once the players have set up all their models, deployment ends and the first battle round begins.

BATTLE LENGTH

At the end of battle round 4, the attacker rolls a D6. The battle continues on a 3+, otherwise the battle ends. At the end of battle round 5, the attacker again rolls a D6. This time the battle continues on a 4+, otherwise the battle ends. The battle automatically ends at the end of battle round 6.

VICTORY CONDITIONS

At the end of the battle, each objective marker is worth 3 victory points to the player who controls it. In addition, the attacker scores 1 victory point for each objective marker they have destroyed, and a player scores 1 victory point if the enemy player's kill team is broken. The player with the most victory points is the winner. If the players have the same number of victory points, the defender wins.

RESOURCES

In a campaign game (see page 202) if the attacker wins the mission, the defender loses 2 Materiel. If the defender wins the mission, the attacker loses 1 Morale.

DISRUPT SUPPLY LINE

Attacker Tactic

Use this Tactic at the end of a battle round. Choose an objective marker you control. You destroy that objective marker – remove it from the battlefield. You can only use this Tactic once per battle round.

1 COMMAND POINT

PROTECT THE ASSETS

Defender Tactic

Use this Tactic at the start of a battle round. Until the start of the next battle round, objective markers may not be destroyed whilst within 2" of any of your models.

2 COMMAND POINTS

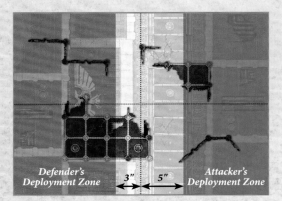

Defender's Deployment Zone — 3" — 5" — *Attacker's Deployment Zone*

AMBUSH

When a choke point is found, a kill team can cause significant damage to a superior force. Canny commanders will send their kill teams to hold these areas, setting ambushes that will restrict enemy movement and potentially cause disproportionate damage to their foes.

THE KILL TEAMS

This is a mission for two players. Choose which player will be the attacker and which will be the defender (roll off if you can't agree – the winner decides). Each player chooses a Faction keyword, and the players reveal their choices at the same time. Then each player chooses a Battle-forged kill team (see page 62) that only includes models with the Faction keyword they chose, but the defender can spend an additional 20 points on their kill team.

THE BATTLEFIELD

Create the battlefield and set up terrain. An example of how you might do this is shown below. The players roll off, and the player that wins chooses which of the short edges of the battlefield their deployment zone is touching.

SCOUTING PHASE

Resolve the Scouting phase as described on page 49.

DEPLOYMENT

The players alternate setting up models, starting with the defender. If a player runs out of models to set up, skip them. Continue setting up models until both players have set up their kill teams. A player's models must be set up wholly within their deployment zone. Once the players have set up all their models, deployment ends and the first battle round begins.

BATTLE LENGTH

If the defender's models are all either shaken, out of action or have escaped (see right) at the end of a battle round, the battle ends. If not, at the end of battle round 4, the attacker rolls a D6. The battle continues on a 3+, otherwise the battle ends. If the battle doesn't end as described above, at the end of battle round 5, the attacker again rolls a D6. This time the battle continues on a 4+, otherwise the battle ends. The battle automatically ends at the end of battle round 6.

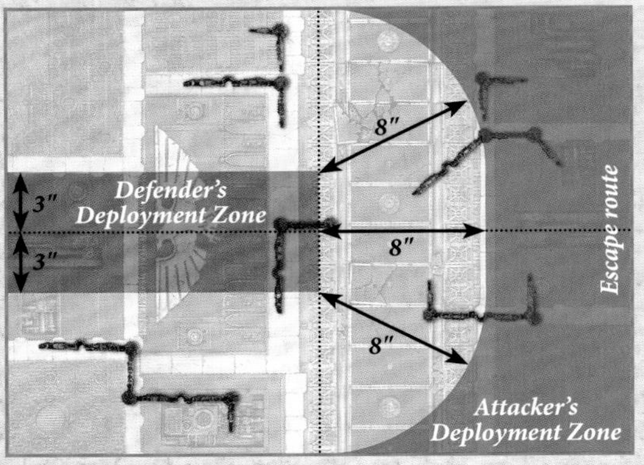

VICTORY CONDITIONS

If, at the end of the battle, more of the defender's models escaped (see below) than did not escape, the defender wins. Otherwise, the attacker wins.

ESCAPE

The defender can move their models off the edge of the battlefield labelled 'escape route' in the Movement phase, if that model's move is sufficient to take it wholly over the edge of the battlefield. A model that escapes this way is not considered to be out of action, but takes no further part in the mission.

RESOURCES

In a campaign game (see page 202) if the attacker wins the mission, the defender loses 1 Intelligence and 1 Territory. If the defender wins the mission, the attacker loses 1 Territory.

YOU'RE GOING NOWHERE

Attacker Tactic

Use this Tactic at the start of the Movement phase. Choose a model from your kill team that is not shaken. Enemy models within 1" of this model cannot Fall Back in this phase.

1 COMMAND POINT

SLINK AWAY

Defender Tactic

Use this Tactic at the start of the Movement phase. Choose a model from your kill team and roll a D6. On a 6, that model is removed from the battlefield and is treated as if it had escaped.

1 COMMAND POINT

Defender's Deployment Zone

Attacker's Deployment Zone

Escape route

3"
3"
8"
8"
8"

NARRATIVE PLAY MISSION
FEINT

By staging a suitably loud, brutal and spectacular attack, a kill team can cause enough disruption and mayhem to make a commander believe they face a much larger force. As they hurriedly reassign troops to where they believe they are needed, the real attack strikes at their most vulnerable spot.

THE KILL TEAMS

This is a mission for two players. Choose which player will be the attacker and which will be the defender (roll off if you can't agree – the winner decides). Each player chooses a Faction keyword, and the players reveal their choices at the same time. Then each player chooses a Battle-forged kill team (see page 62) that only includes models with the Faction keyword they chose.

THE BATTLEFIELD

Create the battlefield and set up terrain. An example of how you might do this is shown below. The players roll off, and the player that wins chooses which of the short edges of the battlefield their deployment zone is touching. Starting with the defender, the players then take it in turn to place an objective marker until each player has placed three objective markers. Each objective marker must be more than 5" from other objective markers and more than 5" from the edge of the battlefield.

SCOUTING PHASE

Resolve the Scouting phase as described on page 49.

DEPLOYMENT

The players roll off, and then alternate setting up models, starting with the player who lost the roll-off. A player's models must be set up wholly within their deployment zone. If a player runs out of models to set up, skip them. Continue setting up models until both players have set up their kill teams. Once the players have set up all their models, deployment ends and the first battle round begins.

BATTLE LENGTH

At the end of battle round 4, the attacker rolls a D6. The battle continues on a 3+, otherwise the battle ends. At the end of battle round 5, the attacker again rolls a D6. This time the battle continues on a 4+, otherwise the battle ends. The battle automatically ends at the end of battle round 6.

VICTORY CONDITIONS

At the end of the battle, the defender scores 2 victory points for each objective marker that is still on the battlefield (see the Cause Mayhem Tactic below). The attacker scores 1 victory point for each objective marker they have destroyed. In addition, the attacker scores 1 victory point if the enemy kill team is broken, and 1 victory point for each enemy specialist that is out of action at the end of the battle. The player with the most victory points is the winner. If the players have the same number of victory points, the defender wins.

RESOURCES

In a campaign game (see page 202) if the attacker wins the mission, the defender loses 1 Materiel and 1 Territory. If the defender wins the mission, the attacker loses 1 Territory.

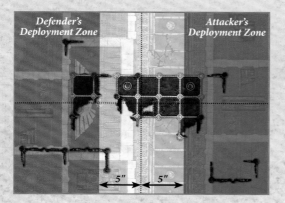

Defender's Deployment Zone   *Attacker's Deployment Zone*

5"   5"

CAUSE MAYHEM

Attacker Tactic

Use this Tactic at the end of a battle round. Choose an objective marker you control. You destroy that objective marker – remove it from the battlefield.

1 COMMAND POINT

REINFORCEMENTS INBOUND

Defender Tactic

Use this Tactic at the beginning of the Morale phase. You can subtract 1 from any Nerve tests you make in this phase.

1 COMMAND POINT

NARRATIVE PLAY MISSION
ASSASSINATE

An army without its commanders is helpless, a beast ready for the slaughter. Kill teams are often despatched with the intent of eliminating enemy leaders, thereby disrupting the war effort in that area so that rapid gains can be made.

THE KILL TEAMS

This is a mission for two players. Choose which player will be the attacker and which will be the defender (roll off if you can't agree – the winner decides). Each player chooses a Faction keyword, and the players reveal their choices at the same time. Then each player chooses a Battle-forged kill team (see page 62) that only includes models with the Faction keyword they chose.

THE BATTLEFIELD

Create the battlefield and set up terrain. An example of how you might do this is shown below. The players roll off, and the player that wins chooses which of the short edges of the battlefield their deployment zone is touching.

SCOUTING PHASE

Resolve the Scouting phase as described on page 49.

DEPLOYMENT

The players roll off, and then alternate setting up models, starting with the player who lost the roll-off. A player's models must be set up wholly within their deployment zone. In addition, the defender's Leader must be set up wholly within 5" of the centre of the defender's deployment zone. If a player runs out of models to set up, skip them. Continue setting up models until both players have set up their kill teams. Once the players have set up all their models, deployment ends and the first battle round begins.

BATTLE LENGTH

If the defender's Leader is taken out of action, the battle ends immediately. If not, at the end of battle round 4, the attacker rolls a D6. The battle continues on a 3+, otherwise the battle ends. If the battle doesn't end as described above, at the end of battle round 5, the attacker again rolls a D6. This time the battle continues on a 4+, otherwise the battle ends. The battle automatically ends at the end of battle round 6.

VICTORY CONDITIONS

If the attacker takes the defender's Leader out of action, the attacker is the winner. Otherwise, the defender wins.

RESOURCES

In a campaign game (see page 202) if the attacker wins the mission, the defender loses 1 Intelligence and 1 Morale. If the defender wins the mission, the attacker loses 1 Morale.

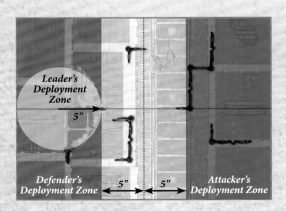

Leader's Deployment Zone

5"

Defender's Deployment Zone 5" 5" Attacker's Deployment Zone

CUT OFF THE HEAD

Attacker Tactic

Use this Tactic at the start of the Shooting phase or Fight phase. For the rest of the phase, you can re-roll wound rolls of 1 for attacks that target the enemy Leader.

1 COMMAND POINT

STAYING LOW

Defender Tactic

Use this Tactic at the start of the Shooting phase. For the rest of the phase, enemy models cannot target your Leader, unless your Leader is the closest enemy model that is visible to them.

2 COMMAND POINTS

MATCHED PLAY MISSION
SWEEP AND CLEAR

When securing territory, it is imperative that all enemy forces are driven out of it, lest lurking saboteurs strike at supposedly safe locations. Kill teams are often employed in this task, sweeping contested areas quickly and stealthily to eliminate any threats that might still be active in the area.

THE KILL TEAMS

This is a mission for two to four players. Each player chooses a Faction keyword, and the players reveal their choices at the same time. Then each player chooses a Battle-forged kill team (see page 62) that only includes models with the Faction keyword they chose.

THE BATTLEFIELD

Create the battlefield and set up terrain. Examples of how you might do this are shown below. Then set up four objective markers midway between the centre of the battlefield and the middle of a battlefield edge, as shown in the deployment maps below.

SCOUTING PHASE

Resolve the Scouting phase as described on page 49.

DEPLOYMENT

The players each roll 2D6. The highest scorer has the greatest strategic advantage in this mission, the next highest gets the second greatest advantage and so on. Any players who roll the same result roll their dice again to determine which of them has a greater advantage. The players then take it in turn, in the order of greatest to least advantage, to choose their deployment zone.

The players then take it in turn to deploy one model from their kill team, in the order of least to greatest advantage. Models must be set up wholly within their own deployment zone. Once all players have set up one model, they do so again in the same order, and so on. If a player runs out of models to set up, skip them. Once the players have set up all their models, deployment ends and the first battle round begins.

BATTLE LENGTH

The battle ends at the end of a battle round if there is only one unbroken kill team on the battlefield. Otherwise, at the end of battle round 4, the player with the greatest advantage rolls a D6. The battle continues on a 3+, otherwise the battle ends. If the battle doesn't end as described above, at the end of battle round 5, the player with the greatest advantage again rolls a D6. This time the battle continues on a 4+, otherwise the battle ends. The battle automatically ends at the end of battle round 6.

VICTORY CONDITIONS

If the battle ends because there is only one unbroken kill team on the battlefield, that kill team's player wins. Otherwise, each player scores 3 victory points for each objective marker that their kill team controls at the end of the battle and 1 victory point for each enemy model taken out of action by one of their model's attacks or psychic powers. The player with the most victory points is the winner. If there is a tie, whichever of those players had the lower Force (see page 19) is the winner. If there is still a tie, the tied players draw and any other players lose.

RESOURCES

In a campaign game (see page 202) the player(s) that lose the mission each lose 2 Territory. If players draw they do not lose Territory.

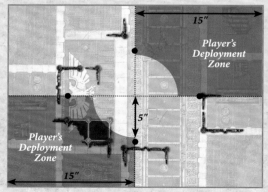

Two-player battlefield using one gameboard

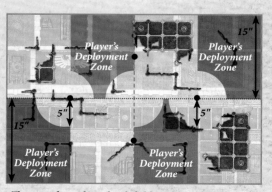

Three- to four-player battlefield using two gameboards

MATCHED PLAY MISSION
TAKE PRISONERS

Kill team operatives are often privy to sensitive information such as the locations of high-ranking personnel, hidden supply caches and secret routes through defensive lines. Rival kill teams may thus seek to seize their enemies alive, so that this vital intelligence can be extracted from them.

THE KILL TEAMS

This is a mission for two to four players. Each player chooses a Faction keyword, and the players reveal their choices at the same time. Then each player chooses a Battle-forged kill team (see page 62) that only includes models with the Faction keyword they chose.

THE BATTLEFIELD

Create the battlefield and set up terrain. Examples of how you might do this are shown below.

SCOUTING PHASE

Resolve the Scouting phase as described on page 49.

DEPLOYMENT

The players each roll 2D6. The highest scorer has the greatest strategic advantage in this mission, the next highest gets the second greatest advantage and so on. Any players who roll the same result roll their dice again to determine which of them has a greater advantage. The players then take it in turn, in the order of greatest to least advantage, to choose their deployment zone.

The players then take it in turn to deploy one model from their kill team, in the order of least to greatest advantage. Models must be set up wholly within their own deployment zone. Once all players have set up one model, they do so again in the same order, and so on. If a player runs out of models to set up, skip them. Once the players have set up all their models, deployment ends and the first battle round begins.

BATTLE LENGTH

At the end of battle round 4, the player with the greatest advantage rolls a D6. The battle continues on a 3+, otherwise the battle ends. At the end of battle round 5, the player with the greatest advantage again rolls a D6. This time the battle continues on a 4+, otherwise the battle ends. The battle automatically ends at the end of battle round 6.

VICTORY CONDITIONS

Each player scores 3 victory points for each enemy Leader that their kill team has captured (see below) and 1 victory point for each other enemy model that their kill team has captured. The player with the most victory points is the winner. If there is a tie, whichever of those players had the lower Force (see page 19) is the winner. If there is still a tie, the tied players draw and any other players lose.

Captured

An enemy model is captured by your kill team if it is taken out of action for whatever reason whilst it is within 1" of a model from your kill team (excluding shaken models) and there are no other enemy models (excluding shaken models) within 2" of your model. Enemy models that go out of action after the battle ends in a campaign game do not count. The enemy model is still considered to be out of action, and in a campaign game the model's player will make a Casualty roll for them as normal.

Resources

In a campaign game (see page 202) the player(s) that lose the mission each lose 1 Materiel and 1 Morale. If players draw they do not lose any resources.

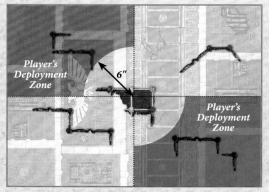

Two-player battlefield using one gameboard

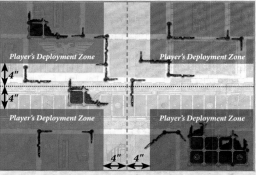

Three- to four-player battlefield using two gameboards

MATCHED PLAY MISSION
RECOVER INTELLIGENCE

Strategic intelligence is a weapon more deadly than any amount of plasma warheads or bolt rifles. It often falls to fast-moving, hard-hitting kill teams to seize the data-augurs, orbital uplinks and the like that contain such data and swiftly exload it so that their commanders can outmanoeuvre the enemy.

THE KILL TEAMS

This is a mission for two to four players. Each player chooses a Faction keyword, and the players reveal their choices at the same time. Then each player chooses a Battle-forged kill team (see page 62) that only includes models with the Faction keyword they chose.

THE BATTLEFIELD

Create the battlefield and set up terrain. Examples of how you might do this are shown below. Set up one objective marker in the centre of the battlefield, and then set four more up; each should be midway between the centre of the battlefield and a corner of the battlefield, as shown on the deployment maps below.

SCOUTING PHASE

Resolve the Scouting phase as described on page 49.

DEPLOYMENT

The players each roll 2D6. The highest scorer has the greatest strategic advantage in this mission, the next highest gets the second greatest advantage and so on. Any players who roll the same result roll their dice again to determine which of them has a greater advantage. The players then take it in turn, in the order of greatest to least advantage, to choose their deployment zone.

The players then take it in turn to deploy one model from their kill team, in the order of least to greatest advantage. Models must be set up wholly in their own deployment zone. Once all players have set up one model, they do so again in the same order, and so on. If

a player runs out of models to set up, skip them. Once the players have set up all their models, deployment ends and the first battle round begins.

BATTLE LENGTH

At the end of battle round 4, the player with the greatest advantage rolls a D6. The battle continues on a 3+, otherwise the battle ends. At the end of battle round 5, the player with the greatest advantage again rolls a D6. This time the battle continues on a 4+, otherwise the battle ends. The battle automatically ends at the end of battle round 6.

VICTORY CONDITIONS

Each player scores victory points for each objective marker their kill team controls at the end of each battle round (keep a score from battle round to battle round). Each player scores 1 victory point for controlling each of the objective markers closest to their deployment zone, 3 victory points if they control the objective marker in the centre of the battlefield, and 2 victory points for each other objective marker they control. The player with the most victory points is the winner. If there is a tie, whichever of those players had the lower Force (see page 19) is the winner. If there is still a tie, the tied players draw and any other players lose.

RESOURCES

In a campaign game (see page 202) the player(s) that lose the mission each lose 2 Intelligence. If players draw they do not lose Intelligence.

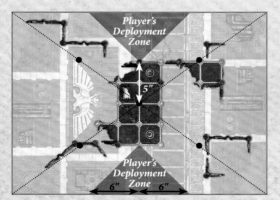

Two-player battlefield using one gameboard

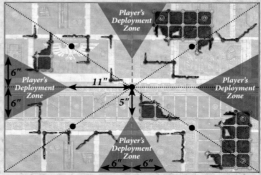

Three- to four-player battlefield using two gameboards

MATCHED PLAY MISSION
TERROR TACTICS

An enemy force whose nerve has failed them is little more than a gaggle of victims waiting to be slaughtered. Some commanders deploy kill teams on dedicated terror raids, their mission to spread as much panic and confusion as possible, scattering the foe and punching through their lines.

THE KILL TEAMS

This is a mission for two to four players. Each player chooses a Faction keyword, and the players reveal their choices at the same time. Then each player chooses a Battle-forged kill team (see page 62) that only includes models with the Faction keyword they chose.

THE BATTLEFIELD

Create the battlefield and set up terrain. An example of how you might do this is shown below.

SCOUTING PHASE

Resolve the Scouting phase as described on page 49.

DEPLOYMENT

The players each roll 2D6. The highest scorer has the greatest strategic advantage in this mission, the next highest gets the second greatest advantage and so on. Any players who roll the same result roll their dice again to determine which of them has a greater advantage. The players then take it in turn, in the order of greatest to least advantage, to choose their deployment zone.

The players then take it in turn to deploy one model from their kill team, in the order of least to greatest advantage. Models must be set up wholly within their own deployment zone. Once all players have set up one model, they do so again in the same order, and so on. If a player runs out of models to set up, skip them. Once the players have set up all their models, deployment ends and the first battle round begins.

BATTLE LENGTH

The battle ends at the end of a battle round if there is only one unbroken kill team on the battlefield.

Otherwise, at the end of battle round 4, the player with the greatest advantage must roll a D6. On a 3+, the game continues, otherwise the game is over. If the battle doesn't end as described above, at the end of battle round 5, the player with the greatest advantage must roll a D6. This time the game continues on a 4+, otherwise the game is over. The battle automatically ends at the end of battle round 6.

VICTORY CONDITIONS

If the battle ends because there is only one unbroken kill team on the battlefield, that kill team's player wins. Otherwise, each player scores 2 victory points for each of their models that have broken through enemy lines (see below), and 1 victory point for each enemy model taken out of action by one of their model's attacks or psychic powers. The player with the most victory points is the winner. If there is a tie, whichever of those players had the lower Force (see page 19) is the winner. If there is still a tie, the tied players draw and any other players lose.

WREAK HAVOC

Any player can move their models off the battlefield edge directly opposite their own deployment zone in the Movement phase, if that model's move is sufficient to take it wholly over that battlefield edge. A model that does so has broken through the enemy lines and takes no further part in the mission (it is not considered to be out of action).

RESOURCES

In a campaign game (see page 202) the player(s) that lose the mission each lose 2 Morale. If players draw they do not lose Morale.

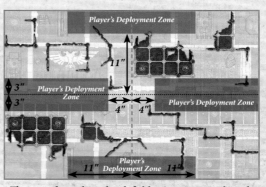

Two-player battlefield using one gameboard | Three- to four-player battlefield using two gameboards

KILL TEAMS

'Each of those valiant Players was
worth one hundred lesser warriors.
When they fought as one in
Cegorach's name, their might was
magnified still further, so that
none could stand against them.'

*- The Lay of the Harlequins' Blades,
from the Song of Decay and Rebirth*

CHOOSING A KILL TEAM

No two kill teams are alike – each is assembled to accomplish a specific vital mission, regardless of the odds or the enemy forces stacked against them, and each contains individuals of exceptional and unique talents that can mean the difference between defeat and victory.

The rules for choosing a kill team are different depending on what kind of game you want to play. The three ways to play Kill Team are described earlier in the book (see page 48). Whichever way you choose to play, you'll complete a datacard (see opposite) for each model in your kill team: this acts as a handy reminder for that model's characteristics, wargear and abilities during the game, and also lets you record details like flesh wounds suffered. For matched play (and narrative play, in some cases) you will also complete a command roster that lists all of the models available for you to choose a kill team from.

Open Play

Simply choose a kill team from the models available to you (using the datasheets included in this book and other Kill Team products), choose one of those models to be the kill team's Leader and fill in a datacard for each of your models. You can use any other of the rules on this page that you and your opponent(s) agree on.

Matched Play

For a matched play game, you need to create a command roster of up to twenty models available to you, all of which must share a Faction keyword. You'll find a blank command roster on page 206. Write the details of each of your models in the spaces provided. Once the mission has been determined, you then choose a Battle-forged kill team (see below) from the models on your command roster.

Battle-forged Kill Team

For your kill team to be Battle-forged, you must adhere to the following restrictions:

- Your kill team must consist of at least three models, and no more than twenty models.
- Your kill team must include one (and only one) Leader – see page 68.
- Your kill team can include up to three other specialists – see page 66.
- Your kill team cannot include more than the maximum of any particular model, as detailed on its datasheet.
- All models must share a Faction keyword – see page 18.
- Your kill team cannot cost more than 100 points. Each model and each of their pieces of wargear has an associated points cost, as detailed in the points section for each Faction. The total cost of your kill team in points is referred to as its 'Force'.

It's a good idea to work out your kill team on a piece of scrap paper first, as you may have to juggle the wargear and models to get as close as you want to the 100-point limit.

Narrative Play

If you want to play a narrative game, the mission may dictate how you choose your kill team, or you may decide to choose a kill team as for open play or matched play, making whatever adjustments you feel are necessary to create the best narrative experience.

In a Kill Team campaign, as described on pages 202-205, you use the command roster to keep track of all the operatives that you have used in your missions. You can choose kill teams from the models on the command roster, but you can also add new models to the roster as the campaign progresses. In addition, during a campaign battle you may wish to make notes on your command roster or datacards to record details such as which specialists have used a Tactic.

Forging a Narrative

We strongly encourage you to come up with some background for your team: their personalities, quirks, names and the like. Tables full of inspiration for this can be found in the Faction sections of this book. Some of these tables require you to roll a D10 – that is, a ten-sided dice. Some others use a D66. To roll a D66, simply roll two six-sided dice, one after the other – the first represents tens, and the second represents digits, giving you a result between 11 and 66.

Datacards

You need to record the details of each of the models in your kill team on datacards. You'll find a photocopiable page of blank datacards for this purpose on page 207. Each datacard has spaces for you to note down all of the most important pieces of information about a model. Each model in your kill team needs to have one of these datacards, and each datacard describes a single, specific model. The example datacard at the bottom of this page is for a Skitarii Ranger.

Command Roster

The command roster contains a summary of all of the models available to you. The example command roster below is for a player partway through a campaign.

COMMAND ROSTER

PLAYER NAME	Anne		RESOURCES		CURRENT KILL TEAM'S FORCE		96 POINTS
FACTION	Adeptus Mechanicus	INTELLIGENCE	8	CURRENT KILL TEAM'S NAME		Team Gamma-Zhul-881	
MISSION	Victory for Logic	MATERIEL	6				
BACKGROUND	Campaign Veterans	MORALE	8				
SQUAD QUIRK	Secretive	TERRITORY	8				

NAME	MODEL TYPE	WARGEAR	EXP	SPECIALISM/ABILITIES	DEMEANOUR	PTS
Dorox-0.4343	Vanguard Alpha	Arc pistol, power sword	2	Leader	Meticulously Observant	10
Sek-XXVII	Vanguard Gunner	Plasma caliver	2	Zealot	Binharic Piety	13
Ar-99	Skitarii Vanguard	Radium carbine	1	Scout	AP Ballistics	9
Kappic-Schoelendt-18.1	Skitarii Ranger	Galvanic rifle	2	Communications	Strategic Chorister	9
Mu-575	Skitarii Vanguard	Radium carbine	2			9
Actus-1111	Skitarii Vanguard	Radium carbine	2			9
Tov-66.75/mk98	Ranger Gunner	Arc rifle	1			10
Xixos-2918	Skitarii Ranger	Galvanic rifle	1			9
Decima-110	Skitarii Ranger	Galvanic rifle	1			9
Gryphonne-Reductus-089	Skitarii Ranger	Galvanic rifle	1			9

KAPPIC-SCHOELENDT-18.1

NAME								9 POINTS	
Skitarii Ranger	M	WS	BS	S	T	W	A	Ld	Sv
	6"	4+	3+	3	3	1	1	6	4+

WEAPON	RANGE	TYPE	S	AP	D	ABILITIES
Galvanic rifle	30"	Rapid Fire 1	4	0	1	Each time you make a wound roll of 6+ for this weapon, that hit is resolved with an AP of -1.

ABILITIES.
Canticles of the Omnissiah, Bionics

SPECIALISM.
Comms – Scanner

DEMEANOUR.
Strategic Chorister

EXPERIENCE
☑ ☑ ☐ ☐ ☐ ☐ ☐ ☐ ☐ ☐ ☐

FLESH WOUNDS ☐ ☐ ☐   **CONVALESCENCE** ☐   **NEW RECRUIT** ☐

COMMAND POINTS AND TACTICS

Having a plan is all very well, but any kill team worthy of the name must be able to adapt to the changing circumstances of their mission – reacting in a split second to a new threat or directive, utilising special equipment or ammunition, or simply digging deep to surpass their mortal limits.

When you choose a Battle-forged kill team, you gain access to Command Points. These can be spent to utilise Tactics, each of which represents a tactical asset available to your kill team.

All Battle-forged kill teams generate 1 Command Point at the beginning of each battle round. In addition, at the start of the first battle round your kill team generates 1 additional Command Point for each 10 points difference between your kill team's Force and that of the kill team with the highest Force (e.g. if your kill team's Force was 19 points lower than that of the kill team with the highest Force, it would generate 1 additional Command Point. If it was 20 points lower, it would generate 2 additional Command Points). Kill teams may have other ways of generating Command Points in addition to this. Unused Command Points can be carried over to subsequent battle rounds until they are spent.

You can spend Command Points to use a Tactic during a battle. Each time you use a Tactic, reduce your Command Points total by the appropriate amount. If you do not have enough Command Points for a specific Tactic, you cannot use it. Unless otherwise stated, you can use the same Tactic multiple times during the

course of a battle, but only once in any given phase. Note that the beginning and end of each battle round are not phases, so you may be able to use certain Tactics multiple times at these points.

The different Tactics available to players depend on the mission they are playing. Players can always use the six Tactics presented on the opposite page. In addition, each specialism has its own Tactics, presented in the following section, each Faction has their own unique Tactics, presented in the Faction sections of this book, and some missions, killzones and expansions may introduce additional Tactics to your battles.

If you are playing an open play or narrative play game, you may choose to use the Command Point rules – simply discuss this with your opponent(s) before the game. Note that some Kill Team open play and narrative missions may include Tactics – it is best to use the Command Point rules in these games!

DECISIVE MOVE

Tactic

Use this Tactic at the start of the Movement phase. Pick a model from your kill team and make a move with it before any other models (including an Advance move, Fall Back move or charge attempt if you wish). If another player uses this Tactic, roll off: the winner goes first.

1 COMMAND POINT

DECISIVE SHOT

Tactic

Use this Tactic at the start of the Shooting phase. Pick a model from your kill team that is eligible to shoot and shoot with it before any other models. If another player uses this Tactic, roll off: the winner goes first.

2 COMMAND POINTS

TACTICAL RE-ROLL

Tactic

Re-roll a single Advance roll, charge roll, Psychic test, Deny the Witch test, hit roll, wound roll, saving throw, Injury roll or Nerve test.

1 COMMAND POINT

DECISIVE STRIKE

Tactic

Use this Tactic at the start of the Fight phase. Pick a model from your kill team that is eligible to fight and fight with it before any other models. If another player uses this Tactic, roll off: the winner goes first.

2 COMMAND POINTS

INSANE BRAVERY

Tactic

Use this Tactic before taking any Nerve tests in the Morale phase. You can automatically pass a single Nerve test for a model from your kill team.

1 COMMAND POINT

GRITTED TEETH

Tactic

Use this Tactic when you choose a model with one or more flesh wounds to shoot in the Shooting phase or fight in the Fight phase. Until the end of the phase, this model's attacks do not suffer any penalty to their hit rolls from this model's flesh wound(s).

1 COMMAND POINT

SPECIALISTS

Each kill team is led by a hard-bitten warrior – a veteran of countless conflicts trusted with command of a vital mission. They are supported by specialists – fighters hand-picked for the mission that are a cut above the rest in their bravery, tenacity or skill.

CHOOSING SPECIALISTS

Experienced warriors are represented in Kill Team with rules for specialisms, which reward you for taking specialists on missions by giving you access to their special abilities and Tactics.

Each model's datasheet tells you which specialisms can be taken by that model. When you add a model to your command roster, you can choose one specialism for it from those listed on its datasheet. When you choose a specialism for a model, note that down on its datacard. You cannot change it later.

Some models can have the Leader specialism. You must include one model with this specialism in your kill team, and this model is your kill team's Leader.

For a Battle-forged kill team, you can include up to three other models with specialisms, aside from your Leader. Each model's specialism must be unique – you cannot have two models with the same specialism in your kill team. Note that you may have more than one of any kind of specialist (including Leaders) on your command roster.

ABILITIES

Each specialist has one or more abilities, depending on how experienced they are. These abilities are set out in an 'ability tree' on that specialism's page. A specialist starts at Level 1, and has the ability shown in the band for that level. In a campaign, specialists gain experience and can advance up to Level 4 (see page 204).

When a specialist advances to Level 2, choose one of the abilities shown in the Level 2 band and make a note of this on their datacard. Be sure to choose carefully, as this will have a bearing on which ability you can choose at Level 3. The specialist gains this ability in addition to the ability gained at Level 1.

When a specialist advances to Level 3, choose one of the abilities shown in the Level 3 band that are connected to the ability you chose at Level 2 and make a note of it on the model's datacard as above – note that you cannot choose abilities connected to the other Level 2 ability.

When a specialist advances to Level 4, you can choose any ability from the ability tree that you have not already chosen for them. They gain this ability in addition to those they already have – make a note of this on their datacard. A specialist cannot advance beyond Level 4.

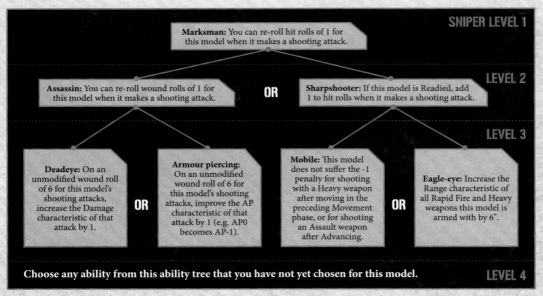

Here is an example of an ability tree – that of Sniper specialists. A Sniper specialist always has the Marksman ability. When a Sniper advances to Level 2, their player chooses whether they gain the Assassin or Sharpshooter ability.

TACTICS

If you have a specialist in your kill team, and they are not currently shaken or out of action, you have access to Tactics that are specific to that model's specialism. Each of these Tactics has a level: the specialist must be that level or higher for you to be able to use that Tactic.

CAREFUL AIM

Level 1 Sniper Tactic

Use this Tactic when you choose a Sniper specialist from your kill team to shoot in the Shooting phase. You can add 1 to hit rolls for that model until the end of the phase.

1 COMMAND POINT

You can use this specialist Tactic if you have a Sniper in your kill team who is not shaken or out of action.

WORTH THEIR WEIGHT

Specialists bring valuable new abilities and Tactics to your kill team. In a Battle-forged kill team, these abilities carry an increased cost for that model, as shown in this table:

Specialist	Cost
Level 1	+0 points
Level 2	+4 points
Level 3	+8 points
Level 4	+12 points

Note that, in a normal matched play game, you can only include Level 1 specialists in your kill team. The points provided for Level 2-4 specialists allow players to choose Battle-forged kill teams including these hard-bitten veterans in Kill Team campaigns.

LEADER SPECIALISTS

A kill team's Leader is its brain and its heart both. Typically the most experienced warrior in the team, the Leader has ultimate responsibility for his warriors' actions on the battlefield, and the success or failure of their mission. With crisp, concise orders or bellowed roars, the Leader inspires courage or terror in his warriors – whatever they require to keep them in the fight and drive them on to overcome their foes. Nor are Leaders simple figureheads. Most are exceptional combatants who can go blade to blade with the finest warriors amongst the enemy ranks. With unparalleled access to some of their forces' most powerful weapons and wargear, these individuals have the power to single-handedly cut a path to victory.

FIRE ON MY TARGET

Level 2 Leader Tactic

Use this Tactic when you pick a Leader of Level 2 or higher from your kill team to shoot in the Shooting phase. Choose another friendly model within 3" of them that is eligible to shoot. You can make a shooting attack with each of these models, in an order of your choice, before the next player's turn.

1 COMMAND POINT

LEAD BY EXAMPLE

Level 1 Leader Tactic

Use this Tactic when you pick a Leader from your kill team to fight in the Fight phase. Choose another friendly model within 3" of them that is eligible to fight. You can fight with each of these models, in an order of your choice, before the next player's turn.

1 COMMAND POINT

FORCE OF WILL

Level 3 Leader Tactic

Use this Tactic at the start of the battle round, if a Leader of Level 3 or higher from your kill team is on the battlefield and not shaken. In this battle round, your kill team does not suffer the penalty for being broken.

1 COMMAND POINT

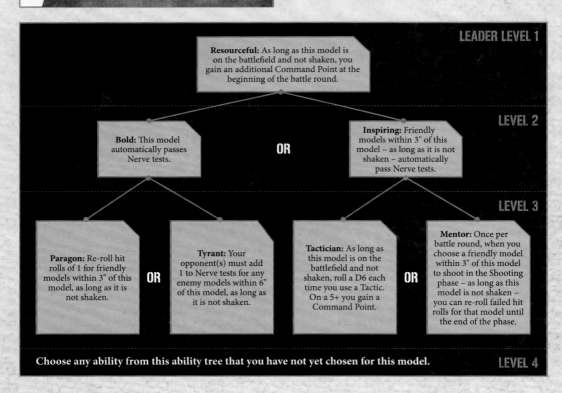

LEADER LEVEL 1

Resourceful: As long as this model is on the battlefield and not shaken, you gain an additional Command Point at the beginning of the battle round.

LEVEL 2

Bold: This model automatically passes Nerve tests.

OR

Inspiring: Friendly models within 3" of this model – as long as it is not shaken – automatically pass Nerve tests.

LEVEL 3

Paragon: Re-roll hit rolls of 1 for friendly models within 3" of this model, as long as it is not shaken.

OR

Tyrant: Your opponent(s) must add 1 to Nerve tests for any enemy models within 6" of this model, as long as it is not shaken.

Tactician: As long as this model is on the battlefield and not shaken, roll a D6 each time you use a Tactic. On a 5+ you gain a Command Point.

OR

Mentor: Once per battle round, when you choose a friendly model within 3" of this model to shoot in the Shooting phase – as long as this model is not shaken – you can re-roll failed hit rolls for that model until the end of the phase.

Choose any ability from this ability tree that you have not yet chosen for this model.

LEVEL 4

COMBAT SPECIALISTS

Some warriors excel in the close-quarters cut and thrust of battle. Whether sublimely skilled bladesmen who fight with absolute composure, berserk savages who live to hack their victims limb from limb, or calculating murderers who know every dirty trick in the book, such warriors are an incredible asset to their comrades. Combat specialists are ideal for leading headlong charges into the heart of the foe, or for rushing to intercept and put down enemies that have broken through their own lines. They swiftly and quietly eliminate enemy sentries, charge down ranged combatants and butcher them up close, and often strike the final blow to break the enemy's nerve altogether.

DEFENSIVE FIGHTER

Level 2 Combat Tactic

Use this Tactic at the start of the Fight phase. Pick a Combat specialist of Level 2 or higher from your kill team. Until the end of the phase, you must subtract 2 from that model's Attacks characteristic (to a minimum of 1), but your opponent(s) must re-roll successful hit rolls made against that model.

1 COMMAND POINT

UP AND AT 'EM!

Level 1 Combat Tactic

Use this Tactic in the Fight phase, after attacking with a model from your kill team. Pick a Combat specialist from your kill team that has not yet attacked this phase: you can immediately fight with them.

1 COMMAND POINT

DEADLY CHARGE

Level 3 Combat Tactic

Use this Tactic when a Combat specialist of Level 3 or higher from your kill team finishes a charge move within 1" of an enemy model. Roll a D6; on a 5+ that enemy model suffers 1 mortal wound.

1 COMMAND POINT

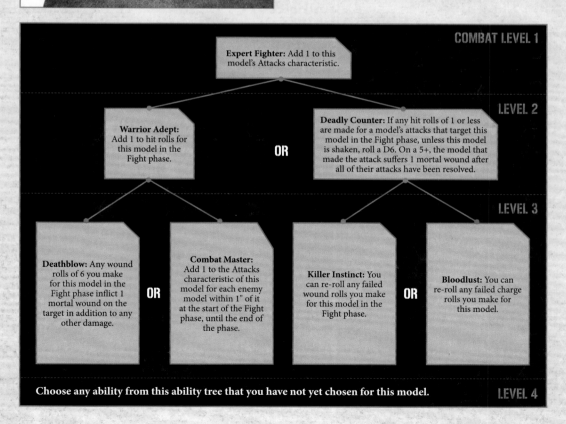

COMBAT LEVEL 1

Expert Fighter: Add 1 to this model's Attacks characteristic.

LEVEL 2

Warrior Adept: Add 1 to hit rolls for this model in the Fight phase.

OR

Deadly Counter: If any hit rolls of 1 or less are made for a model's attacks that target this model in the Fight phase, unless this model is shaken, roll a D6. On a 5+, the model that made the attack suffers 1 mortal wound after all of their attacks have been resolved.

LEVEL 3

Deathblow: Any wound rolls of 6 you make for this model in the Fight phase inflict 1 mortal wound on the target in addition to any other damage.

OR

Combat Master: Add 1 to the Attacks characteristic of this model for each enemy model within 1" of it at the start of the Fight phase, until the end of the phase.

Killer Instinct: You can re-roll any failed wound rolls you make for this model in the Fight phase.

OR

Bloodlust: You can re-roll any failed charge rolls you make for this model.

Choose any ability from this ability tree that you have not yet chosen for this model. **LEVEL 4**

COMMS SPECIALISTS

Some kill teams include a warrior whose area of specialisation is signalling and coordination. Be it an Imperial vox operator, an Ork Mek with a penchant for sowing confusion, or even a Tyranid node-beast capable of sending out powerful synaptic pulses, these warriors can prove potent battlefield assets. Providing their comrades with an eagle-eye view of the battlefield, Comms specialists support and enhance the efforts of the warriors around them. Some relay a constant stream of orders from high command, or beam targeting data directly to their allies, while others jam the enemy's communications and leave them in disarray.

ROUSING TRANSMISSION

Level 1 Comms Tactic

Use this Tactic in the Morale phase before taking any Nerve tests. Until the end of the phase you can subtract 1 from Nerve tests for models from your kill team as though the Comms specialist was within 2" of them.

1 COMMAND POINT

SCANNER UPLINK

Level 2 Comms Tactic

Use this Tactic when you pick a model from your kill team that is within 6" of a friendly Comms specialist of Level 2 or higher to shoot in the Shooting phase. That model can target an enemy model that is not visible to them. If they do so, a 6 is required for a successful hit roll irrespective of the model's Ballistic Skill or any other modifiers, even if that weapon would normally hit automatically. The target is treated as obscured.

2 COMMAND POINTS

NEW INTELLIGENCE

Level 3 Comms Tactic

Use this Tactic at the end of the Movement phase. Pick a model from your kill team within 12" of a friendly Comms specialist of Level 3 or higher. Ready that model.

1 COMMAND POINT

COMMS LEVEL 1

Scanner: Once per Shooting phase, when you pick a model from your kill team to shoot that is within 6" of this model, if this model is not shaken, you can add 1 to hit rolls for that model in this phase.

LEVEL 2

Expert: Roll a D6 at the start of each battle round if this model is not shaken. On a 5+, you gain 1 additional Command Point. This additional Command Point is lost at the end of the battle round if not used.

OR

Static Screech: Once per battle at the start of the Fight phase, if this model is not shaken, subtract 1 from hit rolls for enemy models that make attacks while they are within 6" of this model until the end of the phase.

LEVEL 3

Vox Ghost: Subtract 1 from the Leadership characteristic of enemy models while this model is on the battlefield, as long as it is not shaken.

OR

Command Relay: Roll a D6 each time you use a Tactic while this model is on the battlefield and not shaken. On a 6 the Command Points spent on that Tactic are immediately refunded.

Triangulator: Once per Shooting phase, when you pick a model from your kill team to shoot a Heavy weapon, if this model is not shaken, you can re-roll the dice when determining the number of attacks that model can make.

OR

Vox Hacker: After each battle in which this model was in your kill team, if this model is not in Convalescence (pg 204) or dead, roll a D6. On a 5+ you gain 1 Intelligence.

Choose any ability from this ability tree that you have not yet chosen for this model.

LEVEL 4

DEMOLITIONS SPECIALISTS

There are those warriors for whom the rush of gunfire or bladework simply is not enough, and whose eyes take on a dangerous glint at the mention of high explosives. Such Demolitions specialists excel in the deployment of bombs, grenades and other pyrotechnic munitions, and on a good day they can swiftly be responsible for the explosive demise of swathes of the foe. Fireballs billow to the skies and sundered corpses tumble through the air as the Demolitions specialists ply their lethal trade, and whether they are using carefully laid booby traps, explosive launchers or roaring flamethrowers, Demolitions specialists are terrifying warriors to face.

LUCKY ESCAPE

Level 2 Demolitions Tactic

Use this Tactic at the start of the Shooting phase. Pick a Demolitions specialist of Level 2 or higher from your kill team. Roll a D6 each time that model loses a wound in this phase; on a 5+ that wound is not lost.

1 COMMAND POINT

CUSTOM AMMO

Level 1 Demolitions Tactic

Use this Tactic when you pick a Demolitions specialist from your kill team to shoot in the Shooting phase. You can add 1 to wound rolls for that model's ranged weapons in this phase.

1 COMMAND POINT

HIGH EXPLOSIVE

Level 3 Demolitions Tactic

Use this Tactic when you pick a Demolitions specialist of Level 3 or higher from your kill team to shoot in the Shooting phase. In this Shooting phase, they can only shoot a single weapon, and that weapon can only fire 1 shot (even if it would normally fire more). However, that weapon's Damage characteristic is increased by 2. You cannot use this Tactic in the same battle round as the Custom Ammo Tactic.

1 COMMAND POINT

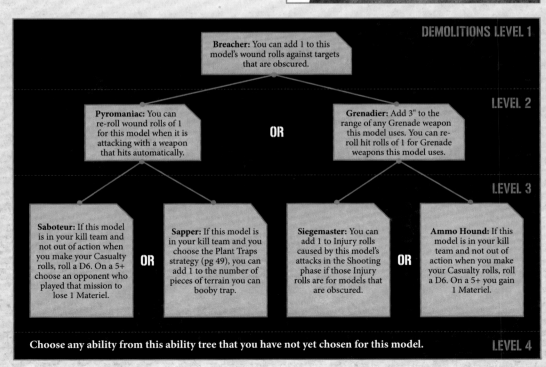

DEMOLITIONS LEVEL 1

Breacher: You can add 1 to this model's wound rolls against targets that are obscured.

LEVEL 2

Pyromaniac: You can re-roll wound rolls of 1 for this model when it is attacking with a weapon that hits automatically.

OR

Grenadier: Add 3" to the range of any Grenade weapon this model uses. You can re-roll hit rolls of 1 for Grenade weapons this model uses.

LEVEL 3

Saboteur: If this model is in your kill team and not out of action when you make your Casualty rolls, roll a D6. On a 5+ choose an opponent who played that mission to lose 1 Materiel.

OR

Sapper: If this model is in your kill team and you choose the Plant Traps strategy (pg 49), you can add 1 to the number of pieces of terrain you can booby trap.

Siegemaster: You can add 1 to Injury rolls caused by this model's attacks in the Shooting phase if those Injury rolls are for models that are obscured.

OR

Ammo Hound: If this model is in your kill team and not out of action when you make your Casualty rolls, roll a D6. On a 5+ you gain 1 Materiel.

Choose any ability from this ability tree that you have not yet chosen for this model.

LEVEL 4

HEAVY SPECIALISTS

In a ferocious firefight between small, elite bands of infantry, a doughty warrior toting a suitably heavy weapon can be every bit as devastating as a battle tank or gun emplacement would in a larger battle. Feet planted, heavy weapon kicking and roaring, the Heavy specialist directs relentless hails of fire into the enemy. Those caught in the open are blown apart, reduced to bloody mist and spinning body parts in the blink of an eye. Even those ducked down in cover can only fire blindly back and scream in terror as their temporary haven is rapidly blasted apart by round after explosive round. Thus does the Heavy specialist act as a lynchpin for their kill team, suppressing and slaughtering the foe while their allies advance.

OVERWHELMING FIREPOWER

Level 2 Heavy Tactic

Use this Tactic when you pick a Heavy specialist of Level 2 or higher from your kill team to shoot in the Shooting phase. That model can shoot twice in this Shooting phase; after they have shot a first time, immediately shoot with them again. You cannot use this Tactic in the same battle round as the More Bullets Tactic.

2 COMMAND POINTS

MORE BULLETS

Level 1 Heavy Tactic

Use this Tactic when you pick a Heavy specialist from your kill team to shoot in the Shooting phase. You can add 1 to the number of shots fired by that model's ranged weapons, with the exception of weapons that would otherwise fire 1 shot (e.g. an Assault 2 weapon would fire 3 shots, but a Rapid Fire 1 weapon at long range would fire 1 shot) in this Shooting phase.

1 COMMAND POINT

UNKILLABLE

Level 3 Heavy Tactic

Use this Tactic at the start of your turn in the Morale phase. Pick a Heavy specialist of Level 3 or higher from your kill team that has one or more flesh wounds. Remove one of that model's flesh wounds.

1 COMMAND POINT

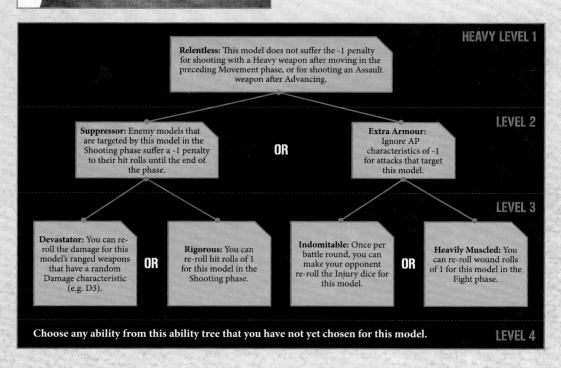

HEAVY LEVEL 1

Relentless: This model does not suffer the -1 penalty for shooting with a Heavy weapon after moving in the preceding Movement phase, or for shooting an Assault weapon after Advancing.

LEVEL 2

Suppressor: Enemy models that are targeted by this model in the Shooting phase suffer a -1 penalty to their hit rolls until the end of the phase.

OR

Extra Armour: Ignore AP characteristics of -1 for attacks that target this model.

LEVEL 3

Devastator: You can re-roll the damage for this model's ranged weapons that have a random Damage characteristic (e.g. D3).

OR

Rigorous: You can re-roll hit rolls of 1 for this model in the Shooting phase.

Indomitable: Once per battle round, you can make your opponent re-roll the Injury dice for this model.

OR

Heavily Muscled: You can re-roll wound rolls of 1 for this model in the Fight phase.

Choose any ability from this ability tree that you have not yet chosen for this model.

LEVEL 4

MEDIC SPECIALISTS

When fighting deep behind enemy lines, squads of warriors must be as self-sufficient as possible, for they have little – if any – hope of receiving support or aid. In such circumstances, a Medic specialist can prove invaluable. Whether they be a highly trained field surgeon, a leering flesh-stitcher or something altogether stranger, Medic specialists concentrate on keeping their comrades in the fight and allowing them to push through terrible injuries to claim victory regardless. Such warriors are instrumental in ensuring the long-term durability of their squad, repairing physical hurts that would otherwise leave permanent injuries, or even fitting whole new augmetics where necessary. Of course, their skills can also be turned to offensive purposes…

PAINKILLER

Level 2 Medic Tactic

Use this Tactic at the end of the Movement phase. Pick a model from your kill team within 2" of a friendly Medic specialist of Level 2 or higher that is not shaken. Add 2 to that model's Toughness characteristic until the end of the battle round.

2 COMMAND POINTS

EMERGENCY RESUSCITATION

Level 3 Medic Tactic

Use this Tactic when a Medic specialist of Level 3 or higher from your kill team that is not shaken is within 2" of another model from your kill team that suffers an Out of Action Injury roll result. That model suffers a Flesh Wound result instead.

2 COMMAND POINTS

STIMM-SHOT

Level 1 Medic Tactic

Use this Tactic at the start of the Movement phase. Pick a model from your kill team within 2" of a friendly Medic specialist that is not shaken. You can add 1 to Advance rolls and charge rolls for that model, and add 1 to that model's Attacks characteristic until the end of the battle round.

1 COMMAND POINT

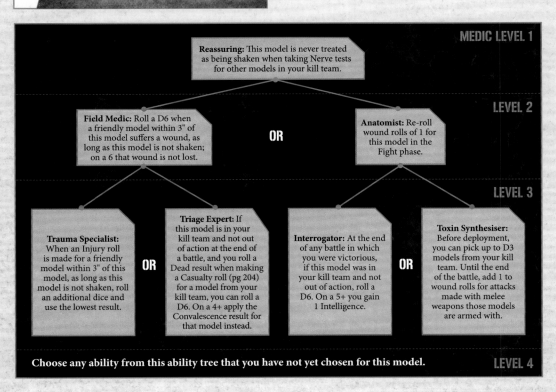

MEDIC LEVEL 1

Reassuring: This model is never treated as being shaken when taking Nerve tests for other models in your kill team.

LEVEL 2

Field Medic: Roll a D6 when a friendly model within 3" of this model suffers a wound, as long as this model is not shaken; on a 6 that wound is not lost.

OR

Anatomist: Re-roll wound rolls of 1 for this model in the Fight phase.

LEVEL 3

Trauma Specialist: When an Injury roll is made for a friendly model within 3" of this model, as long as this model is not shaken, roll an additional dice and use the lowest result.

OR

Triage Expert: If this model is in your kill team and not out of action at the end of a battle, and you roll a Dead result when making a Casualty roll (pg 204) for a model from your kill team, you can roll a D6. On a 4+ apply the Convalescence result for that model instead.

Interrogator: At the end of any battle in which you were victorious, if this model was in your kill team and not out of action, roll a D6. On a 5+ you gain 1 Intelligence.

OR

Toxin Synthesiser: Before deployment, you can pick up to D3 models from your kill team. Until the end of the battle, add 1 to wound rolls for attacks made with melee weapons those models are armed with.

Choose any ability from this ability tree that you have not yet chosen for this model.

LEVEL 4

SCOUT SPECIALISTS

In fast-paced, squad-on-squad combat, information is key. Knowing the enemy's disposition, feeling out their movements, spotting traps and ambushes or locating vital objectives to be eliminated: all of these are the role of the Scout specialist. Ghosting ahead of their comrades, these elite warriors are expert at tracking the enemy to their lair, observing without being observed, and scavenging crucial munitions and wargear that can be turned against their former owners. Many Scout specialists are skilled in evading the enemy's fire, utilising camouflage or natural stealth and agility to defend themselves as effectively as any suit of armour might. Others spread sedition and confusion, ensuring the enemy's plans fall apart even as battle begins.

QUICK MARCH

Level 1 Scout Tactic

Use this Tactic when you pick a Scout specialist from your kill team to move in the Movement phase. You can either increase the model's Move characteristic by 2" this phase or you can re-roll the dice when this model Advances in this phase.

1 COMMAND POINT

MARKED POSITIONS

Level 2 Scout Tactic

Use this Tactic at the start of the Shooting phase. Pick an enemy model within 6" of a Scout specialist of Level 2 or higher from your kill team that is not shaken. You can re-roll hit rolls of 1 for shooting attacks made by models in your kill team that target that enemy model until the end of the phase.

1 COMMAND POINT

MOVE UNSEEN

Level 3 Scout Tactic

Use this Tactic at the start of your turn in the Movement phase. Pick a Scout specialist of Level 3 or higher from your kill team that is not shaken. Remove that model from the battlefield and set it up again anywhere within 18" of its previous position and more than 3" from any enemy models. It is considered to have Advanced.

2 COMMAND POINTS

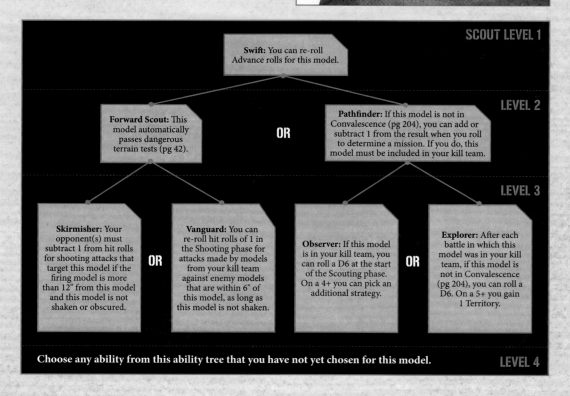

SCOUT LEVEL 1

Swift: You can re-roll Advance rolls for this model.

LEVEL 2

Forward Scout: This model automatically passes dangerous terrain tests (pg 42).

OR

Pathfinder: If this model is not in Convalescence (pg 204), you can add or subtract 1 from the result when you roll to determine a mission. If you do, this model must be included in your kill team.

LEVEL 3

Skirmisher: Your opponent(s) must subtract 1 from hit rolls for shooting attacks that target this model if the firing model is more than 12" from this model and this model is not shaken or obscured.

OR

Vanguard: You can re-roll hit rolls of 1 in the Shooting phase for attacks made by models from your kill team against enemy models that are within 6" of this model, as long as this model is not shaken.

Observer: If this model is in your kill team, you can roll a D6 at the start of the Scouting phase. On a 4+ you can pick an additional strategy.

OR

Explorer: After each battle in which this model was in your kill team, if this model is not in Convalescence (pg 204), you can roll a D6. On a 5+ you gain 1 Territory.

Choose any ability from this ability tree that you have not yet chosen for this model.

LEVEL 4

SNIPER SPECIALISTS

Many kill teams include operatives who excel in the field of ranged combat. More than merely fine shots, these warriors are so skilled that they can pull off feats of marksmanship that appear nigh-on supernatural. Like predators of the battlefield they hunt their targets, lying concealed amidst the shadows for hours, even days at a time. Only when the moment is perfect do they exhale, squeeze the trigger, and place another perfect, killing shot. Of course, every sniper has their own areas of exceptional talent, from shooting with lethal accuracy while on the move, to finding weak spots in enemy armour or slaying targets far beyond what should be extreme range. Whatever their particular skill, all Snipers bring death from afar.

CAREFUL AIM

Level 1 Sniper Tactic

Use this Tactic when you choose a Sniper specialist from your kill team to shoot in the Shooting phase. You can add 1 to hit rolls for that model until the end of the phase.

1 COMMAND POINT

HEADSHOT

Level 2 Sniper Tactic

Use this Tactic when you pick a Sniper specialist of Level 2 or higher from your kill team to shoot in the Shooting phase. Until the end of the phase, when that model shoots at obscured targets they are considered not to be obscured.

1 COMMAND POINT

QUICK SHOT

Level 3 Sniper Tactic

Use this Tactic when you pick a Sniper specialist of Level 3 or higher from your kill team to shoot in the Shooting phase. In this Shooting phase, double the number of shots fired by that model's ranged weapons (e.g. an Assault 2 weapon would fire 4 shots), but subtract 1 from hit rolls for that model. You cannot use this Tactic in the same battle round as the Headshot Tactic.

1 COMMAND POINT

SNIPER LEVEL 1

Marksman: You can re-roll hit rolls of 1 for this model when it makes a shooting attack.

LEVEL 2

Assassin: You can re-roll wound rolls of 1 for this model when it makes a shooting attack.

OR

Sharpshooter: If this model is Readied, add 1 to hit rolls when it makes a shooting attack.

LEVEL 3

Deadeye: On an unmodified wound roll of 6 for this model's shooting attacks, increase the Damage characteristic of that attack by 1.

OR

Armour Piercing: On an unmodified wound roll of 6 for this model's shooting attacks, improve the AP characteristic of that attack by 1 (e.g. AP0 becomes AP-1).

Mobile: This model does not suffer the -1 penalty for shooting with a Heavy weapon after moving in the preceding Movement phase, or for shooting an Assault weapon after Advancing.

OR

Eagle-eye: Increase the Range characteristic of all Rapid Fire and Heavy weapons this model is armed with by 6".

Choose any ability from this ability tree that you have not yet chosen for this model.

LEVEL 4

VETERAN SPECIALISTS

Some kill teams are lucky enough to include a warrior who has fought through dozens of war zones. These Veteran specialists have reaped vast tallies of battlefield experience, and are now able to share this bounty of martial wisdom with their comrades. The Veterans' commanders know that they can be relied upon, absolutely and without exception, to do their duty no matter the circumstances. Veterans know when best to strike at the foe, and exactly where to hit them. They have seen the worst that the galaxy has to offer and fought on regardless, their nerves steely and their hands steady. They know all the most important tricks to survival, and in some cases even personalise and adapt their weapons to be even more lethal.

ADAPTIVE TACTICS

Level 1 Veteran Tactic

Use this Tactic at the start of the first battle round, but before the Initiative phase. Pick a Veteran specialist from your kill team. They can make a normal move or Advance. You can only use this Tactic once per battle.

1 COMMAND POINT

WELL DRILLED

Level 2 Veteran Tactic

Use this Tactic at the start of your turn in the Shooting phase. Pick a Veteran specialist of Level 2 or higher from your kill team. Ready them unless they are within 1" of an enemy. They can shoot in that phase as if they had not moved in the Movement phase.

2 COMMAND POINTS

ROLL WITH THE HITS

Level 3 Veteran Tactic

Use this Tactic during your opponent's turn in the Shooting phase. Pick a Veteran specialist of Level 3 or higher from your kill team that has been Injured, before your opponent makes the Injury roll. Your opponent can only roll a single dice for that Injury roll.

1 COMMAND POINT

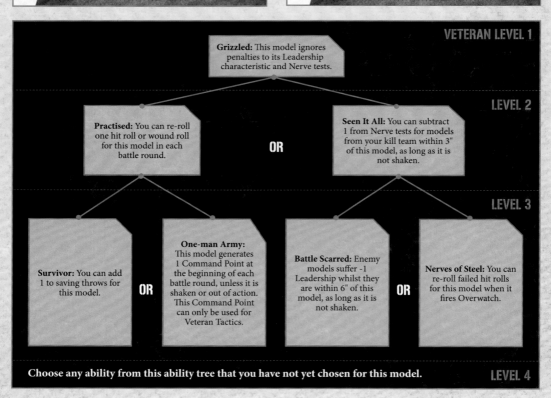

VETERAN LEVEL 1

Grizzled: This model ignores penalties to its Leadership characteristic and Nerve tests.

LEVEL 2

Practised: You can re-roll one hit roll or wound roll for this model in each battle round.

OR

Seen It All: You can subtract 1 from Nerve tests for models from your kill team within 3" of this model, as long as it is not shaken.

LEVEL 3

Survivor: You can add 1 to saving throws for this model.

OR

One-man Army: This model generates 1 Command Point at the beginning of each battle round, unless it is shaken or out of action. This Command Point can only be used for Veteran Tactics.

Battle Scarred: Enemy models suffer -1 Leadership whilst they are within 6" of this model, as long as it is not shaken.

OR

Nerves of Steel: You can re-roll failed hit rolls for this model when it fires Overwatch.

Choose any ability from this ability tree that you have not yet chosen for this model.

LEVEL 4

ZEALOT SPECIALISTS

It is a dark galaxy, and sometimes all the skill and equipment a warrior can possess is simply no match for sheer, bloody-minded faith. Zealots are driven by an absolute belief in their chosen deity or particular world view, their eyes full of fire and their conviction plain for all to see as they storm into battle. It is their deranged fanaticism that allows them to shrug off wounds that ought to have killed them several times over, lends their arm inhuman strength and allows them to inspire their comrades to ever greater feats in battle. In extremis, such warriors think nothing of making the ultimate sacrifice, gladly martyring themselves for the glory of their deity or vindication of their creed.

MARTYR

Level 2 Zealot Tactic

Use this Tactic when a Zealot specialist of Level 2 or higher from your kill team loses their last wound, before any player rolls on the Injury table. You may immediately shoot with one of its weapons as if it were the Shooting phase, or pile in and make one attack as if it were the Fight phase.

2 COMMAND POINTS

KILLING FRENZY

Level 1 Zealot Tactic

Use this Tactic when you pick a Zealot specialist from your kill team to fight in the Fight phase. Until the end of the phase, each time you make a hit roll of 6+ for that model you can make an additional attack with the same weapon against the same target. These attacks cannot themselves generate any further attacks.

1 COMMAND POINT

TERRIFYING RAMPAGE

Level 3 Zealot Tactic

Use this Tactic at the start of the Morale phase. Pick a Zealot specialist of Level 3 or higher from your kill team that took an enemy model out of action in the preceding Fight phase. Each enemy model within 6" of the Zealot must take a Nerve test. If the test is failed the model is shaken.

2 COMMAND POINTS

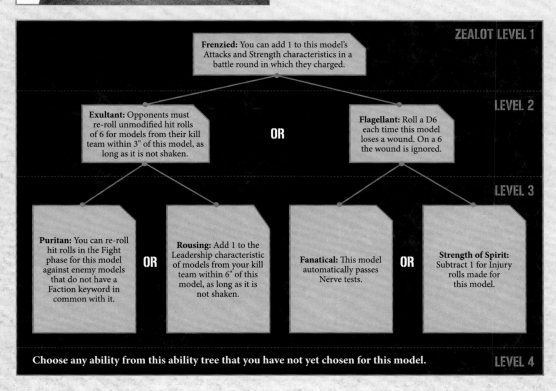

ZEALOT LEVEL 1

Frenzied: You can add 1 to this model's Attacks and Strength characteristics in a battle round in which they charged.

LEVEL 2

Exultant: Opponents must re-roll unmodified hit rolls of 6 for models from their kill team within 3" of this model, as long as it is not shaken.

OR

Flagellant: Roll a D6 each time this model loses a wound. On a 6 the wound is ignored.

LEVEL 3

Puritan: You can re-roll hit rolls in the Fight phase for this model against enemy models that do not have a Faction keyword in common with it.

OR

Rousing: Add 1 to the Leadership characteristic of models from your kill team within 6" of this model, as long as it is not shaken.

Fanatical: This model automatically passes Nerve tests.

OR

Strength of Spirit: Subtract 1 for Injury rolls made for this model.

Choose any ability from this ability tree that you have not yet chosen for this model.

LEVEL 4

ADEPTUS ASTARTES

The Adeptus Astartes are the Imperium's Angels of Death. They descend from the skies upon trails of fire to bring swift and bloody destruction to the enemies of Mankind, for they know no fear. By rolling the appropriate dice on the tables on the following pages, you can generate names and background for your Adeptus Astartes kill teams.

The Adeptus Astartes, more commonly known throughout the Imperium as Space Marines, are Humanity's finest warriors. Each is a genetically modified super-soldier, a warrior of superlative skill, courage, strength and resilience that wields the finest weapons and wargear the Imperium can provide.

Space Marines are organised into Chapters, each a self-contained and autonomous fighting force furnished with its own spacecraft, fleet of armoured combat vehicles and – in most cases – its own world or worlds that it rules and recruits from as the Chapter's masters see fit. Every Chapter has its own warrior culture, its own heraldry and traditions, and its own preferred combat doctrines. In many cases these derive from the tome known as the Codex Astartes, with such exemplary Chapters as the Ultramarines, the Imperial Fists and the Novamarines embodying its strategic tenets. Other Chapters emphasise specific aspects of the Codex's teachings, from the stealth specialists of the Raven Guard and the swift hunters of the White Scars, to the zealous Black Templars, the noble Blood Angels and the ruthlessly logical Iron Hands.

Space Marines are accustomed to fighting in compact, elite strike forces, and thus form kill teams with ease. Each battle-brother brings with him strengths and specialisms honed on battlefields across the galaxy, complementing those of the warriors around him to forge an exceptionally powerful dedicated task force. Whether despatched to assassinate a key enemy leader, secure a site of great strategic importance, or recover a

vital dignitary or sacred artefact, the kill teams of the Adeptus Astartes make use of their unparalleled training and equipment to eliminate any enemy that stands before them, completing their mission with terrifying efficiency in the Emperor's name.

Every battle-brother in an Adeptus Astartes kill team is like an army unto himself, capable of tearing his way through throngs of lesser foes or facing down the most monstrous threats to the Imperium with a broad variety of arms and equipment. Genetic enhancement, psycho-hypnotic indoctrination and unfailing discipline allow these warriors to operate at peak effectiveness for days without rest or sustenance, allowing them to conduct pinpoint strikes or carve paths of destruction deep behind enemy lines, all while adapting with incredible speed to each new threat as it develops.

THE HOLY BOLTER

Of all the weapons used by the Emperor's Space Marines, none are more iconic of their might than those that fire self-propelled micro-missiles known as bolt shells. From the widely used boltgun and the compact but deadly bolt pistol, to the more specialised bolt rifles and bolt carbines of the Primaris Space Marines, variants of bolt weaponry are seen throughout the arsenal of the Adeptus Astartes. Armour piercing and calibrated to detonate inside their target for maximum damage, a salvo of bolt shells can put paid to even the most formidable foes.

D10	MISSION: OATH OF MOMENT
1	**Shock and Awe:** The enemy must be not just defeated, but scattered to the four winds, sent fleeing in mindless terror before the Emperor's wrath.
2	**Assassination:** Whether it be a tainted sorcerer or a xenos war-leader, a crucial enemy target must be eliminated at all costs.
3	**Secure and Control:** The Emperor's Space Marines excel in striking swiftly and utterly dominating crucial battlefield locations.
4	**Hold the Line:** With the enemy pushing hard, this kill team must form an unbreakable line to halt their advance.
5	**Hit and Run:** Moving fast and striking hard, the Space Marines must eliminate their target then disengage before the foe even realises the danger.
6	**Scouting Mission:** These battle-brothers must slip deep behind enemy lines and banish the shadows of ignorance with the Emperor's inescapable light.
7	**Rescue Mission:** With time running out, this kill team must slay the enemy and recover their target before it is too late.
8	**Eliminate Target:** Whether it be a heretical machine, a tainted xenos artefact or a compromised Imperial asset, this kill team must destroy it to keep it from enemy hands.
9	**Line Breakers:** This squad must smash through the foe's lines, breaking through an enemy cordon or punching a hole for a wider Imperial force to exploit.
10	**Speartip:** As a planetary assault begins, this kill team must secure a beachhead for their comrades to exploit.

D10	BACKGROUND: HEROIC ORIGIN
1	**Crusaders:** Driven by their absolute belief in the might of the Imperium, these warriors will stop at nothing to plant the Aquila amidst the corpses of their foes.
2	**Last Survivors:** After months or years of war, only a handful of hardened battle-brothers survives to fight on.
3	**Seekers After Vengeance:** This kill team seek to avenge some unforgivable wrong done to their Chapter.
4	**Oath Sworn:** Bound by mighty oaths, these battle-brothers seek to fulfil a truly monumental task.
5	**Infiltration Specialists:** These warriors slip through the enemy lines like a dagger through the ribs.
6	**Hand-picked Heroes:** This kill team has been assembled by decree of the Chapter Master himself.
7	**Tactical Strike Force:** Versatile and strategically balanced, these warriors can adapt quickly to any situation.
8	**Fire Support:** These warriors specialise in laying down massive volumes of firepower to annihilate the mightiest foes.
9	**Honour Guard:** This kill team represent some of their Chapter's most exceptional warriors, devoted to guarding a single, vital asset.
10	**Extermination Force:** Sometimes the enemy must be annihilated wholesale to ensure victory. This kill team specialises in such merciless actions.

D10	SQUAD QUIRK: CODEX EMPHASIS
1	**Stubborn:** No matter the cost, this squad will not take a step back from the foe.
2	**Dynamic:** Always on the move, these battle-brothers fight on the front foot.
3	**Stealthy:** For all their size and strength, these battle-brothers move through the shadows with barely a whisper.
4	**Zealous:** Unusual amongst their kind, these Space Marines are true believers in the divinity of the Emperor.
5	**Exemplars:** These noble warriors embody everything it means to be Adeptus Astartes, and hold to the Codex in all things.
6	**Selfless:** These warriors believe that their lives are best spent shielding the Emperor's servants from harm.
7	**Merciless:** Not a flicker of compassion lights the eyes of these hardened killers.
8	**Vendetta:** Be it a Traitor Legion or xenos race, a particular foe wronged this squad or their Chapter, and they will not rest until vengeance has been had.
9	**Bloodthirsty:** So ferocious are these battle-brothers that they have to come to resemble the monsters they fight.
10	**Strategists:** With calculated strategies and carefully analysed intelligence, this kill team formulates perfect battle plans to neutralise the foe.

D10	SPECIALISTS' DEMEANOURS
1	**Dour:** Nothing surprises or shocks this warrior, but neither does anything give him joy.
2	**Ebullient:** This battle-brother delights in doing the Emperor's work for the good of all Mankind.
3	**Aggressive:** Always on the attack, this Space Marine presses ever forwards.
4	**Castellan:** This battle-brother excels on the defensive, at digging in and massacring all foes who approach.
5	**Noble:** This warrior will take any risk and pay any price to preserve the lives of his battle-brothers.
6	**Xenophobic:** This battle-brother hates the perfidy of aliens with a particular vehemence, prioritising their demise above all else.
7	**Ferocious:** This battle-brother's wrathful cries and strident oaths ring across the battlefield.
8	**Sombre:** Ever grim, this warrior chants morbid litanies as he fights.
9	**Mysterious:** This battle-brother rarely speaks, and his pronouncements are laced with prophecy and dark insinuation.
10	**Charismatic:** This battle-brother is a figure of courage and inspiration to all.

ULTRAMARINES NAME GENERATOR TABLE

D10	FORENAME	SURNAME
1	Marius	Chronus
2	Agnathio	Tarentus
3	Ollonius	Dysorius
4	Cato	Cassus
5	Titus	Acastian
6	Agies	Varenus
7	Gaius	Apollon
8	Andrus	Aggennor
9	Marcus	Castus
10	Cassius	Poladrus

IMPERIAL FISTS NAME GENERATOR TABLE

D10	FORENAME	SURNAME
1	Lydus	Hagen
2	Darnath	Mirhen
3	Lexandro	Garadon
4	Nereus	Lytanus
5	Tylaeus	Danithor
6	Vorn	Markov
7	Tor	Mordelai
8	Boreas	Julan
9	Jago	Darsway
10	Oreas	Lordann

BLOOD ANGELS NAME GENERATOR TABLE

D10	FORENAME	SURNAME
1	Amareus	Belarius
2	Erasmus	Seraphan
3	Rafael	Moriar
4	Morlaeo	Raneil
5	Leonid	Castivar
6	Faustian	Arteros
7	Donatelus	Redolpho
8	Raelyn	Lorenso
9	Nicodemus	Amuto
10	Furian	Rephas

RAVEN GUARD NAME GENERATOR TABLE

D10	FORENAME	SURNAME
1	Aajz	Kaed
2	Kyrin	Solari
3	Vykus	Solaq
4	Tryris	Qeld
5	Ordias	Korvaedyn
6	Navaer	Vaanes
7	Syras	Torvaec
8	Aevar	Klayde
9	Reszan	Moradus
10	Vorkyl	Ordaris

WHITE SCARS NAME GENERATOR TABLE

D10	FORENAME	SURNAME
1	Anagar	Gatughan
2	Khajog	Yesuberei
3	Suberei	Ghol
4	Khoros	Jaghol
5	Jaygor	Kandakh
6	Seglei	Mologhai
7	Jurgah	Ujumm
8	Kaljyk	Bhangleo
9	Kulghu	J'ungah
10	Saghari	Aghulo

IRON HANDS NAME GENERATOR TABLE

D10	FORENAME	SURNAME
1	Arrven	Feirros
2	Gorrloch	Graevarr
3	Shorrgol	Bannus
4	Galorr	Lydriik
5	Dorrghun	Terrek
6	Kaagos	Korvaan
7	Barrgus	Urloch
8	Ghorrean	Rauth
9	Orros	Varrox
10	Gdolkin	Xeriis

SALAMANDERS NAME GENERATOR TABLE

D10	FORENAME	SURNAME
1	Dak'Lyr	K'Gosi
2	Sho'Tan	Dallor
3	Tsu'Gar	Jurr
4	Fugean	Mir'Shan
5	Xavus	Shenn
6	Nubari	Ta'Phor
7	Vorr'n	Rhoshan
8	Sholta	Antanar
9	Xa'Vor	Shal'Dar
10	Leotrak	Gar'Dos

SPACE WOLVES NAME GENERATOR TABLE

D10	FORENAME	SURNAME
1	Gunnar	Ironaxe
2	Ulfrich	Icefang
3	Laars	Orksbane
4	Sven	the Red
5	Wulfgar	Wyrmslayer
6	Erik	Thunderhowl
7	Dolf	Stormstrider
8	Leif	Stoneshield
9	Olaf	Trollbane
10	Torrvald	Greymane

DARK ANGELS NAME GENERATOR TABLE

D10	FORENAME	SURNAME
1	Azkarael	Zaborial
2	Zakeal	Azdallon
3	Rhellion	Zacahrus
4	Zoreal	Astathor
5	Azathor	Seraphus
6	Shoriel	Zanthor
7	Nemator	Kaelon
8	Ezekial	Namaat
9	Bethor	Soriel
10	Zadakial	Belian

ADEPTUS ASTARTES KILL TEAMS

If every model in your kill team has the ADEPTUS ASTARTES Faction keyword, you can use Adeptus Astartes Tactics.

DEATH TO THE TRAITORS!

Adeptus Astartes Tactic

Use this Tactic when you choose a model from your kill team to fight in the Fight phase. Until the end of that phase, each time you make a hit roll of 6+ for that model and the target is a HERETIC ASTARTES model, you can immediately make an extra attack against the same model using the same weapon. These attacks cannot themselves generate any further attacks.

1 COMMAND POINT

ARMOUR OF CONTEMPT

Adeptus Astartes Tactic

Use this Tactic when a model from your kill team suffers a mortal wound. Roll a D6 for that mortal wound, and each other mortal wound suffered by that model for the rest of the phase; on a 5+ the mortal wound is ignored and has no effect.

1 COMMAND POINT

MASTERFUL MARKSMANSHIP

Adeptus Astartes Tactic

Use this Tactic in the Shooting phase when you choose an INTERCESSOR from your kill team to shoot with a stalker bolt rifle. Until the end of that phase, you can add 1 to hit and wound rolls for that model.

1 COMMAND POINT

HONOUR THE CHAPTER

Adeptus Astartes Tactic

Use this Tactic at the end of the Fight phase. Pick a model from your kill team. That model can immediately fight an additional time.

2 COMMAND POINTS

HELLFIRE SHELLS

Adeptus Astartes Tactic

Use this Tactic when you choose a model in your kill team to shoot with a heavy bolter. You can only make a single hit roll for the weapon this phase, however, if it hits, the target suffers D3 mortal wounds instead of the normal damage.

2 COMMAND POINTS

SHOCK AND AWE

Adeptus Astartes Tactic

Use this Tactic when you declare a REIVER from your kill team will attempt to charge. Before any Overwatch attacks are made, you can make a single shooting attack using this model's shock grenades against a target of the charge. If the attack is successful, that target may not fire Overwatch this phase in addition to the normal effects of the grenade.

2 COMMAND POINTS

'The traitors are dug in, well supplied and heavily armed. They think they're unassailable. What do you say, brothers – shall we disabuse them of that foolish notion?'

- *Ulfrich Wyrmslayer, Space Wolves Reiver Sergeant*

SCOUT

NAME	M	WS	BS	S	T	W	A	Ld	Sv	Max
Scout	6"	3+	3+	4	4	1	1	7	4+	-
Scout Gunner	6"	3+	3+	4	4	1	1	7	4+	2
Scout Sergeant	6"	3+	3+	4	4	1	2	8	4+	1

This model is armed with a boltgun, bolt pistol, frag grenades and krak grenades.
Up to two Scouts in your kill team can be Scout Gunners, and one Scout in your kill team can be a Scout Sergeant.

WARGEAR OPTIONS	• A Scout may replace their boltgun with a combat knife or Astartes shotgun, or a sniper rifle and camo cloak. • A Scout Gunner may replace their boltgun with a heavy bolter or missile launcher, or a sniper rifle and camo cloak. • A Scout Gunner with a missile launcher may take a camo cloak. • A Scout Sergeant may replace their boltgun with an Astartes shotgun or chainsword, or a sniper rifle and camo cloak.
ABILITIES	**And They Shall Know No Fear:** You can re-roll failed Nerve tests for this model. **Transhuman Physiology:** Ignore the penalty to this model's hit rolls from one flesh wound it has suffered.	**Camo Cloak:** When an opponent makes a hit roll for a shooting attack that targets a model equipped with a camo cloak, and that model is obscured, that hit roll suffers an additional -1 modifier.
SPECIALISTS	**Leader** (Sergeant only), **Heavy** (Gunner only), **Comms, Demolitions, Scout, Sniper**
FACTION KEYWORD	**ADEPTUS ASTARTES**
KEYWORDS	**IMPERIUM, INFANTRY, SCOUT**

TACTICAL MARINE

NAME	M	WS	BS	S	T	W	A	Ld	Sv	Max
Tactical Marine	6"	3+	3+	4	4	1	1	7	3+	-
Tactical Marine Gunner	6"	3+	3+	4	4	1	1	7	3+	2
Tactical Sergeant	6"	3+	3+	4	4	1	2	8	3+	1

This model is armed with a boltgun, bolt pistol, frag grenades and krak grenades.
Up to two Tactical Marines in your kill team can be Tactical Marine Gunners, and one Tactical Marine in your kill team can be a Tactical Sergeant.

WARGEAR OPTIONS	• One Tactical Marine Gunner in your kill team may replace their boltgun with a flamer, meltagun, plasma gun or grav-gun. • One Tactical Marine Gunner in your kill team may replace their boltgun with a missile launcher or heavy bolter. • A Tactical Sergeant may replace their bolt pistol and boltgun with a combi-flamer, combi-grav, combi-melta or combi-plasma. Alternatively, he may be armed with a bolt pistol, plasma pistol or grav-pistol, and may also take a chainsword, power fist, power sword or auspex.
ABILITIES	**And They Shall Know No Fear:** You can re-roll failed Nerve tests for this model. **Transhuman Physiology:** Ignore the penalty to this model's hit rolls from one flesh wound it has suffered.	**Auspex:** At the start of the Shooting phase, you can choose another **ADEPTUS ASTARTES** model within 3" of a friendly model equipped with an auspex that is not shaken. That model does not suffer penalties to their hit or injury rolls due to their target being obscured.
SPECIALISTS	**Leader** (Sergeant only), **Heavy** (Gunner only), **Comms, Demolitions, Sniper, Veteran**
FACTION KEYWORD	**ADEPTUS ASTARTES**
KEYWORDS	**IMPERIUM, INFANTRY, TACTICAL MARINE**

REIVER

NAME	M	WS	BS	S	T	W	A	Ld	Sv	Max
Reiver	6"	3+	3+	4	4	2	2	7	3+	-
Reiver Sergeant	6"	3+	3+	4	4	2	3	8	3+	1

This model is armed with a bolt carbine, heavy bolt pistol, frag grenades, krak grenades and shock grenades.
One Reiver in your kill team can be a Reiver Sergeant.

WARGEAR OPTIONS	• A Reiver may replace their bolt carbine with a combat knife. • A Reiver Sergeant may replace their bolt carbine or heavy bolt pistol with a combat knife. • This model may take a grav-chute. • This model may take a grapnel launcher.
ABILITIES	**And They Shall Know No Fear:** You can re-roll failed Nerve tests for this model. **Transhuman Physiology:** Ignore the penalty to this model's hit rolls from one flesh wound it has suffered. **Grapnel Launcher:** A model with a grapnel launcher can climb any distance vertically (up or down) when it makes a normal move – do not measure the distance moved in this way.	**Grav-chute:** A model with a grav-chute never suffers falling damage, and never falls on another model. If it would, instead place this model as close as possible to the point where it would have landed. This can bring it within 1" of an enemy model. **Terror Troops:** Enemy models must subtract 1 from their Leadership if they are within 3" of any Reiver or Reiver Sergeant models.
SPECIALISTS	**Leader** (Sergeant only), **Combat**, **Comms**, **Demolitions**, **Scout**, **Veteran**
FACTION KEYWORD	**Adeptus Astartes**
KEYWORDS	**Imperium, Infantry, Primaris, Reiver**

INTERCESSOR

NAME	M	WS	BS	S	T	W	A	Ld	Sv	Max
Intercessor	6"	3+	3+	4	4	2	2	7	3+	-
Intercessor Gunner	6"	3+	3+	4	4	2	2	7	3+	2
Intercessor Sergeant	6"	3+	3+	4	4	2	3	8	3+	1

This model is armed with a bolt rifle, bolt pistol, frag grenades and krak grenades.
Up to two Intercessors in your kill team can be Intercessor Gunners, and one Intercessor in your kill team can be an Intercessor Sergeant.

WARGEAR OPTIONS	• This model may replace its bolt rifle with an auto bolt rifle or stalker bolt rifle. • An Intercessor Gunner may take an auxiliary grenade launcher. • An Intercessor Sergeant may take a power sword or chainsword, or replace their bolt rifle with a power sword or chainsword.
ABILITIES	**And They Shall Know No Fear:** You can re-roll failed Nerve tests for this model. **Transhuman Physiology:** Ignore the penalty to this model's hit rolls from one flesh wound it has suffered.	**Auxiliary Grenade Launcher:** If a model is armed with an auxiliary grenade launcher, increase the range of any Grenade weapons they have to 30".
SPECIALISTS	**Leader** (Sergeant only), **Demolitions** (Gunner only), **Combat**, **Comms**, **Sniper**, **Veteran**
FACTION KEYWORD	**Adeptus Astartes**
KEYWORDS	**Imperium, Infantry, Primaris, Intercessor**

'Strike swift, brothers, and strike true. Wield your weapons with the Primarch's own might and turn them upon the Emperor's foes until none remain standing to oppose his will.'

- Brother Sergeant Lytornus, Imperial Fists 4th Company during Operation Black Sunrise

RANGED WEAPONS

WEAPON	RANGE	TYPE	S	AP	D	ABILITIES
Astartes shotgun	12"	Assault 2	4	0	1	If the target is within half range, add 1 to this weapon's Strength.
Auto bolt rifle	24"	Assault 2	4	0	1	-
Bolt carbine	24"	Assault 2	4	0	1	-
Bolt pistol	12"	Pistol 1	4	0	1	-
Bolt rifle	30"	Rapid Fire 1	4	-1	1	-
Boltgun	24"	Rapid Fire 1	4	0	1	-
Combi-flamer	When attacking with this weapon, choose one or both of the profiles below. If you choose both, subtract 1 from all hit rolls made for this weapon.					
- Boltgun	24"	Rapid Fire 1	4	0	1	-
- Flamer	8"	Assault D6	4	0	1	This weapon automatically hits its target.
Combi-grav	When attacking with this weapon, choose one or both of the profiles below. If you choose both, subtract 1 from all hit rolls made for this weapon.					
- Boltgun	24"	Rapid Fire 1	4	0	1	-
- Grav-gun	18"	Rapid Fire 1	5	-3	1	If the target has a Save characteristic of 3+ or better, this weapon has a Damage of D3.
Combi-melta	When attacking with this weapon, choose one or both of the profiles below. If you choose both, subtract 1 from all hit rolls made for this weapon.					
- Boltgun	24"	Rapid Fire 1	4	0	1	-
- Meltagun	12"	Assault 1	8	-4	D6	If the target is within half range of this weapon, roll two dice when inflicting damage with it and discard the lowest result.
Combi-plasma	When attacking with this weapon, choose one or both of the profiles below. If you choose both, subtract 1 from all hit rolls made for this weapon.					
- Boltgun	24"	Rapid Fire 1	4	0	1	-
- Plasma gun	24"	Rapid Fire 1	7	-3	1	See plasma gun
Flamer	8"	Assault D6	4	0	1	This weapon automatically hits its target.
Frag grenade	6"	Grenade D6	3	0	1	-
Grav-gun	18"	Rapid Fire 1	5	-3	1	If the target has a Save characteristic of 3+ or better, this weapon has a Damage of D3.
Grav-pistol	12"	Pistol 1	5	-3	1	If the target has a Save characteristic of 3+ or better, this weapon has a Damage of D3.
Heavy bolt pistol	12"	Pistol 1	4	-1	1	-
Heavy bolter	36"	Heavy 3	5	-1	1	-
Krak grenade	6"	Grenade 1	6	-1	D3	-
Meltagun	12"	Assault 1	8	-4	D6	If the target is within half range of this weapon, roll two dice when inflicting damage with it and discard the lowest result.
Missile launcher	When attacking with this weapon, choose one of the profiles below.					
- Frag missile	48"	Heavy D6	4	0	1	-
- Krak missile	48"	Heavy 1	8	-2	D6	-
Plasma gun	When attacking with this weapon, choose one of the profiles below.					
- Standard	24"	Rapid Fire 1	7	-3	1	-
- Supercharge	24"	Rapid Fire 1	8	-3	2	On an unmodified hit roll of 1, the bearer is taken out of action after all of this weapon's shots have been resolved.
Plasma pistol	When attacking with this weapon, choose one of the profiles below.					
- Standard	12"	Pistol 1	7	-3	1	-
- Supercharge	12"	Pistol 1	8	-3	2	On an unmodified hit roll of 1, the bearer is taken out of action.
Shock grenade	6"	Grenade D3	*	*	*	This weapon does not inflict any damage. If an enemy INFANTRY model is hit by any shock grenades, it is stunned; until the end of the next battle round that model cannot fire Overwatch or be Readied, and your opponent must subtract 1 from hit rolls made for the model.
Sniper rifle	36"	Heavy 1	4	0	1	A model firing a sniper rifle does not suffer the penalty to hit rolls for the target being at long range. If you roll a wound roll of 6+ for this weapon, it inflicts a mortal wound in addition to its normal damage.
Stalker bolt rifle	36"	Heavy 1	4	-2	1	-

MELEE WEAPONS

WEAPON	RANGE	TYPE	S	AP	D	ABILITIES
Chainsword	Melee	Melee	User	0	1	Each time the bearer fights, it can make 1 additional attack with this weapon.
Combat knife	Melee	Melee	User	0	1	Each time the bearer fights, it can make 1 additional attack with this weapon.
Power fist	Melee	Melee	x2	-3	D3	When attacking with this weapon, you must subtract 1 from the hit roll.
Power sword	Melee	Melee	User	-3	1	-

KILL TEAM

MODEL	POINTS PER MODEL (Does not include wargear)
Intercessor	15
- Intercessor Gunner	16
- Intercessor Sergeant	16
Reiver	16
- Reiver Sergeant	17
Scout	10
- Scout Gunner	11
- Scout Sergeant	11
Tactical Marine	12
- Tactical Marine Gunner	13
- Tactical Sergeant	13

MELEE WEAPONS

WEAPON	POINTS PER WEAPON
Chainsword	0
Combat knife	0
Power fist	4
Power sword	2

OTHER WARGEAR

WARGEAR	POINTS PER ITEM
Auspex	1
Auxiliary grenade launcher	0
Camo cloak	1
Grapnel launcher	1
Grav-chute	1

RANGED WEAPONS

WEAPON	POINTS PER WEAPON
Astartes shotgun	0
Auto bolt rifle	0
Bolt carbine	0
Bolt pistol	0
Bolt rifle	0
Boltgun	0
Combi-flamer	3
Combi-grav	2
Combi-melta	3
Combi-plasma	4
Flamer	3
Frag grenade	0
Grav-gun	2
Grav-pistol	1
Heavy bolt pistol	0
Heavy bolter	3
Krak grenade	0
Meltagun	3
Missile launcher	5
Plasma gun	3
Plasma pistol	1
Shock grenade	0
Sniper rifle	1
Stalker bolt rifle	0

DEATHWATCH

The Deathwatch is Humanity's shield against xenos horrors. By rolling the appropriate dice on the tables on the following pages, and the name tables from the Adeptus Astartes section, you can generate names and background for your Deathwatch kill teams.

The Deathwatch are the foremost alien hunters in the Imperium. Their ranks comprise the finest warriors of the Adeptus Astartes Chapters, seconded with great honour to serve in the kill teams of the Deathwatch and defend Humanity from the xenos menace.

Deathwatch kill teams make use of every weapon, technology and tactic they can, adapting their way of war to best suit each new foe. They carry a wide variety of armaments, many tailored to the elimination of particular types of enemy, and each warrior's battlefield expertise is leveraged to lethal effect. By combining the greatest strengths of the Space Marine Chapters, and deploying groups of specialist battle-brothers who complement one another's abilities, Deathwatch kill teams have earned their place as one of the most lethal precision tools available to the lords of the Imperium.

Experts at assessing how their might can best be put to use against significantly more numerous enemies, even in large-scale conflicts the Deathwatch will utilise small squads of elite warriors to systematically eradicate their foes. Though they are few in number – even compared to the wider Adeptus Astartes – a single Deathwatch kill team, delivered to the right location at the right moment and equipped with the correct weapons – can change the course of an entire war. They are heroes all, merciless destroyers of the xenos threat, and without their selfless efforts the Imperium would surely have been torn apart long ago.

D10	BACKGROUND: TEAM DOCTRINE
1	**Aquila Kill Team:** This kill team is assembled to deal with any threat, adapting quickly to the developing tactical situation.
2	**Furor Kill Team:** A kill team whose composition and armaments prioritise optimised firepower.
3	**Venator Kill Team:** Fast-moving and deadly, the Venator Kill Team runs its prey to ground with ease.
4	**Dominatus Kill Team:** This kill team specialises in meeting the enemy's elite warriors head-on and slaying them to the last.
5	**Malleus Kill Team:** The monstrous and the mechanical are the chosen prey of this kill team, whose weapons pack a phenomenal punch.
6	**Purgatus Kill Team:** They who strike the head from the body, this kill team excels in taking down alien overlords.
7	**Fortis Kill Team:** Comprising heroic Primaris battle-brothers from the Space Marine Chapters, this kill team can deal with any foe.
8	**Mission Survivors:** The last warriors standing from a larger, now-decimated force, this kill team must fight as one to avenge their fallen.
9	**The Long Hunt:** Brothers have come and gone, but the hunt has endured for decades. Now, at last, this kill team nears its prey.
10	**The Shield that Slays:** Gathering the optimised combination of warriors from all those available, this kill team is perfectly balanced for the conflict at hand.

D6 — MISSION: COVERT OPERATION

1	**Secure and Control:** A dangerous xenos artefact must be either secured for study, or destroyed to prevent corruption.
2	**The Cull:** Xenos numbers in this region must be heavily curtailed before they reach critical mass.
3	**Cut off the Head:** A powerful alien warlord must be slain before they bring a storm of violence down upon the Imperium.
4	**Disrupt the Swarm:** The enemy's advance must be slowed, misdirected and broken apart.
5	**The Heart of the Hive:** Be it a Necron tomb or a xenocult brood-shrine, the source of this region's corruption must be rooted out and put to the torch.
6	**Knowledge is Power:** Even as a campaign progresses against the enemy they must be studied, dissected and catalogued, the better to exploit their weaknesses.

D6 — SQUAD QUIRK: TEAM FACET

1	**Newly Forged:** This kill team has recently been assembled, and its battle-brothers must learn quickly how to fight as one.
2	**Xenovendetta:** Long years of battle against a particular xenos foe have made these warriors expert at their annihilation.
3	**Competitive:** The battle-brothers of this kill team strive not only to win victory for the Imperium, but to best one another in private contests of arms.
4	**Pragmatic:** Comprised of battle-brothers from the more subtle and sombre Chapters, this kill team relies upon their wits and fortitude to win victory.
5	**Bellicose:** Populated by battle-brothers from the most aggressive and feral Chapters, this kill team is a ferocious and aggressive force.
6	**The Bigger Picture:** Knowing full well the wider price of failure, these warriors are willing to commit unconscionable deeds in the name of victory.

D10 — SPECIALISTS' DEMEANOURS

1	**Newcomer:** This warrior replaced a beloved and trusted battle-brother who fell. They seek to prove themselves to their squad.
2	**Black Shield:** Mysterious and insular, this figure's past is a dark secret.
3	**Xenobiologist:** This warrior is fascinated with the workings of xenos anatomy, always ready to carve up aliens to better understand the hated foe.
4	**Fuelled by Hate:** This battle-brother has seen too many comrades fall, too many xenos atrocities, and his hate for all aliens burns hot.
5	**Tactician:** This warrior's mind is a rich repository of tried and tested combat manoeuvres.
6	**Huntsman:** Once this battle-brother sets his eyes upon a particular quarry, he harries them to the exclusion of all else.
7	**Marksman:** This warrior always favours eliminating their enemies at range, and has thus become a truly exceptional shot.
8	**Grim:** This battle-brother is under no illusions that the Imperium is fighting a battle against impossible odds.
9	**Contemptuous:** This warrior has nothing but scorn for xenos and all their works, and his disgust for them finds its purest expression in battle.
10	**Murderous:** So long has this warrior fought alien foes that he cannot restrain his violence against them any more, hacking them to pieces with bloody fury.

DEATHWATCH KILL TEAMS

Deathwatch models in your kill team use the Special Issue Ammunition ability below. If every model in your kill team has the **Deathwatch** Faction keyword, you can use Deathwatch Tactics.

Special Issue Ammunition: When this model fires an auto bolt rifle, bolt carbine, bolt pistol, bolt rifle, boltgun, combi-melta (boltgun profile only), combi-plasma (boltgun profile only), heavy bolt pistol, stalker bolt rifle or stalker pattern boltgun, you can choose one kind of ammunition from the table to the right, and apply the corresponding modifier.

Fortis Kill Team: When you add an Intercessor (pg 85) or a Reiver (pg 85) to your command roster (and create its datacard) you can choose for it to have the **Deathwatch** Faction keyword instead of the **Adeptus Astartes** Faction keyword. If you do so, it gains the Special Issue Ammunition ability but you must use the points values on page 91 for its ranged weapons.

SPECIAL ISSUE AMMUNITION

AMMUNITION	MODIFIER
Dragonfire bolt	Add 1 to hit rolls for this weapon when targeting a model that is obscured.
Hellfire round	This weapon always wounds on a 2+.
Kraken bolt	Add 3" to the range of this weapon if it is a Pistol – or 6" otherwise – and improve the AP of the attack by 1 (e.g. an AP of 0 becomes -1), to a maximum AP of -2.
Vengeance round	Subtract 3" from the range of this weapon if it is a Pistol – or 6" otherwise – and improve the AP of the attack by 2 (e.g. an AP of 0 becomes -2), to a maximum AP of -3.

HELLFIRE SHELL

Deathwatch Tactic

Use this Tactic when you choose a model in your kill team to shoot with a heavy bolter or the heavy bolter profile of an infernus heavy bolter. You can only make a single hit roll with the weapon this phase (subtracting 1 as normal if also firing an infernus heavy bolter's heavy flamer), however, if it hits, the target suffers D3 mortal wounds instead of the normal damage.

1 COMMAND POINT

DECAPITATION DOCTRINE

Deathwatch Tactic

Use this Tactic when a model from your kill team is chosen to attack in the Shooting or Fight phase. Until the end of the phase, re-roll failed wound rolls for that model that target an enemy Leader.

1 COMMAND POINT

ONLY IN DEATH DOES DUTY END

Deathwatch Tactic

Use this Tactic when a model from your kill team is taken out of action; that model summons the strength for one final attack, and can immediately either shoot as if it were your turn in the Shooting phase, or fight as if it were your turn in the Fight phase.

2 COMMAND POINTS

RIVAL CHAPTERS

Deathwatch Tactic

Use this Tactic when a model from your kill team is chosen to attack in the Shooting or Fight phase whilst there is another model from your kill team within 2" of it. Until the end of the phase, re-roll hit rolls of 1 for both models.

1 COMMAND POINT

DEATHWATCH VETERAN

NAME	M	WS	BS	S	T	W	A	Ld	Sv	Max
Deathwatch Veteran	6"	3+	3+	4	4	1	2	8	3+	-
Deathwatch Veteran Gunner	6"	3+	3+	4	4	1	2	8	3+	4
Black Shield	6"	3+	3+	4	4	1	3	8	3+	1
Watch Sergeant	6"	3+	3+	4	4	1	3	9	3+	1

This model is armed with a boltgun, frag grenades and krak grenades.
One Deathwatch Veteran in your kill team can be a Black Shield, up to four Deathwatch Veterans in your kill team can be Deathwatch Veteran Gunners, and one Deathwatch Veteran in your kill team can be a Watch Sergeant.

WARGEAR OPTIONS	• This model may replace its boltgun with a combi-melta, combi-plasma, stalker pattern boltgun, power sword, power maul or storm shield. This model may also take a power sword or power maul; if they are a Watch Sergeant, they may take a xenophase blade instead. • A Deathwatch Veteran may, instead of the above, replace their boltgun with a Deathwatch shotgun or heavy thunder hammer. • A Deathwatch Veteran Gunner may replace their boltgun with a Deathwatch frag cannon or infernus heavy bolter.
ABILITIES	**Special Issue Ammunition** (pg 89) **And They Shall Know No Fear:** You can re-roll failed Nerve tests for this model. **Transhuman Physiology:** Ignore the penalty to this model's hit rolls from one flesh wound it has suffered. **Storm Shield:** A model with a storm shield has a 3+ invulnerable save. **Atonement Through Honour:** You can re-roll failed charge rolls for a Black Shield.
SPECIALISTS	**Leader** (Sergeant only), **Heavy** (Gunner only), **Combat, Comms, Demolitions, Sniper, Veteran, Zealot**
FACTION KEYWORD	DEATHWATCH
KEYWORDS	IMPERIUM, ADEPTUS ASTARTES, INFANTRY, DEATHWATCH VETERAN

RANGED WEAPONS

WEAPON	RANGE	TYPE	S	AP	D	ABILITIES
Boltgun	24"	Rapid Fire 1	4	0	1	-
Combi-melta	When attacking with this weapon, choose one or both of the profiles below. If you choose both, subtract 1 from all hit rolls made for this weapon.					
- Boltgun	24"	Rapid Fire 1	4	0	1	-
- Meltagun	12"	Assault 1	8	-4	D6	If the target is within half range of this weapon, roll two dice when inflicting damage with it and discard the lowest result.
Combi-plasma	When attacking with this weapon, choose one or both of the profiles below. If you choose both, subtract 1 from all hit rolls made for this weapon.					
- Boltgun	24"	Rapid Fire 1	4	0	1	-
- Plasma gun	24"	Rapid Fire 1	7	-3	1	This weapon can be supercharged by the bearer before firing. If they do so, increase the Strength and Damage of the weapon by 1 this turn. On any unmodified hit rolls of 1 when firing supercharge, the bearer is taken out of action after all of the weapon's shots have been resolved.
Deathwatch frag cannon	When attacking with this weapon, choose one of the profiles below.					
- Frag round	8"	Assault 2D6	6	-1	1	This weapon automatically hits its target.
- Shell	24"	Assault 2	7	-2	2	If the target is within half range of this weapon, its attacks are resolved with a Strength of 9 and an AP of -3.
Deathwatch shotgun	When attacking with this weapon, choose one of the profiles below.					
- Cryptclearer round	16"	Assault 2	4	0	1	You can re-roll failed wound rolls for this weapon.
- Xenopurge slug	16"	Assault 2	4	-1	1	If the target is within half range of this weapon, its attacks are resolved with a Damage of 2.
- Wyrmsbreath shell	7"	Assault D6	3	0	1	This weapon automatically hits its target.
Frag grenade	6"	Grenade D6	3	0	1	-
Infernus heavy bolter	When attacking with this weapon, choose one or both of the profiles below. If you choose both, subtract 1 from all hit rolls made for this weapon.					
- Heavy bolter	36"	Heavy 3	5	-1	1	-
- Heavy flamer	8"	Assault D6	5	-1	1	This weapon automatically hits its target.
Krak grenade	6"	Grenade 1	6	-1	D3	-
Stalker pattern boltgun	30"	Heavy 2	4	-1	1	

MELEE WEAPONS

WEAPON	RANGE	TYPE	S	AP	D	ABILITIES
Heavy thunder hammer	Melee	Melee	x2	-3	D6	When attacking with this weapon, you must subtract 1 from the hit roll. Each time you make a wound roll of 6+ with this weapon, that hit is resolved with a Damage of 6.
Power maul	Melee	Melee	+2	-1	1	-
Power sword	Melee	Melee	User	-3	1	-
Xenophase blade	Melee	Melee	User	-3	1	Your opponent must re-roll successful invulnerable saves for wounds caused by this weapon.

KILL TEAM

MODEL	POINTS PER MODEL (Does not include wargear)
Deathwatch Veteran	14
- Deathwatch Veteran Gunner	16
- Black Shield	16
- Watch Sergeant	16

MELEE WEAPONS

WEAPON	POINTS PER WEAPON
Heavy thunder hammer	5
Power maul	2
Power sword	2
Xenophase blade	3

OTHER WARGEAR

WARGEAR	POINTS PER ITEM
Storm shield	3

RANGED WEAPONS

WEAPON	POINTS PER WEAPON
Auto bolt rifle	2
Bolt carbine	2
Bolt pistol	2
Bolt rifle	2
Boltgun	0
Combi-melta	3
Combi-plasma	4
Deathwatch frag cannon	5
Deathwatch shotgun	1
Frag grenade	0
Heavy bolt pistol	2
Infernus heavy bolter	2
Krak grenade	0
Stalker bolt rifle	2
Stalker pattern boltgun	1

GREY KNIGHTS

An ancient order of Space Marines shrouded in mystery and legend, the Grey Knights are Humanity's greatest defence against the threat of daemonkind. By rolling the appropriate dice on the tables on the following pages, you can generate names and background for your Grey Knights kill teams.

Of all the enemies faced by the Imperium, none are a greater threat than the foul Daemons of Chaos. The Grey Knights were created to battle these unnatural terrors, an entire Chapter of psychically gifted Space Marines whose mental, spiritual and physical purity are beyond question. They sally forth from their fortress monastery on Titan in sanctified warships to hunt down daemonic infestations, seal hellish warp portals, and slay those who – through accident or design – threaten to unleash the entities of the empyrean upon realspace.

The Grey Knights' campaigns are aided by the Prognosticars, battle-brothers gifted with the power to scry and to interpret glimpses of the Imperium's future. Grey Knights kill teams are alerted to those locations where especially terrible daemonic incursions or dread daemonic plots are soon to develop, and are given insight into where their strikes can wreak the most damage upon the forces of the enemy. Furthermore, each Grey Knight in a kill team can draw upon their own psychic might to strike at their foes.

Despite their small numbers, Grey Knights kill teams wield exceptional power. Each battle-brother is armed with the specialised wargear of his order – sanctified bolters, psychically charged Nemesis force weapons and warded armour of blessed adamantium and silver. Such a kill team can easily slaughter their way through dozens upon dozens of foes, piling their corpses high until none remain to endanger the Imperium.

BACKGROUND: LEGEND

D6	BACKGROUND: LEGEND
1	**They Hunt the Beast:** This band of warriors pursues a singularly monstrous quarry across the stars.
2	**Those That Remain:** From a larger force, these last few Grey Knights still fight the daemonic hordes.
3	**Purgation Corps:** A kill team gathered to scour all trace of their target from the galaxy by whatever means necessary.
4	**Sworn Guardians:** These Grey Knights are utterly devoted to protecting some dark secret or holy site.
5	**Hand of the Prognosticars:** This elite band act upon the gleanings of the Prognosticars, striking down terrible threats before they can develop.
6	**The Heroic Few:** Though small in number, this band of mighty warriors is more than a match for the most dreadful enemies in the galaxy.

MISSION: QUEST

D6	MISSION: QUEST
1	**End the Nightmare:** Reality is tearing apart; this band of warriors has been sent to seal the breach.
2	**Aquisitus Prohibitum:** This kill team must seize a forbidden relic, and take it back to Titan.
3	**Wield the True Name:** This band of warriors possesses the true name of a Daemon, with which the entity can be destroyed for good. Yet first it must be hunted…
4	**Reap the Tally:** This kill team must strike down a pre-ordained number of enemies in order to complete a purifying ritual.
5	**Scorched Earth:** Nothing may escape the final judgement of the Immortal Emperor of Mankind. Nothing, and no one.
6	**Trial by Blade:** Faced by heretics on every front, this kill team must eliminate the enemy's ringleaders, bringing the Emperor's vengeance down upon those who would defy his will and endanger his realm.

D10 SPECIALISTS' DEMEANOURS

1	**Wrathful:** This warrior's righteous anger drives them ever forwards to the fiercest fights.
2	**Fanatical:** This warrior pursues the daemonic and the unclean and destroys it at the expense of all else.
3	**Mystic:** This warrior's insights border on the prescient, and his utterances are often obscure and unsettling.
4	**Methodical:** This warrior pauses just long enough to carve runes of abnegation into the flesh of each fallen foe, ensuring their cadavers can never be possessed.
5	**Firebrand:** This warrior's holy oratory is legend, and his wrathful utterances ring across the battlefield like a clarion call.
6	**Vengeful:** This warrior pursues a particular Daemon that has done much harm to him and his comrades.
7	**Marksman:** This Grey Knight is an exceptional shot, and uses his skills to cull the most dangerous foes.
8	**Psychic Nexus:** Waves of sanctic energy wash from this warrior's mind, battering at the unholy and the unclean.
9	**Merciless:** There is no act too cruel or unconscionable for this warrior, for he knows the price that the galaxy will pay otherwise.
10	**Stoic:** This proud warrior of Titan is utterly indomitable, and will never yield to any foe.

GREY KNIGHTS NAME GENERATOR TABLE

D10	FORENAME	SURNAME
1	Valdar	Mordrak
2	Kaladour	Torvin
3	Pelenas	Thule
4	Anval	Varn
5	Drystan	Ordan
6	Garran	Gerontas
7	Drako	Solor
8	Caddon	Cromm
9	Arno	Kai
10	Verdan	Trevan

D6 SQUAD QUIRK: VIRTUE

1	**Unyielding:** These warriors never give up, never give ground, and never, ever surrender.
2	**Blessed Aura:** So saturated in holy energies are these warriors that they shine with the light of the Emperor.
3	**Exacting:** Too many times the trickery of Daemons allows them to escape their doom; thus this squad are mercilessly thorough in the destruction of every foe.
4	**Bellicose:** With strident oaths and raking blasts of gunfire, this squad storms into every battle with unstoppable fervour.
5	**Sworn to Purify:** This kill team strongly favours the use of holy fire to scour their enemies from existence.
6	**Dark Lore:** This kill team are versed in many forbidden secrets, and are able to turn their terrible knowledge to their advantage in battle.

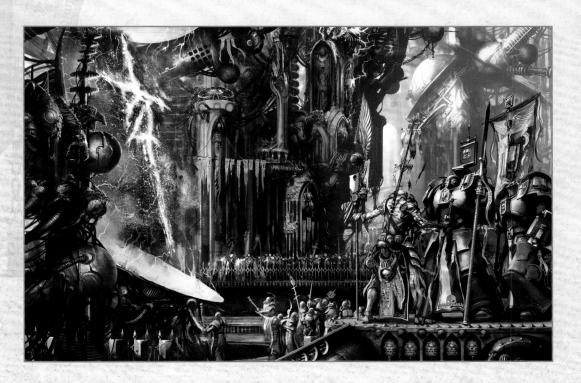

GREY KNIGHTS KILL TEAMS

If every model in your kill team has the GREY KNIGHTS Faction keyword, you can use Grey Knights Tactics.

PSYBOLT AMMUNITION

Grey Knights Tactic

Use this Tactic when you choose a model in your kill team to shoot with a storm bolter. The weapon's Strength characteristic is 5 and its Armour Penetration characteristic is -1 until the end of the phase.

1 COMMAND POINT

PSYCHIC CHANNELLING

Grey Knights Tactic

Use this Tactic when taking a Psychic test for a model from your kill team. Roll three dice rather than two and use the two highest rolls.

2 COMMAND POINTS

HONOUR THE CHAPTER

Grey Knights Tactic

Use this Tactic at the end of the Fight phase. Pick a model from your kill team. That model can immediately fight an additional time.

2 COMMAND POINTS

HEED THE PROGNOSTICARS

Grey Knights Tactic

Use this Tactic at the start of the battle round. Pick a model from your kill team and add 1 to its saving throws until the end of the battle round.

2 COMMAND POINTS

GREY KNIGHT

NAME	M	WS	BS	S	T	W	A	Ld	Sv	Max
Grey Knight	6"	3+	3+	4	4	1	1	7	3+	-
Grey Knight Gunner	6"	3+	3+	4	4	1	1	7	3+	2
Justicar	6"	3+	3+	4	4	1	2	8	3+	1

This model is armed with a Nemesis force sword, storm bolter, frag grenades, krak grenades and psyk-out grenades.
Up to two Grey Knights in your kill team can be Grey Knight Gunners, and one Grey Knight in your kill team can be a Justicar.

WARGEAR OPTIONS	• This model may replace its Nemesis force sword with a Nemesis force halberd, Nemesis Daemon hammer, Nemesis warding stave or two Nemesis falchions. • A Grey Knight Gunner may, instead of the above, replace their Nemesis force sword and storm bolter with an incinerator, psilencer or psycannon.
ABILITIES	**And They Shall Know No Fear:** You can re-roll failed Nerve tests for this model. **Daemon Hunters:** If this model attacks any **DAEMONS** in the Fight phase, you can re-roll failed wound rolls for those attacks. **Transhuman Physiology:** Ignore the penalty to this model's hit rolls from one flesh wound it has suffered. **Rites of Banishment:** When this model manifests the *Psybolt* psychic power it has a range of 12". If *Psybolt* is successfully manifested, and the target model is a **DAEMON**, the target suffers D3 mortal wounds, even if the result of the Psychic test was not 11+.
PSYKER	This model can attempt to manifest one psychic power and attempt to deny one psychic power in each Psychic phase. He knows the *Psybolt* psychic power.
SPECIALISTS	**Leader** (Justicar only), **Heavy** (Gunner only), **Combat**, **Comms**, **Demolitions**, **Veteran**, **Zealot**
FACTION KEYWORD	**GREY KNIGHTS**
KEYWORDS	**IMPERIUM, ADEPTUS ASTARTES, INFANTRY, PSYKER, GREY KNIGHT**

RANGED WEAPONS

WEAPON	RANGE	TYPE	S	AP	D	ABILITIES
Frag grenade	6"	Grenade D6	3	0	1	-
Incinerator	8"	Assault D6	6	-1	1	This weapon automatically hits its target.
Krak grenade	6"	Grenade 1	6	-1	D3	-
Psilencer	24"	Heavy 6	4	0	D3	-
Psycannon	24"	Heavy 4	7	-1	1	-
Psyk-out grenade	6"	Grenade D3	2	0	1	Each time you roll a hit roll of 6+ for this weapon when targeting a **PSYKER** or **DAEMON**, the target suffers a mortal wound instead of the normal damage.
Storm bolter	24"	Rapid Fire 2	4	0	1	-

MELEE WEAPONS

WEAPON	RANGE	TYPE	S	AP	D	ABILITIES
Nemesis Daemon hammer	Melee	Melee	x2	-3	3	When attacking with this weapon, you must subtract 1 from the hit roll.
Nemesis falchion	Melee	Melee	User	-2	D3	If a model is armed with two Nemesis falchions, each time it fights it can make 1 additional attack with them.
Nemesis force halberd	Melee	Melee	+1	-2	D3	-
Nemesis force sword	Melee	Melee	User	-3	D3	-
Nemesis warding stave	Melee	Melee	+2	-1	D3	A model armed with this weapon has a 5+ invulnerable save against attacks made in the Fight phase. If it already has an invulnerable save, add 1 to invulnerable saving throws you make for it in the Fight phase instead.

KILL TEAM

MODEL	POINTS PER MODEL (Does not include wargear)
Grey Knight	18
- Grey Knight Gunner	19
- Justicar	19

RANGED WEAPONS

WEAPON	POINTS PER WEAPON
Frag grenade	0
Incinerator	3
Krak grenade	0
Psilencer	3
Psycannon	2
Psyk-out grenade	0
Storm bolter	0

MELEE WEAPONS

WEAPON	POINTS PER WEAPON
Nemesis Daemon hammer	2
Nemesis falchion	1
Nemesis force halberd	0
Nemesis force sword	0
Nemesis warding stave	0

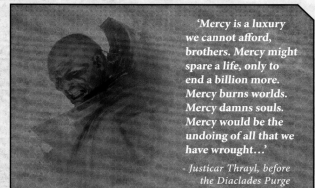

'Mercy is a luxury we cannot afford, brothers. Mercy might spare a life, only to end a billion more. Mercy burns worlds. Mercy damns souls. Mercy would be the undoing of all that we have wrought…'

- Justicar Thrayl, before the Diaclades Purge

ASTRA MILITARUM

The Astra Militarum is the sledgehammer of the Emperor, and its countless armies form the vast majority of the Imperium's military might, relentlessly pounding their enemies with shot and shell until nothing is left but a cratered wasteland. By rolling the appropriate dice on the tables on the following pages, you can generate names and background for your Astra Militarum kill teams.

The Astra Militarum make up the vast bulk of the Imperium's standing armies. Tithed in their billions from worlds across the Imperium, these soldiers undergo swift and brutal training, often en route to their designated war zone. Unlike the more elite arms of the Imperial war machine, the soldiers of the Astra Militarum lack the advantages of genetic enhancement and sophisticated weaponry. Their arms and armour, their battle tanks, artillery pieces and aircraft are all mass-produced and hurled into battle in vast numbers, there to wear the enemy down through attrition and belligerent application of overwhelming firepower.

Casualty rates amongst the Imperial Guard are beyond horrific; if a freshly recruited soldier survives more than their first fifteen hours in battle, they are considered an accomplished veteran. Yet despite the horrors they must face, despite the odds that are stacked against them and the likelihood of their own imminent demise, these courageous men and women follow their orders and march out to fight the Emperor's wars, for they know that the fate of all of Humanity rests upon their shoulders.

The soldiers of an Astra Militarum kill team are equipped with an array of reliable, if basic, weapons and wargear. In order to survive, every Guardsman must learn quickly to wield this weaponry against all manner of fiendish traitor monstrosities and hulking xenos warriors. Faced by such terrifying enemies, these men and women must steel their nerve and stride out to confront these threats to the continued

existence of Mankind. Typically only a fraction of an Astra Militarum kill team's soldiers survive their first excursion, yet through grit, determination and sheer weight of numbers they grind their foes into oblivion.

Astra Militarum kill teams take many forms. Often they are comprised of a team of grizzled veterans supplemented by newer recruits. At other times regimental survivors or scouting troops find themselves fighting behind enemy lines, banding together to increase their chances of survival and victory. Whatever its composition, an Imperial Guard kill team has the numbers, the faith and the firepower to bring down any foe – and though they may face the most dreadful hardships with little more than a lasgun, a bayonet and a whispered benediction to the immortal Emperor, they will pay any cost to secure victory.

THE UBIQUITOUS LASGUN

The lasgun is the standard-issue rifle of the Imperial Guard, and there are many models, marks and patterns in service. The Cadian Shock Troops commonly bear the M36 lasrifle, a weapon well known for its reliability. The Catachan Jungle Fighters use the Mk 4 lascarbine, the hefty power cells of which give the weapon additional clout both as a short-range assault rifle and an improvised club. Many other marks exist throughout the Imperium, from the mass-produced to the exotic, and even weapons for dedicated mechanised or drop regiments.

BACKGROUND: WAR STORY

D10	
1	**Penal Troopers:** Offered one last chance to earn redemption through service, this band of deadly but ill-disciplined soldiers must serve or die.
2	**Hardened Veterans:** Survivors of a dozen war zones, these hard-bitten warriors know all the wily tricks they don't print in the Imperial Primer.
3	**Light Infantry:** Equipped for swift movement and pinpoint combat through dense terrain, these warriors are experts in forward operations.
4	**Sappers:** This squad excels in siege warfare, demolitions, and any other theatre in which the Emperor expects them to blow things sky high.
5	**Elite Guards:** Highly trained and well equipped, these warriors are sworn to give their lives for the great and the good.
6	**Fresh Meat:** Fresh from their first drop and ready to serve the Emperor, how many of these Imperial Guardsmen will survive their 'fifteen hours'?
7	**Drop Troops:** This squad is trained to swoop down upon their objective in fast-moving drop-craft before using rappelling lines and grav-chutes to leap into the action.
8	**Tank Hunters:** Loaded for big game, this team of steely-eyed warriors specialises in eliminating armoured targets.
9	**Shock Troops:** Clad in bulky armour and carrying an array of firearms, this squad is ready for the most intense firefights.
10	**Grizzled Survivors:** The battle has been long, the death toll horrific, yet still this band of warriors fights on in the Emperor's name.

MISSION: DUTY TO THE EMPEROR

D10	
1	**Hold at All Costs:** No matter how many men fall, the enemy must not be allowed to capture or destroy a crucial objective.
2	**Assault:** The foe are at bay; now is the time for a pinpoint strike to shatter their resistance.
3	**Assassinate:** A heretical commander or vile demagogue must be slain, and the duty falls to this band of warriors.
4	**Demolitions:** For the battlefront to advance, an elite team must knock out a key generatorum, gate control, orbital laser or other high-priority target.
5	**Die Well:** The situation is desperate, the enemy advancing. Stand your ground and die well for your Emperor!
6	**Raiders:** An ammo dump, command relay or supply line must be eliminated deep behind enemy lines.
7	**Capture Location:** The value of these coordinates cannot be overstated; they must be seized at any price.
8	**Recon:** With auspex down and the foe on the move, intelligence must be gathered by soldiers on the ground.
9	**Messengers:** Amidst the maelstrom of the battlefield, a crucial message must be borne safely to high command.
10	**Looters:** This squad has gone off the grid, hunting for riches fabled to be lying in no man's land.

SQUAD QUIRK: TRAIT

D10	
1	**Faithful:** These warriors are lent zealous courage by their faith in the Emperor.
2	**Parade Ground Drilled:** This squad is smartly presented and crisply efficient at all times.
3	**Tunnel Fighters:** This squad excels in the hellish confines of ducts, tunnels and crawl-ways.
4	**City Fighters:** These warriors know how to survive and prevail in tangled urban war zones.
5	**Death Worlders:** Many worlds in the Imperium are hazardous in the extreme. This squad hails from such a planet, and its members are renowned for their resulting toughness.
6	**Xenos Hunters:** This squad has fought many battles against a particular alien foe, and has learned how best to kill them.
7	**Seen Too Much:** The mind of man can take only so much horror. These soldiers have been pushed far beyond that line.
8	**Chem-addicts:** The members of this squad habitually use chemical stimms to enhance their strength and banish their fear. Of course, such an addiction has its drawbacks…
9	**Gone Native:** So long has this squad been in the field that its soldiers have become almost feral.
10	**Killer Rep:** Everyone knows that you don't get in this squad's way – not if you value your life.

D10	SPECIALISTS' DEMEANOURS
1	**Dutiful:** Orders must be followed to the letter, for such is the Guardsman's lot.
2	**Haunted:** This warrior can never truly escape the voices of lost comrades. He stares and mutters constantly.
3	**Nerves of Steel:** This soldier is implacably calm and focused no matter the circumstances.
4	**Pious:** This warrior's hymns spill out across the battlefield as he fights.
5	**Eagle-eye:** This warrior is a naturally gifted shot, able to drop an Ork from one hundred yards every time.
6	**Courageous:** A true exemplar of heroism in the face of unimaginable terrors.
7	**Vengeful:** This warrior lost his comrades to a particular race or enemy, and now he hates them with a singular passion.
8	**Psycho:** This knife-wielding madman giggles and shrieks as he slakes his bloodlust amongst the foe.
9	**Expert:** This warrior hasn't survived as long as he has by chance alone. He's the best of the best.
10	**Gung-ho:** The only approach this soldier knows is to kick down the door and storm in with guns blazing.

CADIAN NAME GENERATOR TABLE	
D66	**TROOPER**
11	Jens
12	Karsk
13	Hekler
14	Reeve
15	Pavlo
16	Hektor
21	Nils
22	Thenmann
23	Kyser
24	Erlen
25	Raphe
26	Creed
31	Lasko
32	Ackerman
33	Mattias
34	Mortens
35	Dansk
36	Feodor
41	Tomas
42	Kolson
43	Vance
44	Pask
45	Niems
46	Gryf
51	Willem
52	Sonnen
53	Ekhter
54	Farestein
55	Dekker
56	Graf
61	Arvans
62	Viers
63	Kolm
64	Bask
65	Vesker
66	Pavlo

CATACHAN NAME GENERATOR TABLE	
D66	**TROOPER**
11	Gunnarsen
12	Harker
13	Grytt
14	'Snake' Vandien
15	Greiss
16	Stryker
21	Storm
22	Lance
23	'Crazy' Winters
24	Cage
25	Hammer
26	Cobra
31	'Hardhead' Jackson
32	'Stonefist' Kage
33	'Boss' Stransky
34	'Bomber' Johnson
35	Jacksen
36	Marshall
41	'Fangs' Lorson
42	'Cold-eye' McKay
43	Wolf
44	'Shiv' Frost
45	Brent
46	'Ironheart' McKillen
51	'Killer' Crowe
52	'Wildman' Weiss
53	'Ice' Creek
54	Dane
55	Steeljaw
56	Dransky
61	'Slim' Hasker
62	Mason
63	Hawks
64	Axel
65	Carver
66	Payne

VALHALLAN NAME GENERATOR TABLE	
D66	**TROOPER**
11	Vensk
12	Skarrsen
13	Chernov
14	Dushenko
15	Rynsk
16	Gorska
21	Varence
22	Nyska
23	Putran
24	Dorff
25	Tyvosk
26	Polanski
31	Drekoff
32	Vorn
33	Hapscheldt
34	Olof
35	Trevinska
36	Schonnen
41	Kleiss
42	Borys
43	Ivanek
44	Smirnek
45	Kuzentsev
46	Vasilesnev
51	Petravitch
52	Skolov
53	Fedorev
54	Morazev
55	Volko
56	Lebesnev
61	Egoryn
62	Pavlek
63	Kozlev
64	Stepanovicz
65	Nikoli
66	Orlakev

TALLARN NAME GENERATOR TABLE	
D66	**TROOPER**
11	Alem
12	Hallain
13	Laskair
14	Nathal
15	Altarem
16	Mohal
21	Dharem
22	Hasman
23	Sonnam
24	Ushmet
25	Shadnan
26	Asphret
31	Ushad
32	Tal'hasen
33	Ashmyr
34	Shashlem
35	Haseed
36	Ushar
41	Raheim
42	Dassed
43	Sahleim
44	Alhret
45	Khaleeth
46	Eshmet
51	Ul'shalem
52	Talannar
53	Al'phareim
54	El'shan
55	Khabir
56	Khalym
61	'Swiftrider'
62	'Dunestrider'
63	'Hawkseye'
64	'Sand Devil'
65	'the Mirage'
66	'the Hunter'

ASTRA MILITARUM KILL TEAMS

Astra Militarum Leaders in Kill Team use the Voice of Command ability below. In addition, if every model in your kill team has the **Astra Militarum** Faction keyword, you can use Astra Militarum Tactics.

Voice of Command: Once per battle round, if your Leader is on the battlefield and not shaken, they can issue an order to other members of your kill team at the start of the Shooting phase. To issue an order, pick another friendly **Astra Militarum** model (other than a shaken model) within 12" of your Leader and choose which order you wish to issue from the list opposite. A model may only be affected by one order per battle round.

ASTRA MILITARUM ORDERS

ORDER

Take Aim!: Re-roll hit rolls of 1 for the ordered model until the end of the phase.

Bring it Down!: Re-roll wound rolls of 1 for the ordered model until the end of the phase.

Forwards, for the Emperor!: The ordered model can shoot even if it Advanced in the previous Movement phase.

Get Back in the Fight!: The ordered model can shoot this phase, even if it Fell Back in the Movement phase.

Move! Move! Move!: Instead of shooting this phase, the ordered model immediately makes an Advance move as if it were the Movement phase.

Fix Bayonets!: This order can only be issued to a model within 1" of an enemy model. The ordered model immediately fights as if it were the Fight phase.

DEFENSIVE STAND

Astra Militarum Tactic

Use this Tactic when a charge is declared against a model from your kill team. When that model fires Overwatch this phase, they successfully hit on a roll of 5 or 6.

2 COMMAND POINTS

CUNNING STRATEGY

Astra Militarum Tactic

Use this Tactic after your Leader has issued an order. Your Leader may immediately issue an additional order.

2 COMMAND POINTS

GET DOWN!

Astra Militarum Tactic

Use this Tactic in your opponent's turn in the Shooting phase when they choose a model from your kill team as a target, and your model is obscured. Attacks that target that model in this phase suffer an additional -1 penalty to their hit rolls.

1 COMMAND POINT

RESERVES OF COURAGE

Astra Militarum Tactic

Use this Tactic at the start of your turn in the Morale phase. Pick a model from your kill team that is required to take a Nerve test. Roll a D3 for that model rather than a D6 when taking the test.

1 COMMAND POINT

INFANTRY SQUAD GUARDSMAN

NAME	M	WS	BS	S	T	W	A	Ld	Sv	Max
Guardsman	6"	4+	4+	3	3	1	1	6	5+	-
Guardsman Gunner	6"	4+	4+	3	3	1	1	6	5+	1
Sergeant	6"	4+	4+	3	3	1	2	7	5+	1

This model is armed with a lasgun and frag grenades.
One Guardsman in your kill team can be a Guardsman Gunner, and one Guardsman in your kill team can be a Sergeant. A Sergeant is instead armed with a laspistol, chainsword and frag grenades.

WARGEAR OPTIONS	• One Guardsman in your kill team may take a vox-caster. • A Guardsman Gunner may replace their lasgun with a flamer, grenade launcher, meltagun, plasma gun or sniper rifle. • A Sergeant may replace their laspistol with a bolt pistol or plasma pistol. They may also replace their chainsword with a power sword.
ABILITIES	**Voice of Command** (pg 100) **Vox-caster:** You can re-roll failed Nerve tests for **Astra Militarum** models while a friendly model with a vox-caster is on the battlefield and not shaken.
SPECIALISTS	**Leader** (Sergeant only), **Heavy** (Gunner only), **Comms** (Guardsman with vox-caster only), **Demolitions, Scout, Sniper, Veteran**
FACTION KEYWORD	**Astra Militarum**
KEYWORDS	**Imperium, Infantry, Infantry Squad Guardsman**

SPECIAL WEAPONS SQUAD GUARDSMAN

NAME	M	WS	BS	S	T	W	A	Ld	Sv	Max
Special Weapons Guardsman	6"	4+	4+	3	3	1	1	6	5+	-
Special Weapons Gunner	6"	4+	4+	3	3	1	1	6	5+	3

This model is armed with a lasgun and frag grenades.
Up to three Special Weapons Guardsmen in your kill team can be Special Weapons Gunners.

WARGEAR OPTIONS	• A Special Weapons Gunner may replace their lasgun with a flamer, grenade launcher, meltagun, plasma gun or sniper rifle.
ABILITIES	**Voice of Command** (pg 100)
SPECIALISTS	**Heavy** (Gunner only), **Leader, Comms, Demolitions, Scout, Sniper, Veteran**
FACTION KEYWORD	**Astra Militarum**
KEYWORDS	**Imperium, Infantry, Special Weapons Squad Guardsman**

MILITARUM TEMPESTUS SCION

NAME	M	WS	BS	S	T	W	A	Ld	Sv	Max
Scion	6"	4+	3+	3	3	1	1	6	4+	-
Scion Gunner	6"	4+	3+	3	3	1	1	6	4+	4
Tempestor	6"	3+	3+	3	3	1	2	7	4+	1

This model is armed with a hot-shot lasgun, frag grenades and krak grenades.

Up to four Scions in your kill team can be Scion Gunners, and one Scion in your kill team can be a Tempestor. A Tempestor is instead armed with a hot-shot laspistol, chainsword and frag and krak grenades.

WARGEAR OPTIONS	• One Scion in your kill team may take a vox-caster. • A Scion Gunner may replace their hot-shot lasgun with a flamer, meltagun, plasma gun or hot-shot volley gun. • A Tempestor may replace their hot-shot laspistol with a bolt pistol or plasma pistol. • A Tempestor may replace their chainsword with a power sword or power fist.
ABILITIES	Voice of Command (pg 100) **Vox-caster:** You can re-roll failed Nerve tests for Astra Militarum models while a friendly model with a vox-caster is on the battlefield and not shaken.
SPECIALISTS	**Leader** (Tempestor only), **Demolitions** (Gunner only), **Heavy** (Gunner only), **Comms**, **Medic**, **Scout**, **Sniper**, **Veteran**
FACTION KEYWORD	Astra Militarum
KEYWORDS	Imperium, Militarum Tempestus, Infantry, Militarum Tempestus Scion

RANGED WEAPONS

WEAPON	RANGE	TYPE	S	AP	D	ABILITIES
Bolt pistol	12"	Pistol 1	4	0	1	-
Flamer	8"	Assault D6	4	0	1	This weapon automatically hits its target.
Frag grenade	6"	Grenade D6	3	0	1	-
Grenade launcher	When attacking with this weapon, choose one of the profiles below.					
- Frag grenade	24"	Assault D6	3	0	1	-
- Krak grenade	24"	Assault 1	6	-1	D3	-
Hot-shot lasgun	18"	Rapid Fire 1	3	-2	1	-
Hot-shot laspistol	6"	Pistol 1	3	-2	1	-
Hot-shot volley gun	24"	Heavy 4	4	-2	1	-
Krak grenade	6"	Grenade 1	6	-1	D3	-
Lasgun	24"	Rapid Fire 1	3	0	1	-
Laspistol	12"	Pistol 1	3	0	1	-
Meltagun	12"	Assault 1	8	-4	D6	If the target is within half range of this weapon, roll two dice when inflicting damage with it and discard the lowest result.
Plasma gun	When attacking with this weapon, choose one of the profiles below.					
- Standard	24"	Rapid Fire 1	7	-3	1	-
- Supercharge	24"	Rapid Fire 1	8	-3	2	On an unmodified hit roll of 1, the bearer is taken out of action after all of this weapon's shots have been resolved.
Plasma pistol	When attacking with this weapon, choose one of the profiles below.					
- Standard	12"	Pistol 1	7	-3	1	-
- Supercharge	12"	Pistol 1	8	-3	2	On an unmodified hit roll of 1, the bearer is taken out of action.
Sniper rifle	36"	Heavy 1	4	0	1	A model firing a sniper rifle does not suffer the penalty to hit rolls for the target being at long range. If you roll a wound roll of 6+ for this weapon, it inflicts a mortal wound in addition to its normal damage.

MELEE WEAPONS

WEAPON	RANGE	TYPE	S	AP	D	ABILITIES
Chainsword	Melee	Melee	User	0	1	Each time the bearer fights, it can make 1 additional attack with this weapon.
Power fist	Melee	Melee	x2	-3	D3	When attacking with this weapon, you must subtract 1 from the hit roll.
Power sword	Melee	Melee	User	-3	1	-

KILL TEAM

MODEL	POINTS PER MODEL (Does not include wargear)
Infantry Squad Guardsman	5
- Guardsman Gunner	5
- Sergeant	5
Militarum Tempestus Scion	9
- Scion Gunner	10
- Tempestor	10
Special Weapons Squad Guardsman	5
- Special Weapons Gunner	5

RANGED WEAPONS

WEAPON	POINTS PER WEAPON
Bolt pistol	0
Flamer	3
Frag grenade	0
Grenade launcher	2
Hot-shot lasgun	0
Hot-shot laspistol	0
Hot-shot volley gun	3
Krak grenade	0
Lasgun	0
Laspistol	0
Meltagun	3
Plasma gun	3
Plasma pistol	1
Sniper rifle	1

MELEE WEAPONS

WEAPON	POINTS PER WEAPON
Chainsword	0
Power fist	2
Power sword	1

OTHER WARGEAR

WARGEAR	POINTS PER ITEM
Vox-caster	5

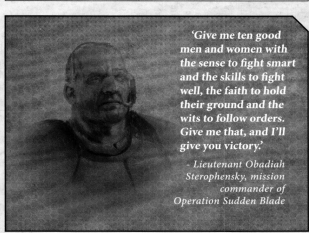

'Give me ten good men and women with the sense to fight smart and the skills to fight well, the faith to hold their ground and the wits to follow orders. Give me that, and I'll give you victory.'

- Lieutenant Obadiah Sterophensky, mission commander of Operation Sudden Blade

ADEPTUS MECHANICUS

The Adeptus Mechanicus is ancient and powerful. Hoarding and ambitious, the Tech-Priests of Mars view the acquisition of knowledge as a holy directive. By rolling the appropriate dice on the tables on the following pages, you can generate names and background for your Skitarii kill teams.

The Adeptus Mechanicus worship the Emperor in his aspect as the Omnissiah, the god of all machines. To the Tech-Priests presiding over their factory-like forge worlds, mortal flesh is weak, and from ruling magi to lowly Servitors the Adeptus Mechanicus augment their bodies with cybernetic components, transcending human emotion and replacing it with cold, inescapable logic.

Their armies are made up of warriors known as Skitarii, whose maniples are part religious procession and part grinding, inexorable war machine. As merciless as the engines they worship, rank upon rank of augmetic warriors advance towards their target with guns blazing. Safely ensconced in orbiting warships or bunker complexes, magi inload doctrina imperatives, control signals that pass through the Skitarii like a religious rapture. Rendered fearless and martially optimised by the commands of their betters, the Skitarii advance gladly into the most hellish war zones, giving no thought to their own survival providing the will of the Machine God is done.

The weapons the Skitarii wield in these wars of auto-religious conquest are ferociously destructive, incorporating technologies so potent that they resemble dark and murderous miracles. Loping war engines and many-legged tanks loom over the Skitarii ranks, their guns spitting atomising beams of pure energy and searing arcs of actinic lightning that pass through the enemy like vengeful ghosts and leave naught but charred corpses in their wake.

Adeptus Mechanicus kill teams scour the galaxy for information and lost archeotech, exterminating any they deem tech-heretics. Composed of warriors who are more machine than man, each kill team is optimised to carry out specific sets of battlefield protocols. With every encounter, the members of a kill team gather more data concerning their enemy, and adapt their subroutines to eliminate any threat.

Adeptus Mechanicus kill teams have access to a wide array of weaponry that is unseen among other Imperial forces. Furthermore, their cybernetics let them wage skirmishing campaigns in environments that would kill unaugmented soldiers, allowing them to infiltrate enemy compounds in rad-blasted wastes or conduct hit-and-run attacks for months on end without sustenance or shelter. This they do for the glory of the Machine God, and they praise him in battle through the incantation of static-ridden psalms.

THE FORGE WORLDS

Though they first rose to prominence on Mars, the priesthood of the Adeptus Mechanicus spread out across the stars during the earliest days of Imperial expansion. They claimed many planets as their own sovereign domains, and these became forge worlds. From Triplex Phall to Ryza, Metalica to Gryphonne IV, each world was transformed from a verdant and resource-rich paradise into a fortress of seething industry, a smog-wreathed temple to the Omnissiah. Many of the forge worlds survive to this day, and are the principal providers of the Imperium's military materiel.

D10 | BACKGROUND: DESIGNATION

D10	
1	**Explorator Team:** The members of this kill team are conquerors who use the light of knowledge to drive back the shadow of ignorance amidst a galaxy of darkness and superstition.
2	**Archeotech Hunters:** These warriors seek ancient lore and holy technologies, such as archeotech troves and sacred STCs.
3	**Elimination Clade:** This kill team has been assembled to neutralise a specific target, be it a sinner in the Omnissiah's eyes or a hated servant of the dreaded Dark Mechanicum.
4	**Campaign Veterans:** These are surviving Skitarii from a long-fought conflict, meshing like cogs to form a deadly machine.
5	**Titan Guards:** These Skitarii are blessed garrison guardians of a mighty god-machine, protecting the colossal war engine while it is quiescent, or striking at some threat beyond its reach.
6	**Rad-zone Corps:** Warriors whose way of war bathes the battlefield in purifying radiation, this kill team seeks to fashion a promised land in which only true servants of the Omnissiah can endure.
7	**Infiltrator Clade:** This is a fast-moving band of elite Skitarii poised to strike at optimal targets, be they communication relays, command centres or the enemy's profane technologies.
8	**Domination Cadre:** A force assembled with endurance in mind, this kill team has been tasked with seizing and holding a specific location or asset, regardless of cost in life.
9	**Itratii Cadre:** Cataloguing the capabilities of the weapons they wield, or the foes they turn them upon, is the speciality of this kill team.
10	**Corpus-Sanctarii Clade:** Elite bodyguards of a high-ranking Tech-Priest, these Skitarii are duty-bound to protect him and his works at all costs.

D10 | MISSION: FUNCTION

D10	
1	**Defend the Sacred Technologies:** The gifts of the Omnissiah must be defended at any cost.
2	**Recover a Holy Prize:** The Omnissiah lays claim to all technologies, whether they are willingly given or no.
3	**Biologis Sample Extraction:** Biosamples must be taken from live subjects to further the Magi Biologis' knowledge.
4	**Strategic Martyrdom:** The Skitarii must march into the guns of the foe, and through their sacrifice reveal where the enemy's defences exhibit exploitable weaknesses.
5	**Smite a Tech-heretic:** Those who profane the holy machine, be they xenos artificers or heretical Warpsmiths, must be slain by its true disciples.
6	**Eliminate Heretical Machineries:** The galaxy is rife with the corrupted technological works of deviants. They must be destroyed, lest they offend the Omnissiah's eyes.
7	**Righteous Auto-castigation:** The Skitarii must prove their faith by unleashing the blessed energies of their sacred electoos.
8	**Root Out Techno-dissidents:** Those ignorant fools that attempt to sabotage the holy machine, or decry its divine nature, must be hunted down and slain.
9	**Eradicate False Testament:** It is not for lesser men to judge the works of the Omnissiah's servants, and without supposed proof there can be no judgement.
10	**Victory for Logic:** A supernatural threat is skewing the cogitations of the Tech-Priests with impossible variables. As it cannot exist in the first place, it must be swiftly eliminated to prevent noospheric corruption.

D10 | SQUAD QUIRK: UNSANCTIONED DIVERGENCE

D10	
1	**Acquisitive:** Offer unto the Omnissiah his due, regardless of the obstacles that stand in your way or the false priorities imposed by those of the flesh.
2	**Jealous Guardians:** None shall lay a hand upon the holy machine, nor even look upon its iron countenance, while you maintain your vigil.
3	**Mindlessly Devout:** You are but cogs, and turn only at the Omnissiah's bidding. You act only when divine guidance strikes.
4	**Requiring Re-sanctification:** Skitarii too long in the field become corrupted by fragments of scrap data that can make them sluggish or unpredictable.
5	**Monotask:** There is purity in a singular obsession, pursued with mechanistic devotion to the exclusion of all else.
6	**Pursuing Auto-perfection:** Whether it be a blade thrust or the pull of a carbine's trigger, a deed must be repeated ad infinitum until it attains the perfection of worship.
7	**Cybernetic Ascension:** Pain, fear, sorrow – all these are weaknesses of the flesh that have long been left behind.
8	**Mercilessly Decisive:** Logic dictates that the enemy must be annihilated regardless of the cost, and to you, logic is all.
9	**Secretive:** Behind screens of stealth technology and auspex-obfuscation, your hidden holy works proceed apace.
10	**Beyond the Crux Mechanicus:** Your warriors are now so blessed that they are more machine than flesh, and all the more resilient for it.

D10 — SPECIALISTS' DEMEANOURS

D10	
1	**Meticulously Observant:** The slightest weakness in the enemy's armour is laid bare to this warrior's augmetic perceptions.
2	**Binharic Piety:** This warrior is given to strident pronunciations in binharic cant whenever they act in anger.
3	**Biologis Cognis:** Databanks singing with holy knowledge of the enemy's biology, this warrior knows just how – and where – to damage their foes the most.
4	**Mechadominus:** Hostile machineries recoil and malfunction in fear at this warrior's autobellicose presence.
5	**Defensor Majoris:** Nothing is more sacred to this warrior than the holy works of the Omnissiah, and he will abandon all other priorities to defend them.
6	**Memeglitch:** With their noospheric intake corrupted by tireless service, this warrior has developed biological tics and twitches they cannot control.
7	**Uncompromator Doctrines:** This warrior is ruthless in the extreme, willing to expend the lives of every comrade they fight with if it will secure victory.
8	**Ironstride:** This warrior is never still, glorying in the perpetual motive force of the Omnissiah.
9	**Strategic Chorister:** Infobanks of oracular and tactico-predictive engrams allow this warrior to constantly exload optimal instructions to their comrades.
10	**Autopuritanical Ballistics:** This warrior preserves the sacred munitions gifted to them by the Omnissiah by ensuring that every round is placed with optimised lethality.

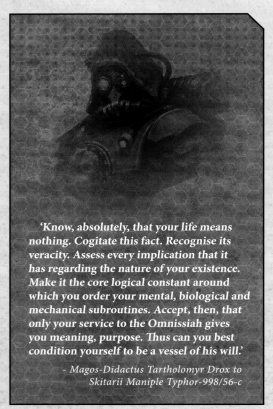

'Know, absolutely, that your life means nothing. Cogitate this fact. Recognise its veracity. Assess every implication that it has regarding the nature of your existence. Make it the core logical constant around which you order your mental, biological and mechanical subroutines. Accept, then, that only your service to the Omnissiah gives you meaning, purpose. Thus can you best condition yourself to be a vessel of his will.'

- Magos-Didactus Tartholomyr Drox to Skitarii Maniple Typhor-998/56-c

SKITARII

D66	ALPHA COMPONENT	BETA COMPONENT
11	Sy-gex	-511
12	Tyr	-1111
13	Dak	-XXVII
14	Ar	-802
15	Kappic-Schoelendt	-323/mk12
16	Tyba	-089
21	Dorox	-744
22	Alb	-VII
23	Zyto-Neumann	-18.1
24	Xixos	-656
25	Kau	-IV
26	Rho	-110
31	Delpha	-0.4343
32	Chu	-97/mk24
33	Ix	-XIX
34	Neng-Pho	-7
35	Bheta	-110100
36	Zhu	-3.16
41	Lho	-961.34254
42	Teppa-Nyxos	-MXV
43	Kor	-99
44	Dox	-2918
45	Sek	-888.88
46	Gryphonne-Reductus	-404
51	Tov	-1010
52	Eq	-0.44//K
53	Mu	-745
54	Rhy	-66.75/mk98
55	Dos	-1/1/2
56	Exitor-Dho	-99941
61	Fel	-83.2
62	Actus	-575
63	Xor	-79.09/5
64	Decima	-668.2
65	Rax	-1/5
66	Kas	-666/2

ADEPTUS MECHANICUS KILL TEAMS

Adeptus Mechanicus models in Kill Team use the Canticles of the Omnissiah ability below. In addition, if every model in your kill team has the Adeptus Mechanicus Faction keyword, you can use Adeptus Mechanicus Tactics.

Canticles of the Omnissiah: At the start of each battle round, pick which Canticle of the Omnissiah from the table opposite is in effect until the end of the battle round. The same Canticle may not be picked twice during the same battle.

Alternatively, you can randomly determine which Canticle of the Omnissiah is in effect by rolling a D6 and consulting the table opposite. Note that if you randomly determine a Canticle, it takes effect even if the same Canticle has been in effect earlier in the battle.

CANTICLES OF THE OMNISSIAH TABLE

D6	CANTICLE
1	**Incantation of the Iron Soul:** You can re-roll failed Nerve tests for models in your kill team.
2	**Litany of the Electromancer:** Roll a D6 for each enemy model within 1" of any models in your kill team at the start of the Fight phase. On a 6, that enemy model suffers 1 mortal wound.
3	**Chant of the Remorseless Fist:** Re-roll hit rolls of 1 for models in your kill team in the Fight phase.
4	**Shroudpsalm:** When an enemy player makes a hit roll for a shooting attack that targets a model from your kill team, and that model is obscured, that hit roll suffers an additional -1 modifier.
5	**Invocation of Machine Might:** Add 1 to the Strength characteristic of models in your kill team.
6	**Benediction of the Omnissiah:** Re-roll hit rolls of 1 for models in your kill team in the Shooting phase.

CONQUEROR DOCTRINA IMPERATIVE

Adeptus Mechanicus Tactic

Use this Tactic when you choose a model in your kill team to fight in the Fight phase. Add 1 to hit rolls for the model until the end of the phase. If the model is within 6" of a friendly model equipped with an enhanced data-tether, you can add 2 to the hit rolls instead.

2 COMMAND POINTS

PROTECTOR DOCTRINA IMPERATIVE

Adeptus Mechanicus Tactic

Use this Tactic when you choose a model in your kill team to shoot in the Shooting phase. Add 1 to hit rolls for the model until the end of the phase. If the model is within 6" of a friendly model equipped with an enhanced data-tether, you can add 2 to the hit rolls instead.

2 COMMAND POINTS

DUNESTRIDER

Adeptus Mechanicus Tactic

Use this Tactic in the Movement phase when a model from your kill team Advances. Roll two dice and pick which result to use when making the Advance roll.

1 COMMAND POINT

GLORIA MECHANICUS

Adeptus Mechanicus Tactic

Use this Tactic after determining which Canticle of the Omnissiah is in effect this battle round. Randomly determine a Canticle of the Omnissiah – that Canticle is in effect instead.

1 COMMAND POINT

SKITARII RANGER

NAME	M	WS	BS	S	T	W	A	Ld	Sv	Max
Skitarii Ranger	6"	4+	3+	3	3	1	1	6	4+	-
Ranger Gunner	6"	4+	3+	3	3	1	1	6	4+	3
Ranger Alpha	6"	4+	3+	3	3	1	2	7	4+	1

This model is armed with a galvanic rifle.
Up to three Skitarii Rangers in your kill team can be Ranger Gunners, and one Skitarii Ranger in your kill team can be a Ranger Alpha.

WARGEAR OPTIONS	• One Skitarii Ranger in your kill team may take an enhanced data-tether or an omnispex. • A Ranger Gunner may replace their galvanic rifle with an arc rifle, plasma caliver or transuranic arquebus. • A Ranger Alpha may replace their galvanic rifle with one of the following pistols and one of the following melee weapons: arc pistol, phosphor blast pistol or radium pistol; arc maul, power sword or taser goad.
ABILITIES	**Canticles of the Omnissiah** (pg 107) **Bionics:** This model has a 6+ invulnerable save. **Enhanced Data-tether:** You can re-roll failed Nerve tests for SKITARII models while a friendly model with an enhanced data-tether is on the battlefield and not shaken.	**Omnispex:** At the start of each Shooting phase, you can choose another SKITARII model within 3" of a friendly model equipped with an omnispex that is not shaken. That model does not suffer penalties to their hit or injury rolls due to their target being obscured.
SPECIALISTS	**Leader** (Alpha only), **Heavy** (Gunner only), **Comms, Scout, Sniper, Zealot**
FACTION KEYWORD	ADEPTUS MECHANICUS
KEYWORDS	IMPERIUM, SKITARII, INFANTRY, SKITARII RANGER

SKITARII VANGUARD

NAME	M	WS	BS	S	T	W	A	Ld	Sv	Max
Skitarii Vanguard	6"	4+	3+	3	3	1	1	6	4+	-
Vanguard Gunner	6"	4+	3+	3	3	1	1	6	4+	3
Vanguard Alpha	6"	4+	3+	3	3	1	2	7	4+	1

This model is armed with a radium carbine.
Up to three Skitarii Vanguard in your kill team can be Vanguard Gunners, and one Skitarii Vanguard in your kill team can be a Vanguard Alpha.

WARGEAR OPTIONS	• One Skitarii Vanguard in your kill team may take an enhanced data-tether or an omnispex. • A Vanguard Gunner may replace their radium carbine with an arc rifle, plasma caliver or transuranic arquebus. • A Vanguard Alpha may replace their radium carbine with one of the following pistols and one of the following melee weapons: arc pistol, phosphor blast pistol or radium pistol; arc maul, power sword or taser goad.
ABILITIES	**Canticles of the Omnissiah** (pg 107) **Bionics:** This model has a 6+ invulnerable save. **Rad-saturation:** Reduce the Toughness characteristic of enemy models by 1 whilst they are within 1" of one or more models with this ability.	**Omnispex:** At the start of each Shooting phase, you can choose another SKITARII model within 3" of a friendly model equipped with an omnispex that is not shaken. That model does not suffer penalties to their hit or injury rolls due to their target being obscured. **Enhanced Data-tether:** You can re-roll failed Nerve tests for SKITARII models while a friendly model with an enhanced data-tether is on the battlefield and not shaken.
SPECIALISTS	**Leader** (Alpha only), **Heavy** (Gunner only), **Comms, Scout, Sniper, Zealot**
FACTION KEYWORD	ADEPTUS MECHANICUS
KEYWORDS	IMPERIUM, SKITARII, INFANTRY, SKITARII VANGUARD

SICARIAN RUSTSTALKER

NAME	M	WS	BS	S	T	W	A	Ld	Sv	Max
Sicarian Ruststalker	8"	3+	3+	4	3	2	3	6	4+	-
Ruststalker Princeps	8"	3+	3+	4	3	2	4	7	4+	1

This model is armed with a transonic razor and chordclaw.
One Sicarian Ruststalker in your kill team can be a Ruststalker Princeps.

WARGEAR OPTIONS	• A Sicarian Ruststalker may replace their transonic razor and chordclaw with transonic blades. • A Ruststalker Princeps may replace their transonic razor with transonic blades.
ABILITIES	**Canticles of the Omnissiah** (pg 107) **Bionics:** This model has a 6+ invulnerable save.
SPECIALISTS	**Leader** (Princeps only), **Combat, Comms, Scout, Veteran, Zealot**
FACTION KEYWORD	ADEPTUS MECHANICUS
KEYWORDS	IMPERIUM, SKITARII, INFANTRY, SICARIAN RUSTSTALKER

SICARIAN INFILTRATOR

NAME	M	WS	BS	S	T	W	A	Ld	Sv	Max
Sicarian Infiltrator	8"	3+	3+	4	3	2	2	6	4+	-
Infiltrator Princeps	8"	3+	3+	4	3	2	3	7	4+	1

This model is armed with a stubcarbine and power sword.
One Sicarian Infiltrator in your kill team can be an Infiltrator Princeps.

WARGEAR OPTIONS	• This model may replace its stubcarbine and power sword with a flechette blaster and taser goad.
ABILITIES	**Canticles of the Omnissiah** (pg 107) **Bionics:** This model has a 6+ invulnerable save. **Neurostatic Aura:** Subtract 1 from the Leadership characteristic of enemy models whilst they are within 3" of one or more models with this ability.
SPECIALISTS	**Leader** (Princeps only), **Combat, Comms, Scout, Veteran, Zealot**
FACTION KEYWORD	ADEPTUS MECHANICUS
KEYWORDS	IMPERIUM, SKITARII, INFANTRY, SICARIAN INFILTRATOR

RANGED WEAPONS

WEAPON	RANGE	TYPE	S	AP	D	ABILITIES
Arc pistol	12"	Pistol 1	6	-1	1	-
Arc rifle	24"	Rapid Fire 1	6	-1	1	-
Flechette blaster	12"	Pistol 5	3	0	1	-
Galvanic rifle	30"	Rapid Fire 1	4	0	1	Each time you make a wound roll of 6+ for this weapon, that hit is resolved with an AP of -1.
Phosphor blast pistol	12"	Pistol 1	5	-1	1	Attacks made with this weapon do not suffer the penalty to hit rolls for the target being obscured.
Plasma caliver	When attacking with this weapon, choose one of the profiles below.					
- Standard	18"	Assault 2	7	-3	1	
- Supercharge	18"	Assault 2	8	-3	2	On an unmodified hit roll of 1, the bearer is taken out of action after all of this weapon's shots have been resolved.
Radium carbine	18"	Assault 3	3	0	1	Each time you make a wound roll of 6+ for this weapon, that hit is resolved with a Damage of 3.
Radium pistol	12"	Pistol 1	3	0	1	Each time you make a wound roll of 6+ for this weapon, that hit is resolved with a Damage of 2.
Stubcarbine	18"	Pistol 3	4	0	1	-
Transuranic arquebus	60"	Heavy 1	7	-2	D3	This weapon cannot be fired if the firing model moved during the Movement phase. A model firing a transuranic arquebus does not suffer the penalty to hit rolls for the target being at long range. Each time you make a wound roll of 6+ for this weapon, it inflicts a mortal wound in addition to the normal damage.

MELEE WEAPONS

WEAPON	RANGE	TYPE	S	AP	D	ABILITIES
Arc maul	Melee	Melee	+2	-1	1	-
Chordclaw	Melee	Melee	User	0	D3	A chordclaw can only be used to make one attack each time this model fights. Each time you make a wound roll of 6+ with this weapon, the target suffers D3 mortal wounds instead of the normal damage.
Power sword	Melee	Melee	User	-3	1	-
Taser goad	Melee	Melee	+2	0	1	Each hit roll of 6+ with this weapon causes 3 hits rather than 1.
Transonic blades	Melee	Melee	+1	0	1	Each time you make a wound roll of 6+ with this weapon, the target suffers a mortal wound instead of the normal damage.
Transonic razor	Melee	Melee	User	0	1	Each time you make a wound roll of 6+ with this weapon, the target suffers a mortal wound instead of the normal damage.

KILL TEAM

MODEL	POINTS PER MODEL (Does not include wargear)
Sicarian Infiltrator	14
- Infiltrator Princeps	15
Sicarian Ruststalker	14
- Ruststalker Princeps	15
Skitarii Ranger	9
- Ranger Gunner	10
- Ranger Alpha	10
Skitarii Vanguard	9
- Vanguard Gunner	10
- Vanguard Alpha	10

RANGED WEAPONS

WEAPON	POINTS PER WEAPON
Arc pistol	0
Arc rifle	0
Flechette blaster	0
Galvanic rifle	0
Phosphor blast pistol	0
Plasma caliver	3
Radium carbine	0
Radium pistol	0
Stubcarbine	0
Transuranic arquebus	5

MELEE WEAPONS

WEAPON	POINTS PER WEAPON
Arc maul	0
Chordclaw	1
Power sword	0
Taser goad	1
Transonic blades	0
Transonic razor	0

OTHER WARGEAR

WARGEAR	POINTS PER ITEM
Enhanced data-tether	5
Omnispex	1

'Detecting a seven-point-three per cent
operational weakness in left flank of enemy
defensive formation. Direct all fire on the
following targeting coordinates for optimal
strategic exploitation…'

- *Vanguard Alpha Dorox-0.4343*

HERETIC ASTARTES

Twisted and corrupt, the Heretic Astartes are traitor Space Marines who have fallen from the Emperor's grace. By rolling the appropriate dice on the tables on the following pages, you can generate names and background for your Heretic Astartes kill teams.

Heretic Astartes are dark mirrors of their loyalist counterparts. Some of these Chaos Space Marines are newly fallen, renegades that have turned their backs upon the Emperor's light in the hopes of personal power. Others are ancient beings, the same warriors that followed the Traitor Primarchs into damnation ten thousand years ago during the days of the Horus Heresy. Many exhibit twisted physiologies and sorcerous talents; others wield strange and terrible weapons, or pursue especially cruel ways of war.

Every Chaos Space Marine fights for themselves, for personal gain and advancement over their peers. Some are self-determining beings that have thrown off the shackles of Imperial rule and seek nothing more than to maraud across the galaxy, wreaking havoc amongst those they were once sworn to defend. Others give their worship to the Dark Gods of Chaos, their every deed calculated to catch the fleeting gaze of their patron deity – or indeed all of the Ruinous Powers – and thus be granted boons of unnatural power beyond the ken of mortal minds.

From the cruel siegemasters of the Iron Warriors and the murderous terror troops of the Night Lords, to the arch-heretics of the Black Legion, the zealous fanatics of the Word Bearers, the duplicitous and cunning Alpha Legion, and many more, each Traitor Legion and Renegade Chapter fights in their own fashion, yet all seek the same end goal: the utter annihilation of the False Emperor's realm. With the emergence of the Great Rift, such is a fate that seems closer to fulfilment than ever before.

Heretic Astartes kill teams vary enormously, dependent upon which Traitor Legion or Renegade Chapter they hail from, and which god or gods they worship. Some are small, elite groups of killers, while others include throngs of chanting cultists amongst their ranks. Many Heretic Astartes kill teams are made up of warriors more like unto maddened bloodhounds than veteran soldiers, whilst those truly touched by the warp are demented and inhuman beyond all reason.

The inconstant nature of the dominions ruled over by the Heretic Astartes breeds strange bedfellows. It is not uncommon to see a kill team made up of worshippers of different Chaos Gods or even the devoted servants of rival Daemons working to outdo one another. Many include mortal Chaos Cultists who strive to impress their masters with their fervour, even as they struggle to keep up with their merciless pace. Only by their leader's sheer willpower and lethality are they bound into a semblance of a unified force. All, however, have an abiding hatred for the Imperium, and a deep-seated desire to put the galaxy to flame.

THE CHAOS GODS

The Chaos Gods lurk in the warp, twisted siblings that vie for power both within their own realms and over the coveted reaches of realspace. Khorne is the Blood God, the Lord of Murder, whose worshippers seek to offer up endless mountains of skulls in his name. Tzeentch is the Great Conspirator, the Architect of Fate and Master of Magic. Nurgle is the God of Plagues, who seeks to spread his foul gifts to all living things, while Slaanesh, the Dark Prince, is the god of excess, whose worshippers inflict the greatest ecstasies and agonies on themselves and their foes.

D10 — BACKGROUND: DARK PACT

D10	
1	**Champions All:** Once part of a far larger warband, these few warriors have endured and prevailed, winning the blessings of the Dark Gods where their comrades were found wanting.
2	**Lost and Damned:** These warriors have lost themselves entirely to madness and mutation.
3	**Veterans of the Long War:** Since the end of the Horus Heresy, these warriors have fought tirelessly for vengeance. They are ancient and filled with hate.
4	**Predators:** Inhuman and terrifying, the members of this kill team act more like beasts hunting prey than trained soldiers.
5	**Warp-infused Warriors:** This band of killers has been saturated with the dark energies of the warp, twisting into bio-mechanical living weapons.
6	**Tzeentch Worshippers:** The members of this kill team are servants of the Great Conspirator, and their way of war is accordingly convoluted and seemingly insane.
7	**Khorne Worshippers:** Blood for the Blood God! Skulls for the Skull Throne! The warriors in this warband are berserk lunatics, and they care not from where the blood flows.
8	**Slaanesh Worshippers:** These warriors exist to experience – and to inflict – the most extreme physical and mental stimuli through the medium of spectacular violence.
9	**Nurgle Worshippers:** This kill team is made up of the diseased and the plague-ridden, foul abominations who exist to spread their god's revolting blessings.
10	**Worldslayers:** This kill team wield weapons of terrible destructive potency, and seek not merely conquest, but the wholesale annihilation of all realspace.

D10 — MISSION: DREAD PURPOSE

D10	
1	**Terror Raid:** The enemy must be driven to such heights of fear and panic that their capacity to resist collapses altogether.
2	**Seed Corruption:** This warband seeks to spread the influence of the Dark Gods, profaning reality and opening the path for the warp to spill forth.
3	**Dark Ritual:** The enemy must be seized and sacrificed to the Dark Gods, and the proper words intoned over their convulsing bodies as they bleed.
4	**Sunder the Gates:** This kill team has been tasked with paving the way for a wider invasion by penetrating the enemy's stronghold and sabotaging its defences.
5	**Arcane Prize:** Despatched by their powerful master, this kill team must acquire an eldritch artefact for him or die in the attempt.
6	**Faithbreakers:** This kill team's mission is to profane the enemy's places of worship, tear down their idols and prove the impotence of their false gods.
7	**Seekers After Glory:** This kill team aims to earn the blessings of the Dark Gods through suitably grand and bloody deeds.
8	**Hand of the Gods:** This warband must strike swiftly and with overwhelming force, eliminating a key strategic asset before vanishing into the shadows.
9	**Dark Guardians:** This band of killers is sworn to protect some great champion or oracle of the Dark Gods, on pain of their immortal souls.
10	**Saboteurs:** Loose behind enemy lines, this kill team seeks targets of opportunity and strikes wherever it can inflict the most damage upon the foe.

D10 — SQUAD QUIRK: TWISTED NATURE

D10	
1	**Embittered:** Hatred fuels these cynical killers, and guides their every deed.
2	**Berserk:** This kill team views the galaxy through a red haze of murder-lust.
3	**Devious:** So long has this kill team used trickery and stealth to achieve their ends that their every act is obscured by lies.
4	**Zealous:** True devotees of the Chaos Gods, these warriors bellow praises to the dark pantheon as they fight.
5	**Cruel:** These warriors live to torment their victims, whether through psychological warfare or taking their time over killing them slowly and painfully at close quarters.
6	**Stolid:** This kill team prefers to use defensive tactics and sheer resilience to win their battles.
7	**Iron Discipline:** Despite their current allegiances, these warriors still fight with all the ferocious efficiency and skill of the Legions of old.
8	**Arrogant:** These warriors consider their enemies to be laughably beneath them, sneering at their every effort to fight back.
9	**Insane:** Perhaps guided by ineffable prophecy, or finally pushed past the final boundary of rational thought, the deeds of this kill team seem like madness to their foes.
10	**Possessed:** These warriors have no will of their own, having surrendered their mortal forms to divine possession by daemonic beings.

D10	SPECIALISTS' DEMEANOUR
1	**Ultimate Veteran:** This warrior has been fighting for many lifetimes of mortals, and has honed their skills to absolute perfection.
2	**Cannibal:** This monstrous renegade stops by each fallen victim to rip gobbets of their flesh free with his fangs, consuming their strength and soul in the process.
3	**Deranged:** Giggling and singing dark, daemonic rhymes, this warrior appears utterly insane.
4	**Blade-master:** This warrior excels in duels, and seeks out the mightiest enemies to humble with his sword.
5	**Visionary:** Guided by portents and omens that only he can see, this warrior seems a superstitious madman or half-intelligible oracle.
6	**Living Canker:** This warrior is corrupt beyond mortal endurance, an avatar of foulness and mutation that taints everything he touches.
7	**Unstoppable Force:** Brutish and monstrous, this warrior smashes through everything in his path.
8	**Twisted:** Jealous and conniving, this warrior is utterly untrustworthy and will see anyone slain, friend or foe, if it is to his benefit.
9	**True Believer:** This warrior's faith in the Dark Gods is unquestioning, his devotion absolute.
10	**On the Brink:** Laden down with dark boons, this warrior is a mere step away from an ascension to daemonhood, or else a debased plunge into spawndom.

BLACK LEGION NAME GENERATOR TABLE

D10	FORENAME	SURNAME
1	Zekyr	Aximand
2	Dreccor	the Vengeful
3	Sorvram	Thrice-Cursed
4	Thallos	Korda
5	Zagator	the Black
6	Korthranus	Daemonsblade
7	Drekva	Orakar
8	Thygmor	Naxos
9	Ashrok	the Mad
10	Azmodial	Faithslayer

ALPHA LEGION NAME GENERATOR TABLE

D10	CODENAME	CYPHER
1	Kyphax	Sheyr
2	Inigo	Dynas
3	Thkeln	Hertzor
4	Sylas	Ranko
5	Armilus	(no cypher)
6	Sheed	23-7
7	Eskyrx	Legion
8	Jaego	Phors
9	Askelitar	Nul
10	Alpharius	(no cypher)

EMPEROR'S CHILDREN NAME GENERATOR TABLE

D10	FORENAME	SURNAME
1	Antinius	Sellion
2	Eidelitor	Thest
3	Ilitoias	Atonian
4	Teloss	Vessatar
5	Abdemis	Bericosian
6	Fabian	Xandassus
7	Julianis	Tresell
8	Abdelis	Vastorius
9	Lycon	Kanasiar
10	Xiander	the Perfect

WORLD EATERS NAME GENERATOR TABLE

D10	FORENAME	HONORIFIC
1	Khargos	Skullfiend
2	Drakh	the Reaper
3	Ashkal	Khorr
4	Gharrax	the Butcher
5	Khorgor	the Furious
6	Sorkhos	Slaughterborn
7	Aggravax	Foe Ripper
8	Ashkorh	the Destroyer
9	Larsakh	the Hound
10	Khaen	Thaxxos

HERETIC ASTARTES KILL TEAMS

If every model in your kill team has the HERETIC ASTARTES Faction keyword, you can use Heretic Astartes Tactics.

VETERANS OF THE LONG WAR

Heretic Astartes Tactic

Use this Tactic when a CHAOS SPACE MARINE model from your kill team is chosen to attack in the Shooting or Fight phase. You can add 1 to wound rolls for the model's attacks that target IMPERIUM models until the end of the phase.

2 COMMAND POINTS

DAEMON SPIRIT

Heretic Astartes Tactic

This Tactic is used at the end of the Movement phase. Pick an enemy model within 1" of your Leader and roll a D6. On a 4+ that enemy model suffers 1 mortal wound.

2 COMMAND POINTS

FURY OF KHORNE

Heretic Astartes Tactic

Use this Tactic at the end of the Fight phase. Pick a KHORNE model from your kill team that is within 1" of an enemy model – your model can immediately fight again.

2 COMMAND POINTS

BESEECH THE GODS

Heretic Astartes Tactic

Use this Tactic at the start of the first battle round. Pick a model from your kill team and roll a D6. On a 1 that model is found unworthy and suffers D3 mortal wounds. On a 2+ add 1 to hit and wound rolls for the model until the end of the battle. You can only use this Tactic once per battle.

2 COMMAND POINTS

CHAOS CULTIST

NAME	M	WS	BS	S	T	W	A	Ld	Sv	Max
Chaos Cultist	6"	4+	4+	3	3	1	1	5	6+	-
Chaos Cultist Gunner	6"	4+	4+	3	3	1	1	5	6+	2
Cultist Champion	6"	4+	4+	3	3	1	2	6	6+	1

This model is armed with an autogun.
Up to two Chaos Cultists in your kill team can be Chaos Cultist Gunners, and one Chaos Cultist in your kill team can be a Cultist Champion.

WARGEAR OPTIONS	• A Chaos Cultist may replace their autogun with a brutal assault weapon and autopistol. • A Chaos Cultist Gunner may replace their autogun with a flamer or heavy stubber. • A Cultist Champion may replace their autogun with a shotgun, or a brutal assault weapon and autopistol.
ABILITIES	**Mark of Chaos:** When you add a model with the <MARK OF CHAOS> keyword to your kill team, you can choose to replace it with one of the following keywords: KHORNE, NURGLE, TZEENTCH or SLAANESH, or you can choose for it to have no mark. If you choose a mark, note this on the model's datacard.
SPECIALISTS	**Leader** (Cultist Champion only), **Heavy** (Gunner only), **Combat, Demolitions, Veteran, Zealot**
FACTION KEYWORD	HERETIC ASTARTES
KEYWORDS	CHAOS, <MARK OF CHAOS>, INFANTRY, CHAOS CULTIST

CHAOS SPACE MARINE

NAME	M	WS	BS	S	T	W	A	Ld	Sv	Max
Chaos Space Marine	6"	3+	3+	4	4	1	1	7	3+	-
Chaos Space Marine Gunner	6"	3+	3+	4	4	1	1	7	3+	2
Aspiring Champion	6"	3+	3+	4	4	1	2	8	3+	1

This model is armed with a boltgun, bolt pistol, frag grenades and krak grenades.
Up to two Chaos Space Marines in your kill team can be Chaos Space Marine Gunners, and one Chaos Space Marine in your kill team can be an Aspiring Champion.

WARGEAR OPTIONS	
	• A Chaos Space Marine may replace their boltgun with a chainsword.
	• One Chaos Space Marine in your kill team may take a Chaos Icon. If they have the **Khorne**, **Tzeentch**, **Nurgle** or **Slaanesh** keyword, they must have the appropriate Icon from the Chaos Icons list below. If they have no mark, they must take an Icon of Vengeance.
	• One Chaos Space Marine Gunner in your kill team may replace their boltgun with a flamer, meltagun or plasma gun.
	• One Chaos Space Marine Gunner in your kill team may replace their boltgun with a heavy bolter.
	• An Aspiring Champion may replace their bolt pistol with a plasma pistol. They may also replace their boltgun with a chainsword, power sword or power fist.

ABILITIES	
	Death to the False Emperor: If a model with this ability makes an attack in the Fight phase which targets an **Imperium** model, each time you roll a hit roll of 6+ you may make an additional attack with the same weapon against the same target. These attacks cannot themselves generate any further attacks. **Mark of Chaos:** When you add a model with the **<Mark of Chaos>** keyword to your kill team, you can choose to replace it with one of the following keywords: **Khorne**, **Tzeentch**, **Nurgle** or **Slaanesh**, or you can choose for it to have no mark. If you choose a mark, note this on the model's datacard. **Transhuman Physiology:** Ignore the penalty to this model's hit rolls from one flesh wound it has suffered.

SPECIALISTS	**Leader** (Aspiring Champion only), **Heavy** (Gunner only), **Demolitions**, **Sniper**, **Veteran**, **Zealot**
FACTION KEYWORD	**Heretic Astartes**
KEYWORDS	**Chaos**, **<Mark of Chaos>**, **Infantry**, **Chaos Space Marine**

CHAOS ICONS

ICON	MODEL	EFFECT
Icon of Wrath	**Khorne** model only	You can re-roll charge rolls for **Khorne** models within 6" of any friendly models equipped with an Icon of Wrath.
Icon of Flame	**Tzeentch** model only	At the start of your turn in the Psychic phase, roll a D6 for each model from your kill team equipped with an Icon of Flame. On a 6 inflict 1 mortal wound on the closest enemy model within 12" of the model being rolled for.
Icon of Despair	**Nurgle** model only	Subtract 1 from the Leadership characteristic of enemy models within 6" of any models equipped with an Icon of Despair.
Icon of Excess	**Slaanesh** model only	The Death to the False Emperor ability of models within 6" of any friendly models equipped with an Icon of Excess takes effect on hit rolls of 5+ rather than 6+.
Icon of Vengeance	Cannot be taken by **Khorne**, **Tzeentch**, **Nurgle** or **Slaanesh** models	Add 1 to the Leadership characteristic of models within 6" of any friendly models equipped with an Icon of Vengeance.

'A single one of us is worth ten of your weakling so-called warriors and more. You stand as much chance of prevailing against us as does your pathetic Imperium against the tide of madness that rises now to engulf it utterly. Kneel before us, mortal, for we are the heralds of your end...'

- Ashrok Korda, Aspiring Champion of the Black Legion

RANGED WEAPONS

WEAPON	RANGE	TYPE	S	AP	D	ABILITIES
Autogun	24"	Rapid Fire 1	3	0	1	-
Autopistol	12"	Pistol 1	3	0	1	-
Bolt pistol	12"	Pistol 1	4	0	1	-
Boltgun	24"	Rapid Fire 1	4	0	1	-
Flamer	8"	Assault D6	4	0	1	This weapon automatically hits its target.
Frag grenade	6"	Grenade D6	3	0	1	-
Heavy bolter	36"	Heavy 3	5	-1	1	-
Heavy stubber	36"	Heavy 3	4	0	1	-
Krak grenade	6"	Grenade 1	6	-1	D3	-
Meltagun	12"	Assault 1	8	-4	D6	If the target is within half range of this weapon, roll two dice when inflicting damage with it and discard the lowest result.
Plasma gun	When attacking with this weapon, choose one of the profiles below.					
- Standard	24"	Rapid Fire 1	7	-3	1	-
- Supercharge	24"	Rapid Fire 1	8	-3	2	On an unmodified hit roll of 1, the bearer is taken out of action after all of this weapon's shots have been resolved.
Plasma pistol	When attacking with this weapon, choose one of the profiles below.					
- Standard	12"	Pistol 1	7	-3	1	-
- Supercharge	12"	Pistol 1	8	-3	2	On an unmodified hit roll of 1, the bearer is taken out of action.
Shotgun	12"	Assault 2	3	0	1	If the target is within half range, add 1 to this weapon's Strength.

MELEE WEAPONS

WEAPON	RANGE	TYPE	S	AP	D	ABILITIES
Brutal assault weapon	Melee	Melee	User	0	1	Each time the bearer fights, it can make 1 additional attack with this weapon.
Chainsword	Melee	Melee	User	0	1	Each time the bearer fights, it can make 1 additional attack with this weapon.
Power fist	Melee	Melee	x2	-3	D3	When attacking with this weapon, you must subtract 1 from the hit roll.
Power sword	Melee	Melee	User	-3	1	-

KILL TEAM

MODEL	POINTS PER MODEL (Does not include wargear)
Chaos Cultist	4
- Chaos Cultist Gunner	5
- Cultist Champion	5
Chaos Space Marine	12
- Chaos Space Marine Gunner	13
- Aspiring Champion	13

OTHER WARGEAR

WARGEAR	POINTS PER ITEM
Icon of Wrath	5
Icon of Flame	1
Icon of Despair	3
Icon of Excess	5
Icon of Vengeance	1

RANGED WEAPONS

WEAPON	POINTS PER WEAPON
Autogun	0
Autopistol	0
Bolt pistol	0
Boltgun	0
Flamer	3
Frag grenade	0
Heavy bolter	3
Heavy stubber	0
Krak grenade	0
Meltagun	3
Plasma gun	3
Plasma pistol	1
Shotgun	0

MELEE WEAPONS

WEAPON	POINTS PER WEAPON
Brutal assault weapon	0
Chainsword	0
Power fist	4
Power sword	2

DEATH GUARD

The Death Guard are foulness made manifest. They are a vision of unnatural corruption, of nobility, courage and strength perverted into rancour, rot and diseased might. By rolling the appropriate dice on the tables on the following pages, you can generate names and background for your Death Guard kill teams.

For ten thousand years, the Death Guard have served the Plague God Nurgle. Once they were a loyalist Space Marine Legion, but during the Horus Heresy they followed their embittered Primarch, Mortarion, into rebellion and gave their souls to the Plague God, Nurgle. Now their bodies are riddled with disease, inured to an impossible level of pain by their bloated, mutated nature. Wreathed in droning clouds of plague flies, wielding revolting weapons that unleash weaponised sicknesses and flesh-eating blights, these Plague Marines spread the countless contagions of Nurgle to every world upon which they set foot.

Death Guard kill teams tend to be compact and incredibly durable. Tough beyond mortal measure and wielding weapons made even deadlier by plague, they sow the seeds of new epidemics and wars wherever Nurgle wills it. They trudge slowly and inexorably towards the foe, arrogant in their sheer resilience and the belief that Grandfather Nurgle has all eternity to lavish his gifts upon the ungrateful foe. Terror, sickness and entropy are the weapons of these foul shock troops – they delight in watching their enemies lose first their nerve, then control of their bodies as the foul contagions of Nurgle take hold, and finally their minds as they realise their inescapable fate. Thus do the Death Guard continue their advance over the bubbling remains of their foes, already seeking new population centres to enlighten with Nurgle's most generous creed.

D6	BACKGROUND: FOUL NATURE
1	**The Virulent:** These warriors are infected with the very foulest of Nurgle's contagions, and have devoted themselves to spreading them far and wide.
2	**Dark Alchemists:** This kill team takes to the battlefield to test the virulent weapons created by the Foul Blightspawn and Biologus Putrifiers.
3	**Trench Fighters:** This kill team is equipped for close-quarters offensives, using sheer endurance and point-blank firepower to drive its enemies from the field.
4	**Mortarion's Chosen:** This band of plague champions was hand-picked by the Daemon Primarch himself.
5	**Reapers:** This kill team fights not merely to defeat the foe, but to effect their utter destruction, to leave nothing but rotting flesh within which Nurgle's pretties can bloom.
6	**Shepherds of the Neverdead:** These warriors herd hordes of Poxwalkers before them into battle, the better to wear down and dismay the foe.

D6	MISSION: GLORIOUS BURDEN
1	**Defilers:** This kill team must sow the foul blessings of Nurgle amongst the enemy ranks to ensure maximum plague saturation.
2	**Seize and Profane:** A vital location or enemy asset must first be captured, and then utterly desecrated with filth.
3	**Victory Through Endurance:** For the glory of the Legion, this kill team must withstand all the enemy can hurl at them and still emerge victorious.
4	**Sevenfold Slaughter:** This kill team must slay seven great enemy champions for the glory of Nurgle.
5	**Fatal Infection:** The masters of the Legion have declared that an enemy leader must die in a truly terrible fashion. This kill team has the honour of doing the deed.
6	**Warp-spores:** These warriors must sow the spores of damnation throughout the region, each fresh canker eroding reality until a full-scale breach into the Garden of Nurgle becomes inevitable.

D6 — SQUAD QUIRK: BLIGHTFUL BOON

D6	
1	**Morbid Mirth:** This band of warriors takes a foul glee in their work, chortling with cruel laughter as they spread sickness and despair.
2	**Justifiable Arrogance:** Revoltingly proud of their Legion, these traitors are determined to uphold its reputation as the galaxy's most unyielding martial force.
3	**Dirgesong:** As they fight, this kill team maintains a sonorous song in praise of Nurgle's foul might.
4	**Vengeful:** These warriors do not take losses well, and will turn their full fury upon any enemy with the temerity to fell one of their own.
5	**Servants of Entropy:** This kill team believes in wearing its enemies down slowly, extracting the most pain and suffering from them before the inevitable end.
6	**Relentless:** These warriors advance as steadily and unstoppably as death itself, laying down a steady hail of fire and never letting up.

DEATH GUARD NAME GENERATOR TABLE

D10	FORENAME	SURNAME
1	Gurloch	Urghe
2	Suppurax	Volghor
3	Golchor	Grulgus
4	Festasmus	the Pestilent
5	Rancidius	the Reeking
6	Mulgh	the Curdled
7	Shurgholgh	Glouch
8	Bubox	Muttermould
9	Pustus	Thrax
10	Malignus	Trudge

D10 — SPECIALISTS' DEMEANOURS

D10	
1	**Drudge:** This warrior trudges into battle with near-mindless stolidity, a living embodiment of misery and despair.
2	**Morbid Fascinations:** This heretic is obsessed with the effects of Nurgle's blessings upon living flesh. They will always seek to get close to their victims, the better to observe the rot setting in.
3	**Jocular:** This warrior delights in spreading the Plague God's foulness, chortling and singing merrily as battle rages around him.
4	**Generous:** This warrior loves to spray plague-impregnated shots into the enemy ranks, indiscriminately spreading his deity's rancid gifts.
5	**Belligerent:** This hulking warrior takes pleasure in bludgeoning his victims into the ground with a steady rain of crushing blows.
6	**Meticulous:** Slow but as relentless as the onset of a fatal disease, this heretic disposes entirely of one luckless victim before moving on to the next.
7	**Deathflinger:** Nothing gives this traitor more pleasure than raining diseased explosives onto the heads of the foe.
8	**Reeking Horror:** The disgusting stench that wafts from this warrior's clammy folds is enough to make an Ogryn vomit themselves unconscious.
9	**Taking Samples:** This warrior collects fluids, organs and particularly delectable sores and buboes from their fallen victims, selecting their treasures with an expert eye.
10	**Stubborn:** Filled with grim determination, this warrior will never give ground.

DEATH GUARD KILL TEAMS

If every model in your kill team has the DEATH GUARD Faction keyword, you can use Death Guard Tactics.

PUTRID SPLATTER

Death Guard Tactic

Use this Tactic when a model from your kill team loses a wound in the Fight phase. Roll a D6 for each enemy model within 1" of that model. On a 6 that enemy model suffers 1 mortal wound after all of its attacks have been resolved.

2 COMMAND POINTS

VETERANS OF THE LONG WAR

Death Guard Tactic

Use this Tactic when a PLAGUE MARINE model from your kill team is chosen to attack in the Shooting or Fight phase. You can add 1 to wound rolls for the model's attacks that target IMPERIUM models until the end of the phase.

2 COMMAND POINTS

NURGLING INFESTATION

Death Guard Tactic

Use this Tactic at the end of the Movement phase. Pick an enemy model within 1" of your Leader and roll a D6. On a 4+ that enemy model suffers 1 mortal wound.

2 COMMAND POINTS

CLOUD OF FLIES

Death Guard Tactic

Use this Tactic at the end of the Movement phase. Pick a model from your kill team. Until the end of the battle round, enemy models can only shoot that model if it is the closest target visible to them.

2 COMMAND POINTS

GRANDFATHER'S BLESSING

Death Guard Tactic

Use this Tactic at the start of the first battle round. Pick a model from your kill team and roll a D6. On a 1 that model is found unworthy and suffers D3 mortal wounds. On a 2+ add 1 to hit and wound rolls for the model until the end of the battle. You can only use this Tactic once per battle.

2 COMMAND POINTS

NURGLE'S GIFT

Death Guard Tactic

Use this Tactic after a POXWALKER from your kill team takes an enemy model out of action in the Fight phase. Roll a D6. On a 4+ you may set up a new Poxwalker within 1" of the Poxwalker that made the attack. The new Poxwalker is treated as a member of your kill team, but is not part of a fire team (pg 204) and is not added to your command roster.

1 COMMAND POINT

PLAGUE MARINE

NAME	M	WS	BS	S	T	W	A	Ld	Sv	Max
Plague Marine	5"	3+	3+	4	5	1	1	7	3+	-
Plague Marine Gunner	5"	3+	3+	4	5	1	1	7	3+	2
Plague Marine Fighter	5"	3+	3+	4	5	1	2	7	3+	2
Plague Champion	5"	3+	3+	4	5	1	2	8	3+	1

This model is armed with a plague knife, boltgun, blight grenades and krak grenades.

Up to two Plague Marines in your kill team can be Plague Marine Gunners, up to two Plague Marines in your kill team can be Plague Marine Fighters, and one Plague Marine in your kill team can be a Plague Champion.

WARGEAR OPTIONS	• A Plague Marine Gunner may replace their boltgun with a plague spewer, plague belcher, blight launcher, meltagun or plasma gun.
	• A Plague Marine Fighter may replace their boltgun with one of the following:
	    - a bubotic axe, great plague cleaver or flail of corruption
	    - a second plague knife
	    - a mace of contagion and bubotic axe
	• A Plague Champion may replace their plague knife with a plaguesword.
	• A Plague Champion may replace their boltgun with a bolt pistol, plasma pistol or plasma gun.
	• A Plague Champion may take a power fist.
	• One Plague Marine in your kill team may take an Icon of Despair.

ABILITIES	**Death to the False Emperor:** If a model with this ability makes an attack in the Fight phase which targets an **Imperium** model, each time you roll a hit roll of 6+ you may make an additional attack with the same weapon against the same target. These attacks cannot themselves generate any further attacks. **Transhuman Physiology:** Ignore the penalty to this model's hit rolls from one flesh wound it has suffered. **Disgustingly Resilient:** Each time a model with this ability loses a wound, roll a D6; on a 5+ the model does not lose that wound. **Icon of Despair:** Subtract 1 from the Leadership characteristic of enemy models within 6" of any models equipped with an Icon of Despair.
SPECIALISTS	**Leader** (Plague Champion only), **Heavy** (Gunner only), **Zealot** (Fighter only), **Combat**, **Demolitions**, **Veteran**
FACTION KEYWORD	**Death Guard**
KEYWORDS	**Chaos, Nurgle, Heretic Astartes, Infantry, Plague Marine**

POXWALKER

NAME	M	WS	BS	S	T	W	A	Ld	Sv	Max
Poxwalker	4"	5+	6+	3	3	1	2	4	7+	-

This model is armed with an improvised weapon.

ABILITIES	**Disgustingly Resilient:** Each time a model with this ability loses a wound, roll a D6; on a 5+ the model does not lose that wound.
SPECIALISTS	**Combat, Zealot**
FACTION KEYWORD	**Death Guard**
KEYWORDS	**Chaos, Nurgle, Heretic Astartes, Infantry, Poxwalker**

'Remember, brothers, that we too were soldiers of the false Imperium before the Primarch opened our eyes. Do not hate your enemy, but rather pity them their ignorance, and be generous with your gifts so that they too might know the glory of Nurgle.'

- Plague Champion Repugnus Grolg of the Sevenfold Stricken

RANGED WEAPONS

WEAPON	RANGE	TYPE	S	AP	D	ABILITIES
Blight grenade	6"	Grenade D6	3	0	1	You can re-roll wound rolls of 1 for this weapon.
Blight launcher	24"	Assault 2	6	-2	D3	You can re-roll wound rolls of 1 for this weapon.
Bolt pistol	12"	Pistol 1	4	0	1	-
Boltgun	24"	Rapid Fire 1	4	0	1	-
Krak grenade	6"	Grenade 1	6	-1	D3	-
Meltagun	12"	Assault 1	8	-4	D6	If the target is within half range of this weapon, roll two dice when inflicting damage with it and discard the lowest result.
Plague belcher	9"	Assault D6	4	0	1	You can re-roll wound rolls of 1 for this weapon. This weapon automatically hits its target.
Plague spewer	9"	Heavy D6	5	-1	1	You can re-roll wound rolls of 1 for this weapon. This weapon automatically hits its target.
Plasma gun	When attacking with this weapon, choose one of the profiles below.					
- Standard	24"	Rapid Fire 1	7	-3	1	-
- Supercharge	24"	Rapid Fire 1	8	-3	2	On an unmodified hit roll of 1, the bearer is taken out of action after all of this weapon's shots have been resolved.
Plasma pistol	When attacking with this weapon, choose one of the profiles below.					
- Standard	12"	Pistol 1	7	-3	1	-
- Supercharge	12"	Pistol 1	8	-3	2	On an unmodified hit roll of 1, the bearer is taken out of action.

MELEE WEAPONS

WEAPON	RANGE	TYPE	S	AP	D	ABILITIES
Bubotic axe	Melee	Melee	+1	-2	1	You can re-roll wound rolls of 1 for this weapon.
Flail of corruption	Melee	Melee	+2	-2	2	You can re-roll wound rolls of 1 for this weapon. Make D3 hit rolls each time you attack with this weapon.
Great plague cleaver	Melee	Melee	x2	-3	D6	You can re-roll wound rolls of 1 for this weapon. When attacking with this weapon, you must subtract 1 from the hit roll.
Improvised weapon	Melee	Melee	User	0	1	-
Mace of contagion	Melee	Melee	+2	-1	3	You can re-roll wound rolls of 1 for this weapon. When attacking with this weapon, you must subtract 1 from the hit roll.
Plague knife	Melee	Melee	User	0	1	You can re-roll wound rolls of 1 for this weapon.
Plaguesword	Melee	Melee	User	0	1	You can re-roll failed wound rolls for this weapon.
Power fist	Melee	Melee	x2	-3	D3	When attacking with this weapon, you must subtract 1 from the hit roll.

KILL TEAM

MODEL	POINTS PER MODEL (Does not include wargear)
Plague Marine	14
- Plague Marine Gunner	15
- Plague Marine Fighter	15
- Plague Champion	15
Poxwalker	3

MELEE WEAPONS

WEAPON	POINTS PER WEAPON
Bubotic axe	2
Flail of corruption	4
Great plague cleaver	4
Improvised weapon	0
Mace of contagion	3
Plague knife	0
Plaguesword	0
Power fist	4

RANGED WEAPONS

WEAPON	POINTS PER WEAPON
Blight grenade	0
Blight launcher	3
Bolt pistol	0
Boltgun	0
Krak grenade	0
Meltagun	3
Plague belcher	3
Plague spewer	4
Plasma gun	3
Plasma pistol	1

OTHER WARGEAR

WARGEAR	POINTS PER ITEM
Icon of Despair	3

THOUSAND SONS

The tang of sorcery taints the air as the Thousand Sons attack. Coruscating bolts of warp energy explode in washes of mutating fire, while hails of ensorcelled rounds mow down the foe in the name of Tzeentch, Chaos God of Change. By rolling the appropriate dice on the tables on the following pages, you can generate names and background for your Thousand Sons kill teams.

The Thousand Sons are the arch-sorcerers of Chaos. Deceit and betrayal led them to a terrible fate, and transformed them into a terrifyingly powerful, but ultimately damned, force of destruction. Thousand Sons warbands launch their assaults from the strange Planet of the Sorcerers, a world that – since the return of their Primarch, Magnus the Red – has blighted the Prospero System and the wider Imperium alike.

The kill teams of the Thousand Sons are often led by potent Sorcerers of Tzeentch, whose command over the energies of the warp allows them to engulf their foes in mutating fires and shield their comrades behind flickering walls of flame. Each kill team's agenda is always to alter the strands of fate to better suit their needs, though sometimes even they do not realise the part their mission plays in Tzeentch's greater plan. Advancing in disturbing synchronicity alongside the kill team's leaders come the Rubric Marines. Reduced millennia ago to little more than armour shells filled with semi-sentient dust thanks to a failed ritual, these incredibly resilient warriors pitilessly turn their enemies to ash with inferno bolts and warpflame. Mutated beasts complete the twisted assemblage – Tzeentch-worshipping Tzaangors that shriek in forbidden tongues as they scavenge arcane treasures from slain foes. These vicious creatures can tear a man in two with sinewy claws, or hack them to pieces with their ornate blades.

D6	BACKGROUND: PATH OF FATE
1	**Heralds of Madness:** This kill team seeks to drive their enemies insane, burning away their wits amidst the fires of magic and mutation.
2	**Seekers After Sorcery:** These warriors were gathered to quest after arcane treasures, going to whatever ends they must to acquire them for their sorcerous masters.
3	**Arch-coven:** This kill team serves an exceptional gathering of psychically gifted warriors.
4	**Relentless Destroyers:** This kill team comprises a hardened core of automaton-like warriors, armed for the extermination of all who stand against them.
5	**Warriors Out of Time:** Trapped on a Daemon world or caught in the warp for millennia, these verdigrised warriors have emerged like risen ghosts to continue the Long War.
6	**Daemonologists:** This kill team's every action is ritual, its every deed calculated to facilitate the summoning of Tzeentch's daemonic servants.

D6	MISSION: INEFFABLE PURPOSE
1	**Ritual Desecration:** This kill team must use sorcery and flame to scour places of enemy faith, the better to weaken their defences against the empyric and the infernal.
2	**Abduction:** This kill team is hunting a specific individual, a luckless victim who must be snatched away to further some esoteric Tzeentchian scheme.
3	**Sowing Sorcery:** Upon the orders of Magnus himself, these warriors must etch glyphs of power across the war zone in sorcerous flame, furthering his enigmatic ends.
4	**Firestorm:** All must burn in the mutating fires of Tzeentch, until nothing but glowing ash and writhing flesh remains.
5	**Vengeance for Prospero:** Never can the offences of the past be forgiven. Ever must the Emperor's servants suffer for what the Thousand Sons lost.
6	**Hands of Fate:** This kill team must perform a series of vital tasks in order to change the fate of worlds, though their deeds would seem almost random to an observer.

D6	SQUAD QUIRK: MYSTERIOUS BOON
1	**Aetheric Coronae:** This kill team advances into battle wreathed in spectral soul-fire.
2	**One Will:** Like puppets marching to a single beat, this kill team acts with eerie coordination.
3	**Single-minded:** The warriors of this kill team show no concern for their own safety, shrugging off incoming fire as they advance relentlessly upon their objective.
4	**Ancient Dust:** The Rubricae of this kill team have begun to lose their grip upon reality, and occasionally pause or wander as though lost.
5	**Superior:** The leaders of this kill team look down upon their foes from towering heights of dark wisdom and arrogance.
6	**Ghosts of the Warp:** So saturated with sorcery are these warriors that they flicker in and out of reality, pale shades one moment, solid and deadly the next.

THOUSAND SONS NAME GENERATOR TABLE

D10	FORENAME	SURNAME
1	Phosis	T'Kor
2	Amonhep	Basth
3	Basteq	Takar
4	Apophitar	Kallisar
5	Thotek	Rhan
6	Kalophis	P'Tra
7	Phael	Manahkmor
8	Thotmas	Shen
9	Imhoden	Apophontar
10	Ankhu	H'Kett

D10	SPECIALISTS' DEMEANOURS
1	**Enigmatic:** This warrior is secretive and strange, their deeds veiled in mystery.
2	**Exacting:** This warrior values precision over all, and will repeat any action until it is perfect.
3	**Ninefold Warrior:** Everything this warrior does must hark back to the sacred number of almighty Tzeentch.
4	**War is an Altar:** This warrior seeks always to bring their enemies to battle in close combat, the better to drive a ritual dagger into their hearts.
5	**The Madness of Tzeentch:** This warrior is truly insane, their words a cascade of babbling nonsense.
6	**Unspeaking:** Not a sound leaves this warrior's lips, not even a shout of anger or cry of pain.
7	**Plans Within Plans:** Nothing this warrior does is as it seems, for their agendas are manifold and many-layered.
8	**Prophesier:** Driven by compulsion, this warrior blurts out dire predictions that every deed their foes attempt will fail.
9	**Pyromaniac:** Wherever possible, this warrior will always use fire as their weapon.
10	**Seething with Change:** This warrior's form writhes and mutates in a constant state of flux.

'Every blow you seek to strike against me, every ploy you attempt and plan you set in motion, know that I have already foreseen them and countered them all. Despair, for fate itself is my weapon.'

- Thanatek P'tor, Aspiring Sorcerer of Tzeentch, Third Magister of the Hidden Path

THOUSAND SONS KILL TEAMS

If every model in your kill team has the THOUSAND SONS Faction keyword, you can use Thousand Sons Tactics.

SORCEROUS FOCUS

Thousand Sons Tactic

Use this Tactic at the start of your turn in the Psychic phase. Pick a PSYKER model from your kill team that is within 2" of at least two other models from your kill team. Add 6" to the range of this model's *Psybolt* psychic power until the end of the phase.

2 COMMAND POINTS

VETERANS OF THE LONG WAR

Thousand Sons Tactic

Use this Tactic when a RUBRIC MARINE model from your kill team is chosen to attack in the Shooting or Fight phase. You can add 1 to wound rolls for the model's attacks that target IMPERIUM models until the end of the phase.

2 COMMAND POINTS

MALICIOUS FAMILIAR

Thousand Sons Tactic

Use this Tactic at the end of the Movement phase. Pick an enemy model within 1" of your Leader and roll a D6. On a 4+ that enemy model suffers 1 mortal wound.

1 COMMAND POINT

IMMOVABLE AUTOMATON

Thousand Sons Tactic

Use this Tactic when a Rubric Marine or Rubric Marine Gunner from your kill team is taken out of action. Roll a D6. On a 4+ that model suffers a flesh wound instead.

2 COMMAND POINTS

CYCLE OF SLAUGHTER

Thousand Sons Tactic

Use this Tactic at the end of the Fight phase. Pick a TZAANGOR from your kill team – that model can immediately fight an additional time.

2 COMMAND POINTS

HUNGERING WARPFLAME

Thousand Sons Tactic

Use this Tactic in the Shooting phase when you choose a model in your kill team to shoot with a warpflamer or warpflame pistol. Until the end of the phase, you can roll two dice when determining the number of attacks made by that weapon and pick the highest result.

1 COMMAND POINT

RUBRIC MARINE

NAME	M	WS	BS	S	T	W	A	Ld	Sv	Max
Rubric Marine	5"	3+	3+	4	4	1	1	7	3+	-
Rubric Marine Gunner	5"	3+	3+	4	4	1	1	7	3+	1
Aspiring Sorcerer	6"	3+	3+	4	4	1	2	8	3+	1

This model is armed with an inferno boltgun.
One Rubric Marine in your kill team can be a Rubric Marine Gunner, and one Rubric Marine in your kill team can be an Aspiring Sorcerer. An Aspiring Sorcerer is instead armed with a force stave and inferno bolt pistol.

WARGEAR OPTIONS	• An Aspiring Sorcerer may replace their inferno bolt pistol with a warpflame pistol. • A Rubric Marine may replace their inferno boltgun with a warpflamer. • A Rubric Marine Gunner may replace their inferno boltgun with a soulreaper cannon. • One Rubric Marine in your kill team may take an Icon of Flame.
ABILITIES	**Death to the False Emperor:** If a model with this ability makes an attack in the Fight phase which targets an **IMPERIUM** model, each time you roll a hit roll of 6+ you may make an additional attack with the same weapon against the same target. These attacks cannot themselves generate any further attacks. **All is Dust:** Add 1 to saving throws for a Rubric Marine or Rubric Marine Gunner if the attack has a Damage characteristic of 1. In addition, the -1 modifier to hit rolls for moving and shooting Heavy weapons does not apply to Rubric Marine Gunners. **Favoured of Tzeentch:** This model has a 5+ invulnerable save. **Icon of Flame:** At the start of your turn in the Psychic phase, roll a D6 for each model from your kill team equipped with an Icon of Flame. On a 6 inflict 1 mortal wound on the closest enemy model within 12" of the model being rolled for. **Transhuman Physiology (Aspiring Sorcerer only):** Ignore the penalty to this model's hit rolls from one flesh wound it has suffered.
PSYKER	An Aspiring Sorcerer can attempt to manifest one psychic power and attempt to deny one psychic power in each Psychic phase. He knows the *Psybolt* psychic power.
SPECIALISTS	**Leader** (Aspiring Sorcerer only), **Heavy** (Gunner only), **Combat**, **Demolitions**, **Veteran**
FACTION KEYWORD	**THOUSAND SONS**
KEYWORDS	**CHAOS, TZEENTCH, HERETIC ASTARTES, INFANTRY, PSYKER** (Aspiring Sorcerer only), **RUBRIC MARINE**

TZAANGOR

NAME	M	WS	BS	S	T	W	A	Ld	Sv	Max
Tzaangor	6"	3+	4+	4	4	1	1	6	6+	-
Twistbray	6"	3+	4+	4	4	1	2	7	6+	1

This model is armed with Tzaangor blades.
One Tzaangor in your kill team can be a Twistbray.

WARGEAR OPTIONS	• This model may replace its Tzaangor blades with an autopistol and chainsword. • One Tzaangor in your kill team may take a brayhorn.
ABILITIES	**Aura of Dark Glory:** This model has a 5+ invulnerable save. **Brayhorn:** Add 1 to Advance and charge rolls made for **TZAANGORS** within 6" of any friendly models equipped with a brayhorn.
SPECIALISTS	**Leader** (Twistbray only), **Comms** (Tzaangor with brayhorn only), **Combat**, **Medic**, **Veteran**, **Zealot**
FACTION KEYWORD	**THOUSAND SONS**
KEYWORDS	**CHAOS, TZEENTCH, HERETIC ASTARTES, INFANTRY, TZAANGOR**

RANGED WEAPONS

WEAPON	RANGE	TYPE	S	AP	D	ABILITIES
Autopistol	12"	Pistol 1	3	0	1	-
Inferno bolt pistol	12"	Pistol 1	4	-2	1	-
Inferno boltgun	24"	Rapid Fire 1	4	-2	1	-
Soulreaper cannon	24"	Heavy 4	5	-3	1	-
Warpflame pistol	6"	Pistol D6	3	-2	1	This weapon automatically hits its target.
Warpflamer	8"	Assault D6	4	-2	1	This weapon automatically hits its target.

MELEE WEAPONS

WEAPON	RANGE	TYPE	S	AP	D	ABILITIES
Chainsword	Melee	Melee	User	0	1	Each time the bearer fights, it can make 1 additional attack with this weapon.
Force stave	Melee	Melee	+2	-1	D3	-
Tzaangor blades	Melee	Melee	User	-1	1	Each time the bearer fights, it can make 1 additional attack with this weapon.

KILL TEAM

MODEL	POINTS PER MODEL (Does not include wargear)
Rubric Marine	16
- Rubric Marine Gunner	16
- Aspiring Sorcerer	17
Tzaangor	7
- Twistbray	8

RANGED WEAPONS

WEAPON	POINTS PER WEAPON
Autopistol	0
Inferno bolt pistol	0
Inferno boltgun	0
Soulreaper cannon	4
Warpflame pistol	1
Warpflamer	4

MELEE WEAPONS

WEAPON	POINTS PER WEAPON
Chainsword	0
Force stave	0
Tzaangor blades	0

OTHER WARGEAR

ITEM	POINTS PER ITEM
Brayhorn	3
Icon of Flame	1

ASURYANI

Vast interstellar arks constructed from living wraithbone, the craftworlds of the Aeldari are marvels of grace and beauty. No less graceful are their occupants, the Asuryani, those members of their race who foresaw the fall of their empire and escaped its death throes. By rolling the appropriate dice on the tables on the following pages, you can generate names and background for your Asuryani kill teams.

The Asuryani are amongst the most ancient of the galaxy's many factions. These Aeldari are sublimely focused and terrifyingly skilled warriors, for whom war is a path that must be trodden with absolute discipline and mastery. For all their martial magnificence, the Asuryani have teetered upon the brink of extinction for millennia. They are but echoes of an empire that once spanned the galaxy, the last survivors sailing through the void aboard immense vessels known as craftworlds.

The ancient Aeldari empire shone incredibly bright at its zenith, yet through obsession and moral deviance it descended into a hellish quagmire from which the Asuryani were amongst the few refugees to escape. So twisted did the ancient Aeldari become that their psychic corruption birthed Slaanesh, the Chaos God of excess. This event, known as the Fall, saw the souls of the ancient Aeldari consumed at a stroke, and left the scattered survivors fleeing from Slaanesh's grip forever more. Only through strict asceticism and psychic scrying of the threads of destiny have the Asuryani avoided the terrible fate of their ancestors, yet still there are many among their race who believe that they are doing little but delaying their inevitable end.

Asuryani kill teams are elite forces of swift and skilful warriors. Each combatant is armed with the optimal weapons and wargear for their tactical niche. Their line troops, the skilled militia known as Guardians, lay down covering fire with hissing shuriken weapons and heavy weapon platforms. Rangers pick off key targets with sniping shots from elegant long-barrelled rifles.

SPIRIT STONES

Upon death, an unguarded Aeldari soul will be drawn into the warp and there consumed by the ever-hungering Slaanesh. To prevent this terrifying fate, the Asuryani have taken to wearing gemstones upon their breasts known as spirit stones. These psycho-receptive crystals capture the soul of the fallen warrior and preserve it in a safe haven until it can be collected and returned to its craftworld. There, the spirit stones are plugged into the infinity circuit, freed to mingle with the souls of their ancestors until the end of time, or until the craftworld's destruction.

Yet it is the warriors of the Dire Avenger Aspect Shrines, with their ritual armaments and honed martial skills, that lead the charge to victory.

Unlike the bands of Aeldari which make up the greater part of the craftworld warhosts, who are grouped together with others that follow the same battle discipline, Asuryani kill teams can include a range of individuals with different specialities fighting as a coherent whole. Often they are the survivors of another conflict, or a company of wanderers long divorced from their homes, for the Asuryani are a race few in number, and necessity binds them together more often than intent. It speaks volumes of the fluid Aeldari mind that a mix of such focused warriors still works as one, achieving the mysterious agendas of its Farseers with a skill and synergy most humans could only dream of.

D10	BACKGROUND: SHARED DESTINY
1	**Gwynt'ar Fue:** The wind that burns or, depending upon tone – vendetta hunters on a mission to slay a specific enemy of the craftworld.
2	**Pre-emptive Strike:** A small team of Asuryani assembled to launch a targeted attack and thereby prevent a terrible future.
3	**Keepers of the Gate:** Warriors sworn to seize and protect an asset, be it a webway tunnel, sacred shrine, or other tactical objective.
4	**The Shrine Ascendant:** As decreed by the Farseers, a warband gathered purely from the Dire Avenger Shrine is assembled to perform a preordained task.
5	**Shadow Squad:** Masters of subtle infiltration and misdirection, who slip behind enemy lines and prepare to strike hard.
6	**Echoes of Greatness:** A force of survivors, fighting on for those they have lost.
7	**Ily'Haeth Khai:** The blade that seeks out weakness – a force assembled to exploit the enemy's every error.
8	**Cleansers:** The members of this warband are united by their hatred of those lesser races who befoul the ancient demesnes of the Aeldari, and their abilities in exterminating them.
9	**The Bladed Mirror:** This kill team is comprised of warriors that excel in the use of misdirection and trickery.
10	**Wardens of the Pivotal Life:** A single warrior can hold in their hands the fate of millions. Such a one was this team assembled to protect.

D10	MISSION: PURPOSE
1	**Enact the Bailic-fen:** This warband must collect the spirit stones of the Aeldari that fell in recent battle.
2	**Surprise Attack:** The enemy are many, the objectives myriad, yet speed and manoeuvrability are the way of the Asuryani – strike quickly and without mercy.
3	**Keepers of the Gate:** This kill team seeks a hidden webway portal leading to a lost spar. It must be sealed from the inside.
4	**Talons of Heg:** This team's mission is one of sabotage and mayhem, using subtle strikes to slow and misdirect the enemy.
5	**Fate's Executioners:** Farseers predict dire events should the enemy leader survive. Hunt down this dangerous commander and alter the skeins of fate in your favour.
6	**Forbidden Ground:** Intruders profane a site of great import. Scour all trace of them from the stars.
7	**The First Wave:** This warband has been sent forth by an Autarch to inflict as much damage as they can before retreating.
8	**Faolchú's Wings:** Deliver the chosen one safely through the war zone, for the Farseers have predicted that only she might know ultimate triumph.
9	**A Greater Foe:** Unbeknownst to any but the Asuryani, a new warp rift will soon open. Ancient technologies can prevent the weakening of reality from becoming a new rent, but only if deployed in the right place at the right time.
10	**Mobile Defence:** Slow, harry, harass – to delay the foe is to win the war.

D10	SQUAD QUIRK: DEEPER NATURE
1	**Close Bonds:** Every member of the squad has close emotional bonds to their comrades, and fights accordingly.
2	**Fickle:** This kill team is perfectly focused on the craft of war, yet fey and whimsy creep into their decisions.
3	**Merciless Hate:** The remembrance of past atrocities spurns the squad to a cold-blooded harshness.
4	**Sorrows Beyond Measure:** Even in triumph, battle losses and the horrors of ruin wrought by barbaric forces are difficult to bear. It is no weakness to weep over the slain.
5	**Psychically Attuned:** This kill team possess sufficient latent psychic potential to exhibit a sort of collective sixth sense, though at the cost of haunting visions.
6	**Uncanny Perfectionists:** The Asuryani in this squad are considered amongst the most sublimely skilled of their kin.
7	**Servants of Prophecy:** This warband follows the directions of a Farseer's scrying. Their deeds may seem strange at times, but they all serve a greater end.
8	**Superior:** Cognisant of their status as members of the sophisticated Aeldari race, these Asuryani are not shy about pointing out the flaws of others and where they might improve.
9	**A Shining Example:** The demands of war are difficult enough, but the grime of battle is simply too much – the entire squad must periodically pause to perform maintenance upon their battle gear until they are, once more, shining and resplendent.
10	**Arrogant and Aloof:** These warriors sneer at their barbaric enemies, and will mercilessly mock any error or misfortune.

D10	SPECIALISTS' DEMEANOURS
1	**Acrobatic:** All Aeldari bear themselves with innate grace, but some raise the artistic bar with their every fluid movement.
2	**Mentally Dexterous:** This warrior's mind moves at lightning speed, enabling them to think, plan, and react with a swiftness far beyond human capacity.
3	**Crystalline Soul:** There is no pain or suffering that cannot be endured.
4	**Damned:** Knowing what the future holds is not always a boon.
5	**Survivor's Guilt:** This warrior has seen all their comrades and loved ones die around them, spurring them to unceasing aggression against the foe.
6	**Absolute Focus:** All Asuryani are supremely focused, but to this warrior there is only the mission, and all will be sacrificed for its success.
7	**Haughty:** This warrior revels in proving their superiority over the lesser races.
8	**Cold as the Void:** Once upon the battlefield, all emotions are suppressed and only the dictates of purest logic will be followed.
9	**Passionate:** This Aeldari is consumed with burning emotions that fuel an intense battle fury.
10	**Grandiloquent:** Verbose, this warrior shouts out loquacious praise and encouragement to comrades while verbally castigating the shortcomings of enemies and dismal surroundings.

ASURYANI NAME GENERATOR TABLE (FEMALE)		
D66	FIRST ELEMENT	SECOND ELEMENT
11	Tenrith	the Fireheart
12	Justune	Kyldroth
13	Aleerith	Tridehlá
14	Yrlla	Who Walks Alone
15	Aileer	of the Flowing Spirits
16	Caslith	Iydoth
21	Tai'shar	Brylliel
22	Jair	Biel-rith
23	Luirth	*(no second appellation)*
24	Aleera	Iyadolath
25	Phyllistra	Last of the House of the Ayandi
26	Myrnoth	the Melancholy
31	Fyrram	Llacharni ('brightheart')
32	Ishylla	the Huntress
33	Tishriel	Aryimelli
34	Aydona	Bringer of Azure Death
35	Galánta	Umachuli
36	Ylleth	Shelwe-hann ('Song of Enlightenment')
41	Giladrea	Serenti ('glory of the setting sun')
42	Osinell	Ullamar
43	Glenoighi	Dystari ('that which will never shatter')
44	Ishtá	Ciaradh
45	Yvraine	Iyadari
46	Intrisiel	Flethál ('Star-pattern of Perfection')
51	Torc	the Whisper of Death
52	Anesh	Hanndroth ('Quest Eternal')
53	Kalistri	Sheersom
54	Alee	Cegodari ('who laughs at despair')
55	Altanish	Ullathani ('she who walks many paths')
56	Gwyth	Corsikanni ('kin to Corsairs')
61	Tyrelli	Yn Farwolloch ('deadly to her enemies')
62	Kaithe	Indomi
63	Galrethi	Saim-Ingrelli ('the grace of the striking snake')
64	Noithi	Ysbwrieli ('Starsplinter')
65	Braesil	Morai-fen
66	Meari	Undomniel

ASURYANI NAME GENERATOR TABLE (MALE)		
D66	FIRST ELEMENT	SECOND ELEMENT
11	Fachean	Son of Coheria
12	Tarvaril	Finarfin
13	Fánai	Eldrion
14	Yrmnoch	the Unyielding Fire
15	Barahir	Glaermril
16	Eldrion	Arronnás
21	Dis'ar	Gloywach ('the Glow Dragon')
22	Eldos	the Uncompromising
23	Kinshar	of the Noble House of Picarothi
24	Rhidhal	Enbrondil
25	Athairnos	Lladronoth
26	Eärandil	Bechareth ('spirit on the wind')
31	Siriolas	Ceifulgaithann ('wind rider')
32	Bahtaam	Undroíl
33	Fian	Caman ('the avenger')
34	Eldroth	Tóir
35	Lorinth	Scion of Rhidmar
36	Illisar	the Wanderer
41	Ealion	of the Clan Randras
42	Elronhir	Llmaea-fen ('born of black suns')
43	Tamishar	Rillietar
44	Arenal	Elarique of Alaitoc
45	Iradil	Sydarus Starstrider
46	Maur	the Implacable
51	Requiel	Ulthos ('speaker of unspeakable truths')
52	Lann	Sharnál
53	Yrule	the Deathly Eloquent
54	Ra'thar	Born of Twilight
55	Las'hár	of the Tower of Stars
56	Arision	Shelwe-nin ('Song of the Fading Star')
61	Ingfhar	the Undaunted
62	Senn	Rhianthari ('starlight partially obscured by nebula')
63	Hal'thar	Eldroneth
64	Yrion	Trithjain ('Storm of the Stars')
65	Silgar	the Rising Star
66	Konrith	Bhanlhar ('avenger of the lost clan')

ASURYANI KILL TEAMS

If every model in your kill team has the ASURYANI Faction keyword, you can use Craftworlds Tactics.

MATCHLESS AGILITY

Craftworlds Tactic

Use this Tactic in the Movement phase when a model from your kill team Advances. Add 6" to the model's Move characteristic for that Movement phase instead of rolling a dice.

1 COMMAND POINT

FEIGNED RETREAT

Craftworlds Tactic

Use this Tactic after a model from your kill team Falls Back. That model can still shoot this battle round.

1 COMMAND POINT

PHANTASM

Craftworlds Tactic

Use this Tactic at the beginning of the first battle round. Pick a model from your kill team and set it up again, anywhere in your deployment zone.

2 COMMAND POINTS

FIRE AND FADE

Craftworlds Tactic

Use this Tactic after a model from your kill team shoots in the Shooting phase. The model can immediately make a normal move of up to 7" as if it were the Movement phase.

1 COMMAND POINT

ASURMEN'S BLESSING

Craftworlds Tactic

Use this Tactic when you choose a **DIRE AVENGER** from your kill team to shoot in the Shooting phase. You can re-roll failed hit rolls for that model until the end of the phase.

1 COMMAND POINT

RUNE OF YNNEAD

Craftworlds Tactic

Use this Tactic when a model from your kill team is taken out of action. Roll a D6. On a 4+ that model suffers a flesh wound instead.

2 COMMAND POINTS

GUARDIAN DEFENDER

NAME	M	WS	BS	S	T	W	A	Ld	Sv	Max
Guardian Defender	7"	3+	3+	3	3	1	1	7	5+	-
Heavy Weapon Platform	7"	6+	3+	3	3	2	1	7	3+	1

This model is armed with a shuriken catapult and plasma grenades.
One Guardian Defender in your kill team can be a Heavy Weapon Platform. A Heavy Weapon Platform is instead armed with a shuriken cannon.

WARGEAR OPTIONS	• A Heavy Weapon Platform may replace its shuriken cannon with an Aeldari missile launcher, bright lance, scatter laser or starcannon.
ABILITIES	**Ancient Doom:** You can re-roll failed hit rolls in the Fight phase for this model in a battle round in which it charges or is charged by a **Slaanesh** model. However, you must add 1 to Nerve tests for this model if it is within 3" of any **Slaanesh** models. **Battle Focus:** If this model moves or Advances in its Movement phase, weapons (excluding Heavy weapons) are used as if the model had remained stationary. **Crewed Weapon:** A Heavy Weapon Platform can only move, Advance, React, shoot or fight if a friendly Guardian Defender that is not shaken is within 3" of it. If a Heavy Weapon Platform shoots, you must choose one such Guardian Defender that could still shoot its own ranged weapons in that phase: that Guardian Defender may not fire any of its own ranged weapons this phase. Heavy Weapon Platforms may not charge, may not be specialists, are not part of a fire team (pg 204) and do not gain experience.
SPECIALISTS	Leader, Comms, Medic, Scout, Veteran
FACTION KEYWORD	**Asuryani**
KEYWORDS (GUARDIAN)	**Aeldari, Warhost, Infantry, Guardian, Guardian Defender**
KEYWORDS (HEAVY WEAPON PLATFORM)	**Aeldari, Warhost, Infantry, Artillery, Guardian, Heavy Weapon Platform**

STORM GUARDIAN

NAME	M	WS	BS	S	T	W	A	Ld	Sv	Max
Storm Guardian	7"	3+	3+	3	3	1	1	7	5+	-
Storm Guardian Gunner	7"	3+	3+	3	3	1	1	7	5+	2

This model is armed with a shuriken pistol, Aeldari blade and plasma grenades.
Up to two Storm Guardians in your kill team can be Storm Guardian Gunners.

WARGEAR OPTIONS	• This model may replace its Aeldari blade with a chainsword. • A Storm Guardian Gunner may replace their shuriken pistol and Aeldari blade with a flamer or fusion gun.
ABILITIES	**Ancient Doom:** You can re-roll failed hit rolls in the Fight phase for this model in a battle round in which it charges or is charged by a **Slaanesh** model. However, you must add 1 to Nerve tests for this model if it is within 3" of any **Slaanesh** models. **Battle Focus:** If this model moves or Advances in its Movement phase, weapons (excluding Heavy weapons) are used as if the model had remained stationary.
SPECIALISTS	Leader, Combat, Comms, Medic, Scout, Veteran
FACTION KEYWORD	**Asuryani**
KEYWORDS	**Aeldari, Warhost, Infantry, Guardian, Storm Guardian**

'These barbarians may outnumber us, but they could never outfight us. We shall flow around their defences as subtle and intangible as starlight, and slay them all before they realise that the fight has even begun.'

- Aleera Iyadari, Dire Avenger Exarch of the Shrine of the Bloodied Moon

RANGER

NAME	M	WS	BS	S	T	W	A	Ld	Sv	Max
Ranger	7"	3+	3+	3	3	1	1	7	5+	-

This model is armed with a shuriken pistol and Ranger long rifle.

ABILITIES	**Ancient Doom:** You can re-roll failed hit rolls in the Fight phase for this model in a battle round in which it charges or is charged by a **SLAANESH** model. However, you must add 1 to Nerve tests for this model if it is within 3" of any **SLAANESH** models.
	Battle Focus: If this model moves or Advances in its Movement phase, weapons (excluding Heavy weapons) are used as if the model had remained stationary.
	Cameleoline Cloak: When an enemy player makes a hit roll for a shooting attack that targets this model, and this model is obscured, that hit roll suffers an additional -1 modifier.
SPECIALISTS	**Leader, Comms, Medic, Scout, Sniper, Veteran**
FACTION KEYWORD	**ASURYANI**
KEYWORDS	**AELDARI, WARHOST, INFANTRY, RANGER**

DIRE AVENGER

NAME	M	WS	BS	S	T	W	A	Ld	Sv	Max
Dire Avenger	7"	3+	3+	3	3	1	1	8	4+	-
Dire Avenger Exarch	7"	3+	3+	3	3	2	2	8	4+	1

This model is armed with an avenger shuriken catapult and plasma grenades.
One Dire Avenger in your kill team can be a Dire Avenger Exarch.

WARGEAR OPTIONS	• A Dire Avenger Exarch may replace their avenger shuriken catapult with one of the following:
	- Two avenger shuriken catapults
	- Shuriken pistol and power glaive
	- Shuriken pistol and diresword
	- Shimmershield and power glaive

ABILITIES	**Ancient Doom:** You can re-roll failed hit rolls in the Fight phase for this model in a battle round in which it charges or is charged by a **SLAANESH** model. However, you must add 1 to Nerve tests for this model if it is within 3" of any **SLAANESH** models.	**Defence Tactics:** When this model fires Overwatch, they successfully hit on a roll of 5 or 6.
		Battle Fortune: A Dire Avenger Exarch has a 4+ invulnerable save.
	Battle Focus: If this model moves or Advances in the Movement phase, weapons (excluding Heavy weapons) are used as if the model had remained stationary.	**Shimmershield: DIRE AVENGER** models within 2" of a friendly model with a shimmershield have a 5+ invulnerable save.
SPECIALISTS	**Leader** (Exarch only), **Combat, Comms, Medic, Scout, Veteran**	
FACTION KEYWORD	**ASURYANI**	
KEYWORDS	**AELDARI, ASPECT WARRIOR, INFANTRY, DIRE AVENGER**	

'Ours is not a fight for conquest, or riches, or glory. It is a fight for the survival of our species, for the right to see another dawn. It is the very desperation of our cause that renders us so dangerous...'

- Iradil the Wanderer, Ranger of Craftworld Alaitoc

RANGED WEAPONS

WEAPON	RANGE	TYPE	S	AP	D	ABILITIES
Aeldari missile launcher	When attacking with this weapon, choose one of the profiles below.					
- Sunburst missile	48"	Heavy D6	4	-1	1	-
- Starshot missile	48"	Heavy 1	8	-2	D6	-
Avenger shuriken catapult	18"	Assault 2	4	0	1	Each time you make a wound roll of 6+ for this weapon, that hit is resolved with an AP of -3.
Bright lance	36"	Heavy 1	8	-4	D6	-
Flamer	8"	Assault D6	4	0	1	This weapon automatically hits its target.
Fusion gun	12"	Assault 1	8	-4	D6	If the target is within half range of this weapon, roll two dice when inflicting damage with it and discard the lowest result.
Plasma grenade	6"	Grenade D6	4	-1	1	-
Ranger long rifle	36"	Heavy 1	4	0	1	A model firing a Ranger long rifle does not suffer the penalty to hit rolls for the target being at long range. Each time you roll a wound roll of 6+ for this weapon, it inflicts a mortal wound in addition to any other damage.
Scatter laser	36"	Heavy 4	6	0	1	-
Shuriken cannon	24"	Assault 3	6	0	1	Each time you make a wound roll of 6+ for this weapon, that hit is resolved with an AP of -3.
Shuriken catapult	12"	Assault 2	4	0	1	Each time you make a wound roll of 6+ for this weapon, that hit is resolved with an AP of -3.
Shuriken pistol	12"	Pistol 1	4	0	1	Each time you make a wound roll of 6+ for this weapon, that hit is resolved with an AP of -3.
Starcannon	36"	Heavy 2	6	-3	D3	-

MELEE WEAPONS

WEAPON	RANGE	TYPE	S	AP	D	ABILITIES
Aeldari blade	Melee	Melee	User	0	1	You can re-roll failed hit rolls for this weapon.
Chainsword	Melee	Melee	User	0	1	Each time the bearer fights, it can make 1 additional attack with this weapon.
Diresword	Melee	Melee	User	-2	1	Each time you make a wound roll of 6+ for this weapon, the target suffers a mortal wound in addition to any other damage.
Power glaive	Melee	Melee	+1	-2	1	-

KILL TEAM

MODEL	POINTS PER MODEL (Does not include wargear)
Dire Avenger	10
- Dire Avenger Exarch	11
Guardian Defender	7
- Heavy Weapon Platform	8
Ranger	11
Storm Guardian	6
- Storm Guardian Gunner	7

MELEE WEAPONS

WEAPON	POINTS PER WEAPON
Aeldari blade	0
Chainsword	0
Diresword	2
Power glaive	1

RANGED WEAPONS

WEAPON	POINTS PER WEAPON
Aeldari missile launcher	5
Avenger shuriken catapult	0
Bright lance	4
Flamer	3
Fusion gun	3
Plasma grenade	0
Ranger long rifle	0
Scatter laser	2
Shuriken cannon	2
Shuriken catapult	0
Shuriken pistol	0
Starcannon	3

OTHER WARGEAR

WARGEAR	POINTS PER ITEM
Shimmershield	4

DRUKHARI

The Drukhari are a race of cruel killers who feed upon agony. From the Dark City of Commorragh, their fleets strike forth in search for new souls to torment. By rolling the appropriate dice on the tables on the following pages, you can generate names and background for your Drukhari kill teams.

The Drukhari are sadists, pirates and murderers all. They are the dark kin of the Asuryani, a subset of the Aeldari race whose peerless skill and mental focus have been bent solely towards hedonism, self-advancement and the infliction of pain. These legendary beings are monsters of nightmare, hyper-intelligent and utterly malevolent. Their technology is akin to sorcery and their physical prowess jaw-dropping. Yet they are hollow creatures, their beauty hiding blackened souls that are constantly draining away like sand through an hourglass. The only way for the Drukhari to recover their waning life force is through feeding off the pain and terror of other beings.

Drukhari raiding parties emerge through webway portals from the Dark City of Commorragh. They launch swift and deadly attacks against settled worlds, not merely for material gain, emerging from the shadows to take slaves and treasures, but more importantly to bathe in the suffering they inflict upon their foes. Such raids are typically led by the vast syndicates known as the Kabals, or the vicious bands of gladiatorial fighters known as the Wych Cults.

The Kabals are something akin to noble houses and paramilitary criminal cartels combined, with every Kabal seeking to clamber to the heights of glory atop the heaped corpses of their rivals. By far the greatest prestige for such organisations can be earned through orchestrating successful raids upon realspace, with Kabals such as the Black Heart, the Poisoned Tongue and the Lords of Iron Thorn leading the greatest of all such invasions. By comparison, the Wych Cults attack

realspace to showcase their martial talents, groups such as the Seventh Woe, the Cult of Strife or the Cult of Red Grief pitting themselves against the greatest enemies they can find, the better to bask in rolling waves of agony and terror.

Drukhari kill teams are built around fiercely competitive cliques of elite killers, each armed for a specialised combat role. Though these individuals often hail from different organisations and subcultures in Commorragh, all rivalries and vendettas are set aside for the duration of the raid. The vicious firepower of the Kabalites combined with the whip-fast combat prowess of the Wyches spreads panic amongst their victims like a raging wildfire. Each kill team strikes with the utmost speed, ferocity and ruthlessness, stealing away screaming captives before vanishing to leave only fear and ruin behind them.

THE DARK CITY

Commorragh is a vast metropolis, scattered across countless different passages of the strange realm known as the webway. It is fractal in complexity, immense beyond imagining and impossible for mortal minds to truly comprehend. From its towering, blade-like spires and lethal arenas to its dark, Haemonculus-haunted oubliettes and shadow-wreathed sub-dimensions, Commorragh is a nightmarish realm in which the Drukhari rule and all other races of the galaxy are but playthings to be tormented, or prey to be hunted and feasted upon at will.

D10	BACKGROUND: SHADOWED ORIGIN
1	**Vanguard Party:** This kill team has been sent as the first wave of a much larger raiding force.
2	**Slave Trialists:** Enslaved by those who destroyed their faction, these warriors have been given a chance to prove their worth in battle, or die trying.
3	**Ascendant Murderers:** Having rising from the ganglands of the Dark City, the members of this kill team now have much greater ambitions.
4	**Enemies of My Enemy:** Though rivals in Commorragh, the members of this kill team work together to slaughter the lesser races.
5	**Avatars of the Arenas:** The wealthy members of this kill team seek nothing more than to recreate in realspace their favourite arena battles.
6	**Slithering Compulsion:** This kill team does the bidding of the Haemonculus who implanted foul parasites in their brains.
7	**Hired Blades:** The warriors of this kill team serve only those who are willing to pay the right price in souls.
8	**Betrayers:** Having angered a powerful Archon, this kill team's only path to survival is through the enemy lines.
9	**One Shall Stand:** Only one member of this kill team will return to Commorragh, taking with them the spoils of their dead allies.
10	**Desolators:** The warriors of this kill team are bound by their shared love of the Dark City's most destructive weaponry.

D10	MISSION: CRUEL INTENT
1	**Probe:** Collect and relay information about the enemy's weaknesses prior to a full-scale raid.
2	**Harvest:** Gather samples of flesh from the warriors of the lesser races.
3	**Interrogate:** Seek out those foes possessed of vital information and pry it from their screaming lips.
4	**Assassinate:** Find the greatest champions of the opposing army and take their heads as trophies.
5	**Deceive:** Sow misinformation and anarchy throughout the ranks of the enemy.
6	**Terrorise:** Breed fear in the minds of the foe to erode their resolve.
7	**Abduct:** Slip from the shadows and steal away the mightiest warriors of realspace for the arenas of Commorragh.
8	**Enslave:** Find those enemy warriors who will fetch a high price in the slave pits, and seize them.
9	**Disembowel:** Gut the enemy forces by savagely butchering their most vital assets.
10	**Revel:** Inflict as much pain as possible upon the foe and bask in their suffering.

D10	SQUAD QUIRK: UNNATURAL PERVERSION
1	**Sinful Focus:** This kill team is guided by the example of their chosen Dark Muse.
2	**Revel in Pain:** The longer and more drawn-out a massacre is, the greater the pleasure this kill team derives from it.
3	**Swift and Deadly:** This kill team enjoys nothing better than rapid, merciless slaughters.
4	**Reckless:** Regardless of their mission, the members of this kill team have their own hedonistic agendas to pursue.
5	**Territorial:** This kill team decorates their battlegrounds with the flayed corpses of their enemies.
6	**Trophy Hunters:** This kill team collects the most aesthetically pleasing heads and body parts of their victims.
7	**Eldritch Cunning:** For every tactic used against them, this kill team has a dozen countermeasures.
8	**Masochistic:** These warriors go out of their way to endure the most nerve-rending pain, for only in this way do they feel alive.
9	**Shadow Stalkers:** This kill team excels at fighting from the shadows, using the enemy's fear and uncertainty against them.
10	**Consummate Provocateurs:** Through sabotage and selective butchery, this band of warriors can wrong-foot an entire army.

'We are the things that haunt the darkest recesses of the nightmares that you cannot face. We are the ones that leer from the shadows and know the fears that you do not admit. We are the predators, you the prey, and we shall make you scream in delicious agony before you meet your end.'

- Thraekynn Neverwhim, Sybarite of the Bladed Curse

D10	SPECIALISTS' DEMEANOURS
1	**Predator's Eye:** No detail is too small to escape this warrior's attention.
2	**Dark Flamboyance:** In both their attire and battle style this Drukhari demonstrates tremendous flair.
3	**Ravenous:** So depraved is this warrior's soul that their hunger for suffering is utterly insatiable.
4	**Extravagant:** This warrior has developed a taste for finery, and they ruthlessly pursue the fulfilment of their desires.
5	**Scheming:** This Drukhari always thinks many steps ahead of their enemies – and their allies.
6	**Mistrustful:** This warrior has survived the intrigues of the Dark City by trusting no one but themselves.
7	**Darkened Soul:** Over long centuries this Drukhari has enacted countless atrocities and is now only rarely amused by them.
8	**Unforgiving:** This warrior strives for perfection, and accepts nothing less from those with whom they fight.
9	**Boundless Ambition:** With each victory, this Drukhari sees themselves climbing higher in the ranks of Commorrite society.
10	**Vindictive:** This warrior never forgets a slight, and will go to any lengths to enact their vengeance.

KABALITE NAME GENERATOR TABLE

D66	TAKEN NAME	KABALITE NAME
11	Anarkyss	Sar'sel
12	Veth'va	Vorpex
13	Mayator	Kreen
14	Quaez	the Bloodbreather
15	Daisan	Maestros
16	Bekliel	Gaarsus
21	Orvak	Ehthrek
22	Narlek	Ghorghast
23	Monsatos	Ignyss
24	Vivithrax	Mohrkhar
25	Drevakh	Thresk
26	Kyzarkh	Scaur
31	Thresyn	the Pale
32	Shylas	Khadylus
33	Lythric	Phrel
34	Kylos	Vulkyriax
35	Theskril	Nul
36	Skythe	the Flenser
41	Akkhar	Poisonblade
42	Kharsac	Barbtongue
43	Nyktos	Xesh
44	Grevyth	the Ravening
45	Thraed	Draeven
46	Sykil	of the Obsidian Needle
51	Khaeyl	Vhrex
52	Madrax	Kaghmyr
53	Akhirion	Thrail
54	Vypus	Flickerblade
55	Ethriliac	Xosh
56	Kheraes	the Bleak
61	Iyshak	Neverbreath
62	Khepres	Skahyl
63	Eldoriac	Verkosian
64	Vrekkus	Ulthurian
65	Thayd	Menesh
66	Xurul	the Cruel

WYCH CULT NAME GENERATOR TABLE

D66	ARENA TITLE	CLIQUE NAME
11	Ariex	La'flenz
12	Melikka	Wysp
13	Grendett	Soriel
14	Vaivel	Oblique
15	Bithandrel	Nervose
16	Ingenue	Mourn
21	Demadyne	Vivicon
22	Laelanyel	Viserhyx
23	Excrucia	Berrebaal
24	Nathra	Vulptuse
25	Vrexith	Ehlynna
26	Thyndrella	Khaur
31	Selithrian	Hexehss
32	Xela	the Crimson
33	Peiythia	Thrix
34	Uless	Khoryssa
35	Skyshrin	Vexx
36	Anielyn	of the Screaming Blade
41	Vyrenik	Khrygg
42	Khatryx	Nichtren
43	Nyssa	Veluxis
44	Phyrix	the Huntress
45	Mellyx	Beastbane
46	Kherissa	the Magnificent
51	Tryxin	Trehll
52	Aniellah	Xyriphraxis
53	Veshtari	Masdruvael
54	Morghynn	Khrone
55	Thrixxesh	the Untouched
56	Thessa	Bloodslyk
61	Xindrell	the Cruel
62	Kladys	Kharavyxis
63	Shemriel	Ynthrekh
64	Lyxanna	Dyvahur
65	Nimhre	Krael
66	Vylekh	the Bloodsister

DRUKHARI KILL TEAMS

DRUKHARI models use the Power From Pain ability below. **WYCHES** in your kill team also use the Combat Drugs ability below. In addition, if every model in your kill team has the **DRUKHARI** Faction keyword, you can use Drukhari Tactics.

Power From Pain: Models with this ability gain a bonus depending upon which battle round it is, as shown in the table below. Note that all bonuses are cumulative; for example, in the second battle round, the model ignores wounds on a roll of 6, and you can re-roll the dice when determining how far the model Advances or charges.

Combat Drugs: Models with this ability gain a bonus during the battle depending on the drugs they have taken. Before the battle, roll on the table below to see which combat drug your kill team is using. This bonus applies to all models in your kill team with the Combat Drugs ability.

POWER FROM PAIN

BATTLE ROUND	BONUS
1	**Inured to Suffering:** Roll a D6 each time this model loses a wound; on a 6 that wound is not lost.
2	**Eager to Flay:** You can re-roll the dice when determining how far this model moves when it Advances or charges.
3	**Flensing Fury:** Add 1 to hit rolls for this model in the Fight phase.
4	**Emboldened by Bloodshed:** Re-roll failed Nerve tests for this model.
5+	**Mantle of Agony:** Subtract 1 from the Leadership characteristic of enemy models that are within 6" of any models from your kill team with this bonus.

COMBAT DRUGS

D6	BONUS
1	**Adrenalight:** +1 to Attacks characteristic
2	**Grave Lotus:** +1 to Strength characteristic
3	**Hypex:** +2 to Move characteristic
4	**Painbringer:** +1 to Toughness characteristic
5	**Serpentin:** +1 to Weapon Skill characteristic (e.g. WS 3+ becomes WS 2+)
6	**Splintermind:** +2 to Leadership characteristic

FIRE AND FADE

Drukhari Tactic

Use this Tactic after a model from your kill team shoots in the Shooting phase. The model can immediately make a normal move of up to 7" as if it were the Movement phase.

1 COMMAND POINT

CRUEL DECEPTION

Drukhari Tactic

Use this Tactic after a model from your kill team Falls Back. That model can still shoot this battle round.

1 COMMAND POINT

PRAY THEY DON'T TAKE YOU ALIVE

Drukhari Tactic

Use this Tactic if a model from your kill team takes an enemy Leader out of action in the Fight phase. For the remainder of the battle, models in that enemy Leader's kill team must subtract 1 from their Leadership characteristic.

2 COMMAND POINTS

TORMENT GRENADE

Drukhari Tactic

Use this Tactic when you choose a model in your kill team to shoot with a phantasm grenade launcher. If an enemy model is hit by any attacks made with that weapon this phase, then, in addition to the normal effects, roll 3D6. If the result is higher than the target's Leadership characteristic, it suffers 1 mortal wound.

2 COMMAND POINTS

'The raiding party bays at our heels, but we
have these few perfect moments where the
enemy are all ours to play with. Let us whip them
into such a frenzy of pain and terror that our
latecomer kin are left with nothing but scraps.'

- *Hekatrix Vylekh the Untouched*

KABALITE WARRIOR

NAME	M	WS	BS	S	T	W	A	Ld	Sv	Max
Kabalite Warrior	7"	3+	3+	3	3	1	1	7	5+	-
Kabalite Gunner	7"	3+	3+	3	3	1	1	7	5+	2
Sybarite	7"	3+	3+	3	3	1	2	8	5+	1

This model is armed with a splinter rifle.
Up to two Kabalite Warriors in your kill team can be Kabalite Gunners, and one Kabalite Warrior in your kill team can be a Sybarite.

WARGEAR OPTIONS	• One Kabalite Gunner in your kill team may replace their splinter rifle with a splinter cannon or dark lance. • One Kabalite Gunner in your kill team may replace their splinter rifle with a shredder or blaster. • A Sybarite may take a power sword or agoniser. • A Sybarite may take a phantasm grenade launcher. • A Sybarite may replace their splinter rifle with a splinter pistol or a blast pistol.
ABILITIES	**Power From Pain** (pg 142)
SPECIALISTS	**Leader** (Sybarite only), **Sniper** (Gunner only), **Comms**, **Scout**, **Veteran**, **Zealot**
FACTION KEYWORD	DRUKHARI
KEYWORDS	AELDARI, INFANTRY, KABALITE WARRIOR

WYCH

NAME	M	WS	BS	S	T	W	A	Ld	Sv	Max
Wych	8"	3+	3+	3	3	1	2	7	6+	-
Wych Fighter	8"	3+	3+	3	3	1	2	7	6+	3
Hekatrix	8"	3+	3+	3	3	1	3	8	6+	1

This model is armed with a splinter pistol, Hekatarii blade and plasma grenades.
Up to three Wyches in your kill team can be Wych Fighters, and one Wych in your kill team can be a Hekatrix.

WARGEAR OPTIONS	• A Wych Fighter may replace their splinter pistol and Hekatarii blade with hydra gauntlets, razorflails, or a shardnet and impaler. • A Hekatrix may replace their Hekatarii blade with a power sword or agoniser. • A Hekatrix may take a phantasm grenade launcher. • A Hekatrix may replace their splinter pistol with a blast pistol.
ABILITIES	**Power From Pain, Combat Drugs** (pg 142) **Dodge:** This model has a 4+ invulnerable save in the Fight phase.	**No Escape:** If an INFANTRY model within 1" of any enemy models with this ability would Fall Back, the controlling players roll off. The model that would Fall Back can only do so if the player controlling it wins the roll-off.
SPECIALISTS	**Leader** (Hekatrix only), **Combat**, **Scout**, **Veteran**, **Zealot**
FACTION KEYWORD	DRUKHARI
KEYWORDS	AELDARI, INFANTRY, WYCH

'Hide, if you think you can. It will make good sport. By all means, raise your walls and bar your gates, double your guards and build your watch-fires high. Lock yourself within your innermost sanctum and cower. When the times comes, little governor, all the walls, and gates, and guns in the galaxy will not protect you.'

- Hekatrix Nyssa Masdruvael to Planetary Governor Tholdh Hekken III,
three days before his hideous death within his code-locked private bunker

RANGED WEAPONS

WEAPON	RANGE	TYPE	S	AP	D	ABILITIES
Blast pistol	6"	Pistol 1	8	-4	D6	-
Blaster	18"	Assault 1	8	-4	D6	-
Dark lance	36"	Heavy 1	8	-4	D6	-
Phantasm grenade launcher	18"	Assault D3	1	0	1	If a model is hit by one or more phantasm grenade launchers, subtract 1 from its Leadership characteristic until the end of the battle round.
Plasma grenade	6"	Grenade D6	4	-1	1	-
Shredder	12"	Assault D6	6	-1	1	When attacking an **INFANTRY** model, re-roll failed wound rolls for this weapon.
Splinter cannon	36"	Rapid Fire 3	*	0	1	This weapon wounds on a 4+.
Splinter pistol	12"	Pistol 1	*	0	1	This weapon wounds on a 4+.
Splinter rifle	24"	Rapid Fire 1	*	0	1	This weapon wounds on a 4+.

MELEE WEAPONS

WEAPON	RANGE	TYPE	S	AP	D	ABILITIES
Agoniser	Melee	Melee	*	-2	1	This weapon wounds on a 4+.
Hekatarii blade	Melee	Melee	User	0	1	Each time the bearer fights, it can make 1 additional attack with this weapon.
Hydra gauntlets	Melee	Melee	User	-1	1	Each time the bearer fights, it can make 1 additional attack with this weapon. You can re-roll failed wound rolls for this weapon.
Power sword	Melee	Melee	User	-3	1	-
Razorflails	Melee	Melee	User	-1	1	Each time the bearer fights, it can make 1 additional attack with this weapon. You can re-roll failed hit rolls for this weapon.
Shardnet and impaler	Melee	Melee	User	-1	2	Each time the bearer fights, it can make 1 additional attack with this weapon.

KILL TEAM

MODEL	POINTS PER MODEL (Does not include wargear)
Kabalite Warrior	7
- Kabalite Gunner	8
- Sybarite	8
Wych	8
- Wych Fighter	9
- Hekatrix	9

MELEE WEAPONS

WEAPON	POINTS PER WEAPON
Agoniser	2
Hekatarii blade	0
Hydra gauntlets	2
Power sword	2
Razorflails	2
Shardnet and impaler	2

RANGED WEAPONS

WEAPON	POINTS PER WEAPON
Blast pistol	2
Blaster	3
Dark lance	4
Phantasm grenade launcher	1
Plasma grenade	0
Shredder	1
Splinter cannon	3
Splinter pistol	0
Splinter rifle	0

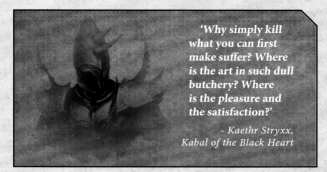

'Why simply kill what you can first make suffer? Where is the art in such dull butchery? Where is the pleasure and the satisfaction?'

- Kaethr Stryxx, Kabal of the Black Heart

HARLEQUINS

To the warrior-acrobats of the Harlequins, who fight for the Laughing God, warfare and art are inseparable disciplines. By rolling the appropriate dice on the tables on the following pages, you can generate names and background for your Harlequin kill teams.

To the Aeldari known as the Harlequins, the acts of waging war and staging a performance are one and the same. They echo the myths of the ancient Aeldari gods in everything they do, with each Player taking on a role in body and soul until the chosen ritualised dance is done. Worshipping the Laughing God, Cegorach, they have a twisted sense of humour, and appreciate irony as a connoisseur does a fine wine – even should it work against them.

All Aeldari loathe and fear Slaanesh, for that fell entity was born from their race's collective psyche, and thirsts for their souls. The Harlequins escape that curse through the worship of the Laughing God. When a Harlequin dies, their soul is snatched up by Cegorach and spirited away, safe into the webway where Slaanesh cannot devour it. Yet there is a price for such salvation; when an Aeldari becomes a Harlequin, they abandon their old life altogether, leaving behind friends, family, responsibilities and everything that once defined them. Instead, they take on their new role within the Troupe, and fight forever more in the name of the Laughing God.

What precisely the Harlequins fight to achieve varies – some seek to defeat Chaos, others to restore the power of the ancient Aeldari, while others still watch over ancient and sacred sites such as the enigmatic Black Library. Yet whatever their aim, all fight with an elegance and grace that is breathtaking to behold, utilising polychromatic domino fields, anti-grav flip belts and an array of lethal close-range weaponry to confound and outfight their foes.

THE WEBWAY

The webway is a labyrinth dimension that exists between realspace and the warp. Though damaged by the ravages of time, this interstellar maze allows travel across space with impossible swiftness; journeys that would take starships many weeks or months to complete can be made on foot via its twisting passages in a matter of hours. Yet the webway is dangerous. The Harlequins of the Laughing God are the only faction in the galaxy who can tread its pathways without fear, and even they treat their strange realm with a respectful wariness.

Harlequin Troupes – each effectively a kill team in its own right – travel across time and space, using the secret labyrinth dimension of the webway to strike suddenly at critical targets, falling upon their prey in a storm of acrobatic attacks and graceful sword blows. As a Troupe, they will take on an aspect of the Light, the Dark, or the Twilight that exists between the two. As individuals, each Harlequin's role will dictate their fighting style – the Hidden Prince, for example, will use his flip belt to descend from above before neatly taking his foe's head in a single stroke, whereas the Bladed Fool will caper and prance, untouched by any attempted reprisals, until he 'accidentally' slashes the throat of his foe. The ancestral enemies of all Harlequin Troupes are the scions of the Dark Gods, and those of Slaanesh in particular, but any who stand in their path risk being artfully despatched.

D6 · BACKGROUND: THE CAST

1 The Swords of Khaine: These warriors give worship to sundered Khaine by hurling themselves into close-quarters battle with wrathful arrogance.

2 Webway Wanderers: The members of this kill team are nomadic warriors who wander the webway according to the whims of Cegorach, and slay those who threaten his labyrinth realm.

3 The Solitary: Sundered from their masque by death or lonely narrative, these Harlequins dance the steps of their saedath alone.

4 Fate's Messengers: This band of Harlequins has come together to deliver a particular message or lesson, or to protect its bearer.

5 Sinister Killers: The Players of this kill team bear the most horrific weapons available to them, and aim to spread terror and panic with their every deed.

6 Guardians of the Black Library: This kill team consists of Harlequins sworn to protect the Black Library, and to eliminate threats to that shadowy repository of lore.

D6 · SQUAD QUIRK: THE AFFECTATION

1 Warriors of the Light: These Harlequins are predominantly heroic and dynamic Players of the Light.

2 Blades of the Twilight: This kill team is made up of the enigmatic and transitory Players of the Twilight.

3 Talons of the Dark: Sinister and malevolent, this kill team comprises Players of the Dark.

4 Swift as the Wind: Even by the standards of their kind, the Players of this kill team are remarkably agile and athletic.

5 Cruelly Mocking: As part of the roles they play, these Harlequins bait their enemies mercilessly, and pour scorn on their endeavours.

6 Starlight Stride: These warriors are always on the move, their feet seeming to dance through the air with incredible swiftness, their every motion a brilliantly choreographed combination of martial prowess and elegant dance.

D6 · MISSION: THE TALE

1 The Dance of the Thief's Reward: This kill team seeks to locate and punish one who took something they should not have from the Black Library.

2 The Dance of Kurnous' Gate: Somewhere in this war zone lies a webway gate that must be protected or sealed to prevent unwanted intruders in Cegorach's domain.

3 The Dance of the Crimson Reaping: This kill team is performing a protracted saedath that requires it to fell a total of one-score-and-ten enemies in battle

4 The Dance of the Veiled Blade: These Harlequins seek to misdirect and confuse their enemies before striking the killing blow from an unexpected angle.

5 The Dance of the Starving Ygghs: This kill team maraud behind the enemy lines, seeking to ritually destroy their stockpiles and supply lines.

6 The Dance of Vaul's Tempering: These Harlequins must engage as many foes as they can in contests of close-quarters skill, duelling and defeating them one-on-one.

D10 · SPECIALISTS' DEMEANOURS

1 Heroic Protagonist: This Player's role requires them to be ever brave and noble.

2 Malicious Antagonist: This Harlequin plays the villain in all situations.

3 Bladed Fool: This Player adopts a ridiculous role until the precise moment they strike.

4 Sorrowful Killer: This Harlequin laments every blow they strike with woeful and dramatic gestures.

5 Gleeful Maniac: This Harlequin's persona requires them to be forever maniacal, revelling in anarchy and bloodshed.

6 Relentless Destroyer: Embodying a character like Khaine or Ulthanash, this Harlequin harries their enemies with tireless aggression.

7 Sombre Executioner: This Player grimly slays their foes one by one, embodying death itself.

8 Fate's Herald: This Harlequin's role requires them to kill from afar, singling out their targets and slaying them at the most dramatic moment.

9 The Eternal Wanderer: The role of this Player requires them to be always on the move, never stopping for even a moment.

10 The Harmonious Herald: This Harlequin sings in a strange, lilting tongue as they fight, and may never stop their song.

HARLEQUIN NAME GENERATOR TABLE

D10	DRAMATIC MANTLE	RITUAL PERSONA
1	The Sun	King
2	The Star	Queen
3	The Shadow	Prince
4	The Void	Knave
5	The Sky	Witch
6	The Redtide	Judge
7	The Moon	Executioner
8	The Highborn	Seer
9	The Leering	Ghoul
10	The Bladed	Crone

HARLEQUIN KILL TEAMS

If every model in your kill team has the HARLEQUINS Faction keyword, you can use Harlequins Tactics.

PRISMATIC BLUR

Harlequins Tactic

Use this Tactic in the Movement phase when a model from your kill team Advances. That model has a 3+ invulnerable save until the start of the next battle round.

1 COMMAND POINT

WARRIOR ACROBATS

Harlequins Tactic

Use this Tactic in the Movement phase when a model from your kill team Advances. Add 6" to the model's Move characteristic for that Movement phase instead of rolling a dice.

1 COMMAND POINT

FIRE AND FADE

Harlequins Tactic

Use this Tactic after a model from your kill team shoots in the Shooting phase. The model can immediately make a normal move of up to 7" as if it were the Movement phase.

1 COMMAND POINT

CEGORACH'S JEST

Harlequins Tactic

Use this Tactic after an enemy model has Fallen Back from a model from your kill team. Provided no other enemy models are within 1" of your model, it can shoot at the model that Fell Back as if it were the Shooting phase.

2 COMMAND POINTS

WAR DANCERS

Harlequins Tactic

Use this Tactic at the end of the Fight phase. Pick a model from your kill team that has already fought this phase. That model can immediately fight an additional time.

2 COMMAND POINTS

MIRTHLESS HATRED

Harlequins Tactic

Use this Tactic when a model from your kill team is chosen to fight. Re-roll failed hit rolls and failed wound rolls for this model's attacks that target SLAANESH models until the end of the phase.

1 COMMAND POINT

PLAYER

NAME	M	WS	BS	S	T	W	A	Ld	Sv	Max
Player	8"	3+	3+	3	3	1	4	8	6+	-

This model is armed with a shuriken pistol, Harlequin's blade and plasma grenades.

WARGEAR OPTIONS	• This model may replace its shuriken pistol with a neuro disruptor or fusion pistol. • This model may replace its Harlequin's blade with a Harlequin's embrace, Harlequin's caress or Harlequin's kiss.
ABILITIES	**Flip Belt:** This model can move across other models and terrain as if they were not there. In addition, it never suffers falling damage, and never falls on another model. If it would, instead place this model as close as possible to the point where it would have landed. This can bring it within 1" of an enemy model. **Holo-suit:** This model has a 4+ invulnerable save.	**Rising Crescendo:** You may roll 3D6 instead of 2D6 for this model when making a charge roll, and may choose an enemy model within 18" of this model as the target of a charge, rather than 12".
SPECIALISTS	**Leader, Combat, Medic, Scout, Veteran, Zealot**
FACTION KEYWORD	**HARLEQUINS**
KEYWORDS	**AELDARI, INFANTRY, PLAYER**

RANGED WEAPONS

WEAPON	RANGE	TYPE	S	AP	D	ABILITIES
Fusion pistol	6"	Pistol 1	8	-4	D6	If the target is within half range of this weapon, roll two dice when inflicting damage with it and discard the lowest result.
Neuro disruptor	12"	Pistol 1	3	-3	D3	-
Plasma grenade	6"	Grenade D6	4	-1	1	-
Shuriken pistol	12"	Pistol 1	4	0	1	Each time you make a wound roll of 6+ for this weapon, that hit is resolved with an AP of -3.

MELEE WEAPONS

WEAPON	RANGE	TYPE	S	AP	D	ABILITIES
Harlequin's blade	Melee	Melee	User	0	1	-
Harlequin's caress	Melee	Melee	+2	-2	1	-
Harlequin's embrace	Melee	Melee	+1	-3	1	-
Harlequin's kiss	Melee	Melee	+1	-1	D3	-

KILL TEAM

MODEL	POINTS PER MODEL (Does not include wargear)
Player	12

RANGED WEAPONS

WEAPON	POINTS PER WEAPON
Fusion pistol	3
Neuro disruptor	2
Plasma grenade	0
Shuriken pistol	0

MELEE WEAPONS

WEAPON	POINTS PER WEAPON
Harlequin's blade	0
Harlequin's caress	3
Harlequin's embrace	2
Harlequin's kiss	4

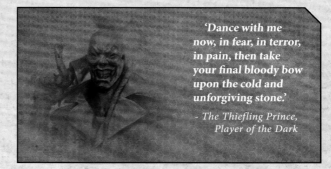

'Dance with me now, in fear, in terror, in pain, then take your final bloody bow upon the cold and unforgiving stone.'

- The Thiefling Prince, Player of the Dark

NECRONS

Advancing in inexorable lockstep come the deathless legions of the Necrons, eldritch energy crackling from their ancient weapons. They have risen to reclaim the stars, and none shall stand in their way. By rolling the appropriate dice on the tables on the following pages, you can generate names and background for your Necrons kill teams.

Ancient beyond reckoning and utterly without mercy, the Necrons are soulless creatures whose skeletal bodies are formed from living metal. In aeons past these beings ruled the galaxy with an iron fist, until the accumulated losses of their ceaseless wars of conquest forced them to retire to stasis-crypts deep beneath the surfaces of the planets under their sovereignty. There they slumbered, awaiting a time when their many enemies were weak and ripe for domination. Millions of years later the Necrons have emerged, and their multitudinous legions march forth across the galaxy at the behest of the proud and imperious Necron Overlords.

When the Necrons vanished into their hidden stasis crypts more than sixty million years ago, they were counted amongst the most powerful species in the galaxy, and their worlds spread across the stars in great profusion. Through the long millennia, many of these tomb worlds have been lost to catastrophe, while others have undergone such radical shifts in climate or geology that the tomb complexes beneath their surfaces have been irreparably damaged or destroyed.

Yet many more have merely been settled by the galaxy's younger races, who now find strange ruins and the yawning mouths of glowing crypts rising from beneath their feet. The Necrons are awakening to discover that their empire of old teems with what they see as nothing more than fleshy vermin. They have little patience for such creatures, with the vast majority seeking simply to eradicate the infestations as their first step upon the road of restoring their glories of old.

Necron kill teams are chosen by an Overlord from amongst his most favoured warriors. They are invariably led by elite troops such as Immortals, for unlike the mindless Warriors such Necrons have retained some of their individuality and extensive combat experience during the long sleep. That said, the unthinking foot soldiers of the dynastic legions have their uses – the leader of a Necron kill team can trust these automatons to march into the thickest hails of enemy fire in order to capture vital locations, or retrieve objects of value desired by their master. For more delicate missions – whether assassination, the gathering of subjects for mindshackle interrogation or perhaps the violent humiliation of a rival – the Necron Lord will make use of more specialised troops. Thus, Necron kill teams can vary greatly in composition, though their predominant strategy is to obliterate their foes from afar with a relentless storm of atomising gauss energy.

GIFTS OF THE CRYPTEKS

Necron technology is so incredibly potent that to many races it appears indistinguishable from sorcery. Created by the technomancers known as Crypteks, it enables their armies of conquest to teleport to and from the battlefield seemingly at will, and allows grievously damaged Necron warriors to rapidly self-repair or even phase out of reality altogether. Most terrifying of all, it provides Necron soldiery with weapons that can flay their victims apart on an atomic level, wreathe them in arcs of lethal energy, or reduce them to glowing ashes in the blink of an eye.

D10 — BACKGROUND: ANCIENT ORIGINS

D10	
1	**Harbingers:** This kill team is just the tip of the iceberg, the first encroaching warband to break this world's surface and the spearhead for a far greater emergence.
2	**Tomb Guardians:** These warriors have stood sentry over their tomb complex for countless long years, unsleeping, unfaltering, ever vigilant.
3	**Invaders from Beyond:** This kill team is part of a wider planetary invasion, forerunners paving the way for a larger assault.
4	**The Phaeron's Chosen:** These hand-picked warriors are the elite guards and finest agents of their Overlord.
5	**Scouring Party:** This kill team is equipped to exterminate the vermin that have infested the demesnes of the Necrontyr.
6	**Code-bound:** This kill team cleaves to the ancient codes of the Triarch, and would never stoop to the use of dishonourable weapons or tactics.
7	**Assassins:** These warriors have been drawn together by their unscrupulous Overlord and charged with eliminating key enemies through use of whatever tactics they see fit.
8	**Ghoulish Nightmares:** This kill team consists of ghastly flesh-draped Necrons who spread terror amongst the enemy ranks.
9	**Mindless Martyrs:** This kill team has been constructed specifically to wear down the foe through sheer relentlessness, impassively soaking up firepower only to return from apparent demise again and again.
10	**Domination Force:** This kill team comprises those warriors that can best – and most violently – demonstrate the Necrons' utter superiority over the lesser races.

D10 — MISSION: GLORIOUS TASK

D10	
1	**The Cull:** All sentient non-Necron lifeforms must be exterminated without mercy or exception.
2	**Mindthieves:** A prominent enemy leader has been slated for mental domination through the application of mindshackle scarabs. This kill team must perform the forced indoctrination.
3	**Servants of the Crypteks:** This kill team has been charged with testing the deadly weapons of the Crypteks upon a variety of living specimens and reporting the results.
4	**Heralds of the Uprising:** In order to awaken a major tomb complex, specific locations above ground must be seized and invested with Necron technologies.
5	**Chrono-aquisitors:** Below the planet's surface, a tomb complex stirs. This kill team must disrupt the lesser races and, in so doing, buy time for the awakening to proceed.
6	**Fractal Disruption:** Following an exacting, hyper-logical plan, this kill team must eliminate a series of enemy supply and control assets to cripple the foe.
7	**Punishment Detail:** These warriors have failed their Overlord in some way and, on his whim, have been sent on a desperate mission to atone or be destroyed.
8	**Relentless War:** This kill team has been prioritised for resurrection protocols, and charged with fighting a rigged war of attrition with the enemy forces in this war zone.
9	**The Phaeron's Blade:** The Necron war effort will be rendered three hundred per cent more efficient if a specific enemy defensive asset or leader is mercilessly eliminated by this kill team.
10	**The Phaeron's Curse:** Some insolent member of the lesser races was fool enough to invade a tomb complex and steal a priceless artefact. This kill team will reclaim that artefact, and administer a suitably horrific punishment to the transgressor.

D10 — SQUAD QUIRK: GIFT OF AEONS

D10	
1	**The Curse of Time:** So ancient are these warriors, so many times have they been resurrected, that they have become somewhat faltering and unreliable.
2	**Wreathed in Power:** Some artifice of the Crypteks ensures that these warriors' bodies crackle with a constant energised halo.
3	**Deadly Automata:** These warriors stalk into battle without hesitation, single-mindedly focused on their objective and untroubled by the incoming fire of the foe.
4	**Dark Sentience:** These Necrons are more self-aware and intelligent than most of their kind, able to reason, react and hate…
5	**Ether-flux:** These warriors have slipped slightly out of sync with time, and flicker in and out of reality like a mirage.
6	**Skin-takers:** These Necrons are driven to flense their victims at close-quarters.
7	**Arrogant Hunters:** This kill team looks down upon the lesser races as game-animals to be hunted.
8	**Deranged:** The Great Sleep has scrambled the mental engrams of these warriors, leaving their actions random and strange.
9	**Unfeeling:** Hollow and robotic, these warriors show no sign of emotion, personality or conscious thought.
10	**Favoured Warriors:** The warriors of this kill team have been decorated to demonstrate their Overlord's power and wealth, and their wargear is of the highest standard.

D10 SPECIALISTS' DEMEANOURS

D10	
1	**Menacing:** This warrior has a ghastly aspect that spreads fear amongst the foe.
2	**Maniacal:** What remains of this warrior's personality has been corrupted so far that they do little but emit a terrible, grating laughter.
3	**Strategic:** Whether by dint of strategic sub-engrams or memory artefacts, this warrior is a sound battlefield tactician.
4	**Nihilist:** This Necron simply wishes to see a destructive end to all things.
5	**Tormentor:** This warrior takes a sadistic delight in inflicting pain upon the lesser races.
6	**Glitching:** This warrior's movements are stilted and halting, and they emit blurts of partial vocalisation as they act.
7	**Obsessive:** Whatever this warrior does, they do repeatedly and to violent excess.
8	**Delusional:** This warrior is convinced that they are still flesh and blood, fighting in an ancient war now long gone.
9	**Acquisitive:** To this warrior, the Necrons are the rightful inheritors of everything in the galaxy; they take trophies and steal wargear with a compulsive urgency.
10	**Necrochirurgeon:** This warrior is fascinated with the effects that Necron weaponry have upon the flesh of living things, and the transition from life to final death.

IMMORTAL / FLAYED ONE / DEATHMARK NAME GENERATOR TABLE

D66	BEQUEATHED NAME	MAGNIFICENT TITLE
11	Ankhep	the Unliving
12	Tamonhak	the Gilded
13	Eknotath	the Great
14	Khotek	the Exalted
15	Thanatar	the Loyal
16	Amhut	the Cruel
21	Karok	the Storm's Eye
22	Zan-Tep	the Bloodied
23	Unakh	the Mighty
24	Khophec	the Relentless
25	Tzantath	the Unforgiving
26	Tahar	the Merciless
31	Imonekh	the Glorious
32	Trazat	the Devoted
33	Xeoptar	the Victorious
34	Hamanet	the Destroyer
35	Oberek	the Shrouded
36	Banatur	the Flenser
41	Ahmnok	the Unstoppable
42	Kophesh	the Beheader
43	Teznet	the Impaler
44	Odakhar	the Magnificent
45	Kythok	the Illuminated
46	Eknothet	the Executioner
51	Anubitar	the Phaeron's Hand
52	Anokh	the Guardian
53	Thotep	the Gatekeeper
54	Anhutek	the All-seeing
55	Ikhatar	the All-knowing
56	Thotmek	the Starwalker
61	Ramatek	the Starkiller
62	Homanat	the Lifetaker
63	Taknophet	the Godbreaker
64	Makhret	the Torchbearer
65	(no first appellation)	the Stormbringer
66	Zanatek	the Colossus

NECRON KILL TEAMS

If every model in your kill team has the NECRONS Faction keyword, you can use Necrons Tactics.

PRIME REANIMATION PROTOCOLS

Necrons Tactic

Use this Tactic when an Injury roll is made for a model from your kill team. Roll an additional dice and apply the lowest result.

2 COMMAND POINTS

TARGETING ROUTINES

Necrons Tactic

Use this Tactic when you choose a model in your kill team to shoot in the Shooting phase. Add 1 to hit rolls for that model against targets which are obscured.

1 COMMAND POINT

FLENSING FURY

Necrons Tactic

Use this Tactic when you choose a **FLAYED ONE** in your kill team to fight in the Fight phase. Until the end of the phase, each time you make a wound of 6+ for that model's flayer claws, add 1 to the Damage characteristic of the weapon for that attack.

1 COMMAND POINT

DISRUPTION FIELDS

Necrons Tactic

Use this Tactic when you choose a model in your kill team to fight in the Fight phase. Increase the Strength characteristic of that model by 1 until the end of the phase.

1 COMMAND POINT

MINDSHACKLE SCARABS

Necrons Tactic

Use this Tactic at the start of the Shooting phase. Pick an enemy model within 6" of a model from your kill team and roll 2D6. If the result is higher than the enemy model's Leadership characteristic, you can immediately make a shooting attack with one of that model's ranged weapons as if it were a model from your kill team.

2 COMMAND POINTS

OVERCHARGED DISINTEGRATION

Necrons Tactic

Use this Tactic in the Shooting phase when you choose a model in your kill team to shoot with a gauss flayer or gauss blaster. Improve the Armour Penetration characteristic of that weapon by 1 until the end of the phase (e.g. AP-1 becomes AP-2, AP-2 becomes AP-3).

2 COMMAND POINTS

'We have awoken, we who are the rightful rulers of the stars themselves. We shall ascend, now, to retake our rightful place, and these vermin that scurry and grub and make their nests amidst the ruins of our former glories, they shall hinder us not.'

- Overlord Azmartek, the Ever-Glorious, Prince of the Thousand Moons, Dominator of the Ancient Realms, He Who Strides Between the Stars and Before Whom the Gods Themselves Shall Surely Kneel

NECRON WARRIOR

NAME	M	WS	BS	S	T	W	A	Ld	Sv	Max
Necron Warrior	5"	3+	3+	4	4	1	1	10	4+	-

This model is armed with a gauss flayer.

ABILITIES	**Reanimation Protocols:** When an Injury roll is made for this model, on an unmodified roll of 6 the model is not taken out of action and does not suffer a flesh wound. Instead it is restored to 1 wound remaining with no flesh wounds.
SPECIALISTS	**Leader, Comms, Veteran**
FACTION KEYWORD	**Necrons**
KEYWORDS	**Infantry, Necron Warrior**

IMMORTAL

NAME	M	WS	BS	S	T	W	A	Ld	Sv	Max
Immortal	5"	3+	3+	4	4	1	1	10	3+	-

This model is armed with a gauss blaster.

WARGEAR OPTIONS	• This model may replace its gauss blaster with a tesla carbine.
ABILITIES	**Reanimation Protocols:** When an Injury roll is made for this model, on an unmodified roll of 6 the model is not taken out of action and does not suffer a flesh wound. Instead it is restored to 1 wound remaining with no flesh wounds.
SPECIALISTS	**Leader, Comms, Veteran, Zealot**
FACTION KEYWORD	**Necrons**
KEYWORDS	**Infantry, Immortal**

FLAYED ONE

NAME	M	WS	BS	S	T	W	A	Ld	Sv	Max
Flayed One	5"	3+	6+	4	4	1	3	10	4+	-

This model is armed with flayer claws.

ABILITIES	**Reanimation Protocols:** When an Injury roll is made for this model, on an unmodified roll of 6 the model is not taken out of action and does not suffer a flesh wound. Instead it is restored to 1 wound remaining with no flesh wounds.
SPECIALISTS	**Leader, Combat, Veteran, Zealot**
FACTION KEYWORD	NECRONS
KEYWORDS	INFANTRY, FLAYED ONE

DEATHMARK

NAME	M	WS	BS	S	T	W	A	Ld	Sv	Max
Deathmark	5"	3+	3+	4	4	1	1	10	3+	-

This model is armed with a synaptic disintegrator.

ABILITIES	**Reanimation Protocols:** When an Injury roll is made for this model, on an unmodified roll of 6 the model is not taken out of action and does not suffer a flesh wound. Instead it is restored to 1 wound remaining with no flesh wounds.
SPECIALISTS	**Leader, Comms, Scout, Sniper, Veteran**
FACTION KEYWORD	NECRONS
KEYWORDS	INFANTRY, DEATHMARK

RANGED WEAPONS

WEAPON	RANGE	TYPE	S	AP	D	ABILITIES
Gauss blaster	24"	Rapid Fire 1	5	-2	1	-
Gauss flayer	24"	Rapid Fire 1	4	-1	1	-
Synaptic disintegrator	24"	Rapid Fire 1	4	0	1	A model firing a synaptic disintegrator does not suffer the penalty to hit rolls for the target being at long range. Each time you roll a wound roll of 6+ for this weapon, the target suffers a mortal wound in addition to any other damage.
Tesla carbine	24"	Assault 2	5	0	1	Each hit roll of 6+ with this weapon causes 3 hits.

MELEE WEAPONS

WEAPON	RANGE	TYPE	S	AP	D	ABILITIES
Flayer claws	Melee	Melee	User	0	1	Re-roll failed wound rolls for this weapon.

KILL TEAM

MODEL	POINTS PER MODEL (Does not include wargear)
Deathmark	15
Flayed One	10
Immortal	16
Necron Warrior	12

RANGED WEAPONS

WEAPON	POINTS PER WEAPON
Gauss blaster	0
Gauss flayer	0
Synaptic disintegrator	0
Tesla carbine	0

MELEE WEAPONS

WEAPON	POINTS PER WEAPON
Flayer claws	0

'This world is ours in perpetuity, as decreed by the Triarch and ratified by the Silent King. You are trespassers upon a sovereign domain that was already old when these stars were young. That you were ignorant of this is the only reason you still live. My lord and master offers you a single chance to remove yourselves and all your works from his world or be eradicated. You have one solar cycle to comply.'

- Zanatek the Beheader to the populace of Thesvor II

'Our enemies seek to do battle with us, yet they do not realise that they have already lost. How can beings so crude, from a culture so primitive and immature, hope to battle such as we? This is not war, it is eradication of vermin…'

- *Xeoptar the Great upon the Plains of Desolation*

ORKS

The Orks are the most belligerent and resourceful race in the galaxy. Rampaging across the void in their billions, the greenskins devastate everything in their path. By rolling the appropriate dice on the tables on the following pages, you can generate names and background for your Ork kill teams.

The Orks are a galactic menace, a race of hulking, bellicose aliens who love nothing more than a good fight, and will devastate entire star systems in their attempts to find a battle worthy of their time. Their cobbled-together vehicles and weapons appear crude in design, but that does not make them any less destructive on the battlefield – to stand against an Ork assault is to be enveloped by a tidal wave of primal ferocity that is as unstoppable as it is terrifying.

Orks are exceptionally straightforward creatures, whose culture is as robust as it is simple. In greenskin society, might makes right, and so the largest and strongest Ork inevitably bullies his way to the top of the heap. Thus, the Boss Nobz that rule over mobs of greenskins are muscle-bound, thick-skinned brutes, while the Warbosses that in turn rule over them are truly monstrous creatures that command entire tribes or – in the case of the mightiest leaders – a star-spanning military migration known as a Waaagh!.

Beyond this simple societal structure, Orks are further divided into a number of clans, each of which has distinguishing features, a favoured colour and glyph, and certain specialities on and off the battlefield. Whether it be the Evil Sunz, who paint everything red and are obsessed with speed, the brutal Goffs with their black armour and love of close-quarters violence, the rich and showy Bad Moons, the light-fingered looters of the Deathskulls, the atavistic and tough Snakebites or the oddly disciplined – and universally mistrusted – Blood Axes, each Ork clan has its place in Ork society, and its own favourite ways of making war.

GORK AND MORK

The Orks worship a pair of rumbustious and belligerent gods known as Gork and Mork, who embody the greenskin love of violence for violence's sake. Gork is said by the Orks to be brutal but kunnin', a hulking warrior god who likes nothing more than to take the most direct route into the biggest fight he can find. Meanwhile, his brother Mork is kunnin' but brutal, a massive war club hidden just behind his back where it can be swiftly whipped out and brought crashing down on his enemies' heads the moment they look the other way.

An Ork kill team is comprised of a raucous mob of greenskins who delight in the rush and crunch of battle. Its leader is always the biggest and meanest Ork around, accompanied by those he has managed to bully, cajole or threaten into following him. Like a green wrecking ball, this gathering will smash aside anything in its path. Hollering Orks will fill the air with storms of lead from their crude shootas, while towering brutes lumber forwards through the carnage of battle, hacking, bashing and blasting their foes apart with murderous glee.

The Orks' great strength and durability make them excellent hand-to-hand fighters, and most Ork kill teams eschew such a tedious concern as marksmanship in favour of closing with the enemy as quickly and violently as possible, swarming them with sheer numbers. However, what the greenskins lack in accuracy they make up for in weight of fire, and their foes should not discount the cumulative devastation unleashed by a dozen shootas and burnas blazing away in deafening unison.

D10	BACKGROUND: DA LADZ
1	**Gung-ho!:** This kill team are glory seekers out to prove themselves, wishing to stand out from their horde-mates with their deeds of battle and kunnin'.
2	**Filled with Waaagh!:** The violent energies of the Waaagh! have filled these greenskins with unnatural enthusiasm for battle.
3	**Skraphuntaz:** These Orks are driven to hoard scrap, and even if it is bolted down these ladz will steal it (along with the bolts).
4	**The Shootiest:** When it comes to dakka, these greenskins know how to lay it down, for they love firepower the way Squiggoths love to eat.
5	**Sneaky Gits!:** This kill team firmly believes that attacking from unexpected quarters is not only thrilling, but good for laughs when they see the panic in their doomed enemies' eyes.
6	**Brutal:** These Orks like to fight up-close and personal, preferring to pummel their foes in hand-to-hand combat.
7	**Kunnin':** These Orks know how to rig cruel traps of every variety, and are well known amongst their brethren for using other sneaky tricks like hiding behind cover when the enemy shoots at them.
8	**Internal Rivalries:** The Orks in this mob are constantly trying to outdo one another, whether because they belong to different tribes or clans, or just because one of the ladz said he was 'da best' and the others are going to prove him wrong or die trying.
9	**Addicted to Destruction:** These Orks are so keen to wreck everything they see that they will even blast apart terrain if there are no better targets.
10	**Spreaders of the Waaagh!:** This kill team believes that the best way to spread the Waaagh! is with shockingly brutal acts of violence inflicted upon the foe.

D10	MISSION: DA PLAN
1	**Kill Their Bosses:** This kill team is out to hunt down and kill enemy leaders and specialists.
2	**Get Stuck In:** Hit 'em hard and keep moving forwards: it's the greenskin way.
3	**Salvage:** This kill team must pick over every fallen corpse and piece of machinery to grab everything they can for the Meks.
4	**'Andz off:** These ladz are out to protect something the Meks built, and that the enemy want to steal or destroy.
5	**We'll Show 'Em:** Each Ork vies to be the one that can 'bag da most trophies', with 'trophies' here meaning 'enemy heads'.
6	**Da Ambush:** The foe is surrounded; now the fun begins. This kill team must launch a surprise attack to wipe out the enemy.
7	**Speed Is Its Own Reward:** For these Orks, its all about going as fast as they can, because the fastest ladz win.
8	**Sneak About:** Only Blood Axes leaders would worry about 'scoutin' da foe', and on their orders a small team has been sent out to reconnoitre the area.
9	**Fist of Gork (or Mork):** As the speartip of a larger attack, this kill team must clear the way for the hordes that follow.
10	**Plant da Flag:** To claim an area the Orks must wipe out the foe and then ensure all know who did it in the brashest and most unsubtle way possible.

D10	SQUAD QUIRK: DA KNOW-WOTZ
1	**Loud and Tuneless:** From amped-up weaponry to deafening warshouts and bellowed Freebooterz space-shanties, this entire squad values making as much noise as possible.
2	**Boastful:** Full of bravado and braggadocio, this squad never shuts up about their own violent accomplishments, pointing out and extolling at length each and every one.
3	**Itchy:** Some sort of rash has been making even the Orks' leathery hides feel all scratchy, often at the least convenient times…
4	**Madboyz:** Possibly it was the recent 'ead-butting contest, but the loud, raucously shouted war cries of this crew are entirely incomprehensible, and their behaviour rather strange.
5	**Krumpin' Krew:** This squad revels in the biggest and loudest-struck blows, and have become experts at winding up and delivering the most brutal of close-combat hits.
6	**Hard-bitten:** The Orks in this mob boast iron gobs, steel teef or incredibly powerful jaws with which they like to 'leave their mark' upon any who fight them.
7	**Lucky Gitz:** Whether by sacred keepsakes or lucky blue tattoos, this entire mob has proven to be blessed with good fortune by Gork and Mork themselves.
8	**Pyromaniacs:** Every member of this mob enjoys setting things ablaze and knows 'a burny fing is a good fing'.
9	**Buzzsquigs:** This mob is overhyped on Buzzsquigs – small snack-sized creatures that boost greenskin energies beyond even their usual maniacal levels.
10	**Praktical Jokers:** Whether it's stingjaws placed in their fellows' trousers, slugga-grips loosened while the owner is distracted, or the explosives in a stikkbomb replaced with stink-squigs, this mob will go to any lengths to mess with each other.

D10 SPECIALISTS' DEMEANOURS

1	**Thick-headed:** While this warrior is not overly bright, they can deliver an 'eadbutt that will dent a plascrete-reinforced bunker.
2	**Heavily Scarred:** Other greenskins view so much battle damage in the same way other races might gaze upon veterans bedecked with military medals, ribbons, and honours.
3	**Stubborn:** With single-minded determination this Ork is set on accomplishing every task in their own way.
4	**Light-fingered:** This Ork is a master pilferer and they snatch, steal and loot at all times, ensuring they have plenty of extra gear should the need arise.
5	**Violent Loon:** Even by greenskin standards this warrior is full of aggression, and he does not know the meaning of the word overkill.
6	**Resilient:** Too angry to know pain, too full of fight to slow down, this warrior can shrug off any wound, at least for a time.
7	**Beady-eyed:** This Ork is so shrewd that no small detail escapes his low kunnin, and he knows just where to place his shot or drive his choppa for maximum effect.
8	**Too Dumb to Know Fear:** Nothing could dissuade this Ork from attacking.
9	**Foul Gob:** None can challenge or taunt the foe with as much zeal and mockery as this Ork.
10	**Big and Brawny:** When this Ork bellows the whole battlefield can hear it, and he looms over his mates like a monster.

ORK NAME GENERATOR TABLE

D66	FRONT BIT	UVVER BIT
11	Urzog	Drakka
12	Snikrat	Grug
13	Krogskull	Gitstompa
14	Gorgrok	Skullcrusha
15	Droknog	Facekrumpa
16	Grodd	the 'Ard
21	Zogwarp	Grot Kicker
22	Gitzog	da Shiv
23	Ruggat	*(no uvver bit)*
24	Zargruk	Blaktoof
25	Stugbrog	da Hammer
26	Snarkrat	Ghazbhag
31	Zagblag	Steelfang
32	Bokgrobber	Daggafist
33	Zarknutz	Squigbiter
34	Dhakadak	da Stompy
35	Nargrunt	da Facegrinda
36	Farksnot	Loudgob
41	Gharagh	Facebiter
42	Urlakk	da Maniak
43	Zogger	Steelbootz
44	Slazbag	Ripblade
45	Squigface	'Umiechewa
46	Ugul	Ironboot
51	Tuska	Flame Spitta
52	Nakboz	Wurldkilla
53	Skarzot	Stompkrumpa
54	Kroggler	Spleenrippa
55	Grukk	Bigfangz
56	Fragbad	Badfang
61	Traknug	Snotkicka
62	Grizgutz	Brewguzzla
63	Shrokbog	Bonesplitta
64	Kraznag	'Eadkrakka
65	Gragnatz	Madeye
66	Blokrotz	Trakeye

ORK KILL TEAMS

If every model in your kill team has the ORKS Faction keyword, you can use Orks Tactics.

KRUMP 'EM!

Orks Tactic

Use this Tactic when you choose a model in your kill team to fight in the Fight phase. Increase the Strength characteristic of that model by 1 until the end of the phase.

1 COMMAND POINT

GNASHER SQUIG

Orks Tactic

Use this Tactic at the start of the Fight phase. Pick an enemy model that is within 1" of any of your models and roll a D6. On a 4+, that enemy model suffers 1 mortal wound.

2 COMMAND POINTS

DAKKA DAKKA DAKKA

Orks Tactic

Use this Tactic after a model from your kill team shoots in the Shooting phase. You can immediately shoot an additional time with that model.

1 COMMAND POINT

JUST A FLESH WOUND

Orks Tactic

Use this Tactic when a model from your kill team is taken out of action. Roll a D6. On a 4+ that model suffers a flesh wound instead.

2 COMMAND POINTS

GROT SHIELD

Orks Tactic

Use this Tactic at the start of the Shooting phase. Pick a model from your kill team that is within 2" of a **GRETCHIN** model. Until the end of the phase, while that Gretchin model is on the battlefield, any attacks which target the chosen model are resolved against that Gretchin model instead.

2 COMMAND POINTS

MEK'S SPECIAL STIKKBOMB

Orks Tactic

Use this Tactic when you choose a model from your kill team to attack with a stikkbomb. Until the end of the phase, change the weapon's type to Grenade D3 and add 1 to its Strength and Damage characteristics.

2 COMMAND POINTS

'Right ladz, listen up. Da humies 'ave got a big shiny box an' it's powerin' all their gubbinz. Da plan is, we'ze goin' to kick da door in, give 'em all sum dakka, chuck rokkits about 'til da box blows up like Mugrot's buggy in dat minefield, and bosh, job's a good 'un! Any questions? Nah? Good, didn't fink so... Let's get stuck in den boyz! WAAAGH!'

– Boss Nob Gazrot Gitstompa just minutes before the infamous Meltdown Catastrophe of Generatorum Beta-2

ORK BOY

NAME	M	WS	BS	S	T	W	A	Ld	Sv	Max
Ork Boy	5"	3+	5+	4	4	1	2	6	6+	-
Ork Boy Gunner	5"	3+	5+	4	4	1	2	6	6+	2
Boss Nob	5"	3+	5+	5	4	2	3	7	6+	1

This model is armed with a slugga, choppa and stikkbombs.
Two Ork Boys in your kill team can be Ork Boy Gunners, and one Ork Boy in your kill team can be a Boss Nob.

WARGEAR OPTIONS	• This model may replace its slugga and choppa with a shoota. • An Ork Boy Gunner may replace their slugga and choppa with a big shoota or rokkit launcha. • A Boss Nob may replace their slugga with a kombi-weapon with rokkit launcha or kombi-weapon with skorcha. • A Boss Nob may replace their choppa with a big choppa or a power klaw.
ABILITIES	'Ere We Go: Re-roll failed charge rolls for a model with this ability.
SPECIALISTS	**Leader** (Boss Nob only), **Heavy** (Gunner only), **Combat**, **Demolitions**, **Veteran**
FACTION KEYWORD	ORKS
KEYWORDS	INFANTRY, ORK BOY

GRETCHIN

NAME	M	WS	BS	S	T	W	A	Ld	Sv	Max
Gretchin	5"	5+	4+	2	2	1	1	4	6+	-

This model is armed with a grot blasta.

SPECIALISTS	**Leader**, **Scout**
FACTION KEYWORD	ORKS
KEYWORDS	INFANTRY, GRETCHIN

KOMMANDO

NAME	M	WS	BS	S	T	W	A	Ld	Sv	Max
Kommando	6"	3+	5+	4	4	1	2	6	6+	-
Kommando Boss Nob	6"	3+	5+	5	4	2	3	7	6+	1

This model is armed with a slugga, choppa and stikkbombs. One Kommando in your kill team can be a Kommando Boss Nob.

WARGEAR OPTIONS	• A Kommando Boss Nob may replace their choppa with a power klaw.
ABILITIES	**'Ere We Go:** Re-roll failed charge rolls for a model with this ability. **Sneaky Gits:** When an enemy player makes a hit roll for a shooting attack that targets this model, and this model is obscured, that hit roll suffers an additional -1 modifier.
SPECIALISTS	**Leader** (Kommando Boss Nob only), **Combat, Demolitions, Scout, Veteran**
FACTION KEYWORD	ORKS
KEYWORDS	INFANTRY, KOMMANDO

BURNA BOY

NAME	M	WS	BS	S	T	W	A	Ld	Sv	Max
Burna Boy	5"	3+	5+	4	4	1	2	6	6+	-
Burna Spanner	5"	3+	5+	4	4	1	2	6	6+	3

This model is armed with a burna and stikkbombs.
Up to three Burna Boys in your kill team can be Burna Spanners. Burna Spanners are instead armed with a big shoota and stikkbombs.

WARGEAR OPTIONS	• A Burna Spanner may replace their big shoota with a kustom mega-blasta or rokkit launcha.
ABILITIES	**'Ere We Go:** Re-roll failed charge rolls for a model with this ability.
SPECIALISTS	**Comms** (Burna Spanner only), **Leader, Combat, Demolitions, Veteran, Zealot**
FACTION KEYWORD	ORKS
KEYWORDS	INFANTRY, BURNA BOY

LOOTA

NAME	M	WS	BS	S	T	W	A	Ld	Sv	Max
Loota	5"	3+	5+	4	4	1	2	6	6+	-
Loota Spanner	5"	3+	5+	4	4	1	2	6	6+	3

This model is armed with a deffgun and stikkbombs.
Up to three Lootas in your kill team can be Loota Spanners. Loota Spanners are instead armed with a big shoota and stikkbombs.

WARGEAR OPTIONS	• A Loota Spanner may replace their big shoota with a kustom mega-blasta or rokkit launcha.
ABILITIES	**'Ere We Go:** Re-roll failed charge rolls for a model with this ability.
SPECIALISTS	**Comms** (Loota Spanner only), **Leader, Combat, Demolitions, Heavy, Veteran**
FACTION KEYWORD	ORKS
KEYWORDS	INFANTRY, LOOTA

'Orks. Are there any more dangerous or belligerent enemies in all the wide, dark galaxy? Has Humanity ever encountered an enemy more difficult to eradicate, more senselessly violent and needlessly destructive than the greenskin menace? I highly doubt it...'

- General Grumman van der Vosteen, 884th Brachtovarian Dragoons

RANGED WEAPONS

WEAPON	RANGE	TYPE	S	AP	D	ABILITIES
Big shoota	36"	Assault 3	5	0	1	-
Burna		This weapon can be used as a ranged weapon and a melee weapon. When making shooting attacks or firing Overwatch with this weapon, use the ranged profile; when making close combat attacks, use the melee profile.				
- Ranged	8"	Assault D3	4	0	1	This weapon automatically hits its target.
- Melee	Melee	Melee	User	-2	1	-
Deffgun	48"	Heavy D3	7	-1	2	-
Grot blasta	12"	Pistol 1	3	0	1	-
Kombi-weapon with rokkit launcha		When attacking with this weapon, choose one or both of the profiles below. If you choose both, subtract 1 from all hit rolls made for this weapon.				
- Rokkit launcha	24"	Assault 1	8	-2	3	-
- Shoota	18"	Assault 2	4	0	1	-
Kombi-weapon with skorcha		When attacking with this weapon, choose one or both of the profiles below. If you choose both, subtract 1 from all hit rolls made for this weapon.				
- Shoota	18"	Assault 2	4	0	1	-
- Skorcha	8"	Assault D6	5	-1	1	This weapon automatically hits its target.
Kustom mega-blasta	24"	Assault 1	8	-3	D3	On an unmodified hit roll of 1, the bearer suffers a mortal wound.
Rokkit launcha	24"	Assault 1	8	-2	3	-
Shoota	18"	Assault 2	4	0	1	-
Slugga	12"	Pistol 1	4	0	1	-
Stikkbomb	6"	Grenade D6	3	0	1	-

MELEE WEAPONS

WEAPON	RANGE	TYPE	S	AP	D	ABILITIES
Big choppa	Melee	Melee	+2	-1	2	-
Choppa	Melee	Melee	User	0	1	Each time the bearer fights, it can make 1 additional attack with this weapon.
Power klaw	Melee	Melee	x2	-3	D3	When attacking with this weapon, you must subtract 1 from the hit roll.

KILL TEAM

MODEL	POINTS PER MODEL (Does not include wargear)
Burna Boy	12
- Burna Spanner	10
Gretchin	3
Kommando	8
- Kommando Boss Nob	12
Loota	12
- Loota Spanner	10
Ork Boy	6
- Ork Boy Gunner	7
- Boss Nob	10

RANGED WEAPONS

WEAPON	POINTS PER WEAPON
Big shoota	0
Burna	0
Deffgun	0
Grot blasta	0
Kombi-weapon with rokkit launcha	3
Kombi-weapon with skorcha	4
Kustom mega-blasta	0
Rokkit launcha	3
Shoota	0
Slugga	0
Stikkbomb	0

MELEE WEAPONS

WEAPON	POINTS PER WEAPON
Big choppa	2
Choppa	0
Power klaw	4

'Come on ladz, push 'em back! Dat's right, get some fire in there an' burn 'em up good! They thought they woz gonna ambush us did they, the sneaky gitz? Well now they're gonna see wot a proppa fight looks like!'

- *Krogskull Drakka*

T'AU EMPIRE

The T'au Empire is a rising force in the galaxy. United by the Greater Good, the T'au strive to bring enlightenment to other races, by force if necessary. By rolling the appropriate dice on the tables on the following pages, you can generate names and background for your T'au Empire kill teams.

The T'au are a young and dynamic race who seek to spread word of their unifying philosophy – the *T'au'va*, or the Greater Good – throughout the stars. Guided by the mysterious spiritual leaders known as Ethereals, the T'au sweep aside any who would deny this universal truth with the power of their superior technology. Compared to many species in the galaxy, the T'au race is still in its infancy, yet the pace at which T'au technology advances is truly ferocious. Unified by their belief in the Greater Good, the T'au set aside personal gain and internal strife, instead pouring all of their considerable intellect and manufacturing genius into creating ever more advanced machineries, artificial intelligences and devastating weapons of war.

The T'au Empire's efforts at colonisation are similarly fast-paced and single-minded; each new world encountered by the T'au is swiftly surveyed and assessed for assimilation into the latest T'au Sphere. Any indigenous, sentient beings are offered a simple choice – join the glory of the Greater Good, contribute to spreading its light across the stars, or be evicted through swift and targeted military action. It is this uncompromising stance that has brought the T'au into conflict with many of the galaxy's older races, but to their credit they continue to push their empire's borders ever outwards.

As befitting the T'au Empire's highly organised and adaptable forces, T'au kill teams tend to be perfectly specialised and equipped for their task. The soldiers

of the Fire caste – the military arm of the empire – are well used to forming teams comprised of a mix of troop types in order to maximise combat efficiency. It is common for the warriors of these kill teams to undergo the bonding ritual known as *ta'lissera* – a pact where each T'au pledges unconditional support to their comrades. This is the highest form of T'au commitment to another, and it symbolises the sacrifice of the individual to become part of a greater whole.

Specialists within a T'au kill team will be combined and utilised at the discretion of the T'au officer given command of the mission – most often a veteran Shas'ui or Shas'vre. In battle, these kill teams operate as a microcosm of the greater T'au war machine. They prioritise swift movement and superior firepower, unbalancing the enemy with cunning counter-attacks, flanking assaults and ambushes. Melee combat is generally regarded as a desperate last resort.

DRONES

The T'au make prolific use of artificial intelligences in every aspect of their society, including dexterous mechanised assistants in operating theatres and laboratories, training units in military academies, and a range of anti-gravitic support drones that aid their warriors upon the field of battle. Combat support drones range from simple gun-bearing modules that add their firepower to that of their assigned squad, to units that can lock and transmit targeting data, surround their assigned squad with a protective force field, interpose themselves like shields between their operators and imminent danger, or even send out thrumming gravitic pulses that drive back charging foes.

D10	BACKGROUND: BOND
1	**Survivors:** This kill team comprises the few remaining survivors of a battle that wiped out an entire cadre.
2	**Stealth Experts:** This kill team excels at ranging behind enemy lines and destroying mission-critical targets.
3	**Prototype Weapons Testers:** This kill team has been assigned the mission of testing bleeding-edge Earth caste munitions in the field.
4	**Edification Team:** This kill team has been despatched by their Ethereal council to ensure that their comrades do not stray from the T'au'va.
5	**Urban Combat Specialists:** This kill team has trained extensively in close-combat tactics and breaching techniques.
6	**Heroes of the Greater Good:** This kill team is renowned across the Empire for its heroic actions, and has been the subject of several propaganda campaigns.
7	**Bodyguard Retinue:** This kill team has been seconded to the retinue of a blessed Ethereal, tasked with protecting its ward unto death.
8	**Elite of the Academies:** This kill team has been hand-picked from the Fire caste academies for their tactical innovation and strategic genius.
9	**Fourth Sphere Veterans:** This kill team was part of the fateful Fourth Sphere Expansion, and their traumatic experiences have left them with a deep distrust of non-T'au species.
10	**Sniper Team:** This kill team is comprised of expert sharpshooters whose pinpoint shots can bring down any foe.

D10	MISSION: SERVICE TO THE GREATER GOOD
1	**Bait the Trap:** Using strike-and-fade attacks, this kill team must draw the enemy into the jaws of a trap.
2	**Mark the Target:** This kill team must range into enemy territory and lay down beacons for an AX39 Sun Shark bombing mission.
3	**Destroy the Enemy Supplies:** An enemy cannot fight on will alone – this kill team must rob the opposing army of vital supplies and ammunition.
4	**Assassination:** The enemy commander inspires great devotion. Their death will send the opposition into disarray.
5	**Ambush:** This kill team seeks to launch an ambush that will cut the heart from the enemy force.
6	**Extract the Target:** An important T'au official is trapped behind enemy lines. They must be recovered and extracted at any cost.
7	**Weapons Test:** The Earth caste science divisions require live holo-footage and statistical analysis of their weapons in action.
8	**Seize Vital Intel:** T'au High Command requires intelligence regarding the enemy's strategic disposition and intentions – this kill team must raid the opposition's command post and acquire this data.
9	**Forward Reconnaissance:** The Kauyon requires patience and foresight. This kill team seeks to push into enemy territory and observe their movement.
10	**Defend Strategic Asset:** The enemy is launching probing assaults against vital T'au holdings. This kill team must engage and repel the attackers, and hold the objective at all costs.

D10	SQUAD QUIRK: PHILOSOPHY
1	**Honourable Warriors:** This kill team strictly adheres to the Code of Fire, and always treats defeated opponents with respect and honour.
2	**Vengeful:** This kill team has suffered a great loss at the hands of a particular alien race, and wishes to revisit their suffering in kind.
3	**Unyielding:** True adherents of the T'au'va, this kill team will stand and die rather than giving a single inch to their foes.
4	**Students of Kauyon:** Careful and cunning, the warriors of this kill team embody the way of the Patient Hunter.
5	**Students of Mont'ka:** This kill team is filled with aggressive, hot-blooded warriors who excel at the killing strike of the Mont'ka.
6	**Canny Tacticians:** This kill team excels at luring the enemy into ill-advised actions, launching strike-and-fade attacks to draw their quarry into deadly ambushes.
7	**No Heroes:** This kill team gladly carries out the most unpleasant and distasteful missions, knowing that they do so in the name of the Greater Good.
8	**Tech-minded:** The warriors of this kill team are constantly re-calibrating and adjusting their weaponry and equipment in order to improve combat performance.
9	**Ghosts:** The warriors of this kill team never speak in battle, instead utilising a complex system of visual signifiers, comm clicks and hand gestures that they have developed over many years of fighting together.
10	**No One Left Behind:** The ta'lissera bond within this kill team is so strong that its warriors would never abandon a comrade in peril, even at the cost of their own lives.

SPECIALISTS' DEMEANOURS

1	**Scholar of Puretide:** This warrior has memorised the teachings and aphorisms of the legendary Commander Puretide, and recites favoured passages to his comrades in the heat of battle.
2	**Pragmatic:** This warrior understands that sometimes difficult choices and unpalatable actions must be made in service of the Greater Good.
3	**Precise:** This warrior never utilises more force than is necessary to achieve the desired objective.
4	**Hot-Blooded:** This warrior is prone to bold – perhaps even rash – action.
5	**Wise Veteran:** This warrior is an experienced and well-respected veteran of the Fire caste who acts as a steadying hand to his younger comrades.
6	**Unflappable:** Even under the most intense pressure, this warrior maintains a cool head and a steady aim.
7	**Perceptive:** This sharp-eyed warrior is constantly on the lookout for incoming threats, and is almost impossible to catch off-guard.
8	**Dishonoured:** This warrior was once a highly regarded officer, but after committing an unknown act of subversion they were subjected to the punishment ritual of Malk'la and returned to the ranks. They fight fiercely to erase the stain of this dishonour.
9	**Farsight Sympathiser:** The legendary Commander Farsight has been named traitor by the Ethereals, but there are still those within the Fire caste who venerate his legacy.
10	**Monat:** Quiet and withdrawn, this warrior practises the philosophy of the Monat – embracing the path of the lone hunter rather than fighting as one with his bonded kin.

D66 **T'AU INDIVIDUAL NAME GENERATOR TABLE**

11	Sul'an	41	Ren'as
12	Ho'sen	42	Lor'ma
13	Atsumo	43	Tash'lor
14	N'ea	44	Watana
15	Els'im	45	Nomura
16	K'yen	46	Nishino
21	Or'os	51	D'tano
22	Pashera	52	Xo'yima
23	Rais	53	T'suka
24	Sel'tas	54	Kais
25	Be'tol	55	Shamasa
26	E'yaal	56	Pu'jato
31	Murakan	61	Ju'yem
32	To'jo	62	Ga'mo
33	Kurami	63	Kasashi
34	U'so	64	Lamano
35	Lorresa	65	Mi'daro
36	Paluto	66	Uvash'a

CASTES	RANKS	SEPTS		
The first component of a T'au name. Unless in exceptional circumstances, all T'au in a kill team will be Fire caste.	The second component in a T'au name. Most T'au in a kill team will have their ranks clearly indicated in their title.	The third component in a T'au name. This indicates the sept in which they were born, raised and trained.		
Shas – Fire (soldiers and warriors)	'la – Warrior	T'au	Au'taal	Fi'rios
Fio – Earth (engineers and scientists)	'ui – Veteran	Dal'yth	Tash'var	Mu'gulath Bay
Kor – Air (pilots and starfarers)	'vre – Hero	T'au'n	N'dras	Fe'saan
Por – Water (diplomats and merchants)	'el – Noble (possibly knight)	Fal'shia	Vash'ya	Kor'tal
	'o – Commander	D'yanoi	Ke'lshan	Yo'vai
		Vior'la	T'olku	Sa'cea
		Bork'an	Elsy'eir	Ksi'm'yen

T'AU EMPIRE KILL TEAMS

Some T'au Empire models are armed with markerlights, which work differently to normal weapons – the rules for these can be found below. In addition, if every model in your kill team has the T'AU EMPIRE Faction keyword, you can use T'au Empire Tactics.

Markerlights: If a model fires a markerlight, it cannot fire any other weapons in that phase. When a model is hit by a markerlight, place a counter next to it for the remainder of the phase. The table below describes the benefits models from your kill team receive when shooting at a model that has markerlight counters. All benefits are cumulative.

MARKERLIGHT TABLE

MARKERLIGHTS	BENEFIT
1	You can re-roll hit rolls of 1 for attacks that target this model.
2	Add 1 to hit rolls for attacks that target this model if it is obscured.
3	Models attacking this model do not suffer the penalty for moving and firing Heavy weapons or Advancing and firing Assault weapons.
4 or more	Add 1 to hit rolls for attacks that target this model.

UPLINKED MARKERLIGHT

T'au Empire Tactic

Use this Tactic after an enemy model has been hit by a markerlight fired by a model from your kill team. Place D3+1 markerlight counters next to that model instead of only 1.

2 COMMAND POINTS

BREACH AND CLEAR

T'au Empire Tactic

Use this Tactic in your turn in the Shooting phase, when a FIRE WARRIOR BREACHER from your kill team targets an enemy model that is obscured. Re-roll failed wound rolls made for the FIRE WARRIOR BREACHER against that enemy model until the end of this phase.

1 COMMAND POINT

RECON SWEEP

T'au Empire Tactic

Use this Tactic in the Shooting phase when you pick a PATHFINDER from your kill team to shoot. Instead of shooting, that model can immediately make a normal move as if it were the Movement phase, but instead of moving up to their Move characteristic they move up to 2D6".

1 COMMAND POINT

STIMULANT INJECTOR

T'au Empire Tactic

Use this Tactic when a model from your kill team (other than a DRONE) loses a wound. Roll a D6 for that wound, and each other wound lost by that model for the rest of the phase; on a 5+ that wound is not lost.

1 COMMAND POINT

FIRE WARRIOR

NAME	M	WS	BS	S	T	W	A	Ld	Sv	Max
Shas'la	6"	5+	4+	3	3	1	1	6	4+	-
Shas'ui	6"	5+	4+	3	3	1	2	7	4+	1
DS8 Tactical Support Turret	-	-	4+	3	3	1	0	4	4+	1

A Shas'la or Shas'ui is equipped with a pulse rifle and photon grenades.
One Shas'la in your kill team can be a Shas'ui.

WARGEAR OPTIONS	• A model may replace its pulse rifle with a pulse carbine. • A Shas'la or Shas'ui may take a pulse pistol. • A Shas'ui may instead replace its pulse rifle with a pulse pistol. • A Shas'ui may take a markerlight. • One Shas'la in your kill team may be accompanied by a DS8 Tactical Support Turret. A DS8 Tactical Support Turret is equipped with either a missile pod or smart missile system.
ABILITIES	**For the Greater Good:** When an enemy model declares a charge against a model from your kill team, models from your kill team with this ability within 6" of one of the charging model's targets may fire Overwatch as if they were also targeted. Once a model has done so, they cannot fire Overwatch or Retreat for the rest of the phase. **Bonding Knife Ritual:** You can subtract 1 from Nerve tests for Shas'las or Shas'uis from your kill team within 3" of any friendly models with this ability that are not shaken.	**DS8 Tactical Support Turret:** A Tactical Support Turret is set up within 2" of the model it accompanies when that model is set up on the battlefield. It is treated as a separate model, but cannot move for any reason. If this model is more than 2" from the model it accompanies at any point, it is removed from the battlefield. It does not count as having been taken out of action. Tactical Support Turrets may not be specialists, are not part of a fire team (pg 204) and do not gain experience.
SPECIALISTS	**Leader** (Shas'ui only), **Comms**, **Medic**, **Scout**, **Sniper**, **Veteran**
FACTION KEYWORD	T'au Empire
KEYWORDS	Infantry, Fire Warrior

PATHFINDER

NAME	M	WS	BS	S	T	W	A	Ld	Sv	Max
Pathfinder	7"	5+	4+	3	3	1	1	6	5+	-
Pathfinder Gunner	7"	5+	4+	3	3	1	1	6	5+	3
Pathfinder Shas'ui	7"	5+	4+	3	3	1	2	7	5+	1

This model is armed with a pulse carbine, markerlight and photon grenades.
Up to three Pathfinders in your kill team can be Pathfinder Gunners, and one Pathfinder in your kill team can be a Pathfinder Shas'ui.

WARGEAR OPTIONS	• A Pathfinder Gunner may replace their pulse carbine and markerlight with an ion rifle or rail rifle. • A Pathfinder Shas'ui may take a pulse pistol.
ABILITIES	**For the Greater Good:** When an enemy model declares a charge against a model from your kill team, models from your kill team with this ability within 6" of one of the charging model's targets may fire Overwatch as if they were also targeted. Once a model has done so, they cannot fire Overwatch or Retreat for the rest of the phase.	**Bonding Knife Ritual:** You can subtract 1 from Nerve tests for Pathfinders, Pathfinder Gunners or Pathfinder Shas'uis from your kill team within 3" of any friendly models with this ability that are not shaken.
SPECIALISTS	**Leader** (Pathfinder Shas'ui only), **Sniper** (Gunner only), **Comms**, **Demolitions**, **Medic**, **Scout**, **Veteran**
FACTION KEYWORD	T'au Empire
KEYWORDS	Infantry, Pathfinder

FIRE WARRIOR BREACHER

NAME	M	WS	BS	S	T	W	A	Ld	Sv	Max
Breacher Shas'la	6"	5+	4+	3	3	1	1	6	4+	-
Breacher Shas'ui	6"	5+	4+	3	3	1	2	7	4+	1
DS8 Tactical Support Turret	-	-	4+	3	3	1	0	4	4+	1

A Breacher Shas'la or Breacher Shas'ui is armed with a pulse blaster and photon grenades.
One Breacher Shas'la in your kill team can be a Breacher Shas'ui.

WARGEAR OPTIONS	• A Breacher Shas'la or Breacher Shas'ui may take a pulse pistol. • A Breacher Shas'ui may instead replace its pulse blaster with a pulse pistol. • A Breacher Shas'ui may take a markerlight. • One Breacher Shas'la in your kill team may be accompanied by a DS8 Tactical Support Turret. A DS8 Tactical Support Turret is equipped with either a missile pod or smart missile system.
ABILITIES	**For the Greater Good:** When an enemy model declares a charge against a model from your kill team, models from your kill team with this ability within 6" of one of the charging model's targets may fire Overwatch as if they were also targeted. Once a model has done so, they cannot fire Overwatch or Retreat for the rest of the phase. **Bonding Knife Ritual:** You can subtract 1 from Nerve tests for Breacher Shas'las or Breacher Shas'uis from your kill team within 3" of any friendly models with this ability that are not shaken.	**DS8 Tactical Support Turret:** A Tactical Support Turret is set up within 2" of the model it accompanies when that model is set up on the battlefield. It is treated as a separate model, but cannot move for any reason. If this model is more than 2" from the model it accompanies at any point, it is removed from the battlefield. It does not count as having been taken out of action. Tactical Support Turrets may not be specialists, are not part of a fire team (pg 204) and do not gain experience.
SPECIALISTS	**Leader** (Breacher Shas'ui only), **Comms**, **Demolitions**, **Medic**, **Scout**, **Veteran**
FACTION KEYWORD	T'AU EMPIRE
KEYWORDS	INFANTRY, FIRE WARRIOR BREACHER

XV25 STEALTH BATTLESUIT

NAME	M	WS	BS	S	T	W	A	Ld	Sv	Max
Stealth Shas'ui	8"	5+	4+	4	4	2	2	7	3+	-
Stealth Shas'vre	8"	5+	4+	4	4	2	3	8	3+	1

This model is armed with a burst cannon.
One Stealth Shas'ui in your kill team can be a Stealth Shas'vre.

WARGEAR OPTIONS	• One Stealth Shas'ui or Stealth Shas'vre in your kill team may replace its burst cannon with a fusion blaster. • A Stealth Shas'vre may take a markerlight and target lock.
ABILITIES	**For the Greater Good:** When an enemy model declares a charge against a model from your kill team, models from your kill team with this ability within 6" of one of the charging model's targets may fire Overwatch as if they were also targeted. Once a model has done so, they cannot fire Overwatch or Retreat for the rest of the phase. **Bonding Knife Ritual:** You can subtract 1 from Nerve tests for Stealth Shas'uis or Stealth Shas'vres from your kill team within 3" of any friendly models with this ability that are not shaken.	**Target Lock:** A model with a target lock does not suffer the penalty to their hit rolls for Advancing and firing Assault weapons. **Camouflage Fields:** Your opponent must subtract 1 from all hit rolls for attacks that target this model.
SPECIALISTS	**Leader** (Stealth Shas'vre only), **Comms**, **Heavy**, **Scout**, **Veteran**
FACTION KEYWORD	T'AU EMPIRE
KEYWORDS	BATTLESUIT, INFANTRY, JET PACK, FLY, XV25 STEALTH BATTLESUIT

DRONE

NAME	M	WS	BS	S	T	W	A	Ld	Sv	Max
MV1 Gun Drone	8"	5+	5+	3	4	1	1	6	5+	-
MV4 Shield Drone	8"	5+	5+	3	4	1	1	6	5+	-
MV7 Marker Drone	8"	5+	5+	3	4	1	1	6	5+	-
MV36 Guardian Drone	8"	5+	5+	3	4	1	1	6	5+	1
MV33 Grav-inhibitor Drone	8"	5+	5+	3	4	1	1	6	5+	1
MV31 Pulse Accelerator Drone	8"	5+	5+	3	4	1	1	6	5+	1
MB3 Recon Drone	8"	5+	5+	4	4	2	1	6	5+	1

An MV1 Gun Drone is equipped with two pulse carbines.
- Any MV1 Gun Drone can be an MV4 Shield Drone. An MV4 Shield Drone is equipped with a shield generator instead of two pulse carbines.
- Any MV1 Gun Drone can be an MV7 Marker Drone. An MV7 Marker Drone is equipped with a markerlight instead of two pulse carbines.
- If your kill team includes any **Fire Warrior Breachers** or **Fire Warriors**, one MV1 Gun Drone in your kill team can be an MV36 Guardian Drone. An MV36 Guardian Drone has no equipment.
- If your kill team includes any **Pathfinders**, one MV1 Gun Drone in your kill team can be an MV33 Grav-inhibitor Drone, one MV1 Gun Drone in your kill team can be an MV31 Pulse Accelerator Drone and one MV1 Gun Drone in your kill team can be an MB3 Recon Drone. An MV33 Grav-inhibitor Drone has no equipment. An MV31 Pulse Accelerator Drone has no equipment. An MB3 Recon Drone is equipped with a burst cannon instead of two pulse carbines.

ABILITIES	
	Support Subroutines: Drones cannot be specialists, are not part of a fire team and cannot gain experience. **For the Greater Good:** When an enemy model declares a charge against a model from your kill team, models from your kill team with this ability within 6" of one of the charging model's targets may fire Overwatch as if they were also targeted. Once a model has done so, they cannot fire Overwatch or Retreat for the rest of the phase. **Saviour Protocols:** If a **Drone** is within 3" of a friendly **T'au Empire Infantry** model when an enemy attack successfully wounds it, you can inflict a mortal wound on the Drone, and the target model does not suffer any damage from this attack. **Guardian Fields (Guardian Drone only):** A Guardian Drone has a 5+ invulnerable save. Friendly **T'au Empire** models within 6" of this model have a 6+ invulnerable save.	**Gravity Wave Projector (MV33 Grav-inhibitor Drone):** Enemy models beginning a charge move within 12" of any Grav-inhibitor Drones reduce their charge distance by D3". **Pulse Accelerator (MV31 Pulse Accelerator Drone only):** Whilst a **T'au Empire Infantry** model is within 3" of a friendly Pulse Accelerator Drone, increase the Range characteristic of that model's pulse pistol, pulse carbine or pulse rifle by 6". **Recon Suite (MB3 Recon Drone only):** At the start of the Shooting phase, you can choose a **Pathfinder** from your kill team within 6" of a friendly Recon Drone. Until the end of the phase, that model does not suffer penalties to their hit and Injury rolls due to their target being obscured. **Shield Generator:** A model with a shield generator has a 4+ invulnerable save.
FACTION KEYWORD	T'au Empire
KEYWORDS	Fly, Drone

MV1 Gun Drone

MV4 Shield Drone

MV7 Marker Drone

MV36 Guardian Drone

MV33 Grav-inhibitor Drone

MV31 Pulse Accelerator Drone

MB3 Recon Drone

RANGED WEAPONS

WEAPON	RANGE	TYPE	S	AP	D	ABILITIES
Burst cannon	18"	Assault 4	5	0	1	-
Fusion blaster	18"	Assault 1	8	-4	D6	If the target is within half range of this weapon, roll two dice when inflicting damage with it and discard the lowest result.
Ion rifle		When attacking with this weapon, choose one of the profiles below.				
- Standard	30"	Rapid Fire 1	7	-1	1	-
- Overcharge	30"	Heavy D3	8	-1	2	If you make one or more unmodified hit rolls of 1, the bearer suffers a mortal wound after all of this weapon's shots have been resolved.
Markerlight	36"	Heavy 1	-	-	-	Markerlights (pg 169)
Missile pod	36"	Assault 2	7	-1	D3	-
Photon grenade	12"	Grenade D6	-	-	-	This weapon does not inflict any damage. Your opponent must subtract 1 from hit rolls made for INFANTRY models that have suffered any hits from photon grenades until the end of the battle round.
Pulse blaster		When attacking with this weapon, choose one of the profiles below.				
- Close range	5"	Assault 2	6	-2	1	-
- Medium range	10"	Assault 2	5	-1	1	-
- Long range	15"	Assault 2	4	0	1	-
Pulse carbine	18"	Assault 2	5	0	1	-
Pulse pistol	12"	Pistol 1	5	0	1	-
Pulse rifle	30"	Rapid Fire 1	5	0	1	-
Rail rifle	30"	Rapid Fire 1	6	-4	D3	For each wound roll of 6+ made for this weapon, the target model suffers a mortal wound in addition to the normal damage.
Smart missile system	30"	Heavy 4	5	0	1	This weapon can be fired at models that are not visible to the bearer. If the target is not visible to the bearer, a 6 is required for a successful hit roll, irrespective of the firing model's Ballistic Skill or any modifiers.

KILL TEAM

MODEL	POINTS PER MODEL (Does not include wargear)
Shas'la	8
- Shas'ui	8
- DS8 Tactical Support Turret	0
Breacher Shas'la	8
- Breacher Shas'ui	8
- DS8 Tactical Support Turret	0
Pathfinder	6
- Pathfinder Gunner	7
- Pathfinder Shas'ui	7
Stealth Shas'ui	20
- Stealth Shas'vre	20

RANGED WEAPONS

WEAPON	POINTS PER WEAPON
Burst cannon	0
Fusion blaster	4
Ion rifle	3
Markerlight	0
Missile pod	7
Photon grenade	0
Pulse blaster	0
Pulse carbine	0
Pulse pistol	0
Pulse rifle	0
Rail rifle	5
Smart missile system	5

KILL TEAM DRONES

MODEL	POINTS PER MODEL (Includes wargear)
MV1 Gun Drone	7
- MV4 Shield Drone	7
- MV7 Marker Drone	7
- MV36 Guardian Drone	7
- MV33 Grav-inhibitor Drone	7
- MV31 Pulse Accelerator Drone	7
- MB3 Recon Drone	7

OTHER WARGEAR

WARGEAR	POINTS PER ITEM
Target lock	1

TYRANIDS

Driven by an all-consuming imperative to feed, the Tyranids devour entire worlds, leaving them as little more than barren rocks devoid of all life. By rolling the appropriate dice on the tables on the following pages, you can generate names and background for your Tyranids kill teams.

The Tyranids are an utterly alien race that is inimical to all other forms of life. Sailing the void in vast living craft known as hive ships, billions of Tyranid bioforms wait in suspended animation to be woken once more as a new prey world heaves into view. Guided by the godlike meta-sentience known as the Hive Mind, countless splinter fleets of hive ships push into the galaxy from every direction, tendrils questing through the outer dark until they find a living, breathing world to wrap themselves around so that it may be fed upon.

When a Tyranid fleet locates a new world or system to attack, the immense swarms of weaponised lifeforms aboard each craft awaken. Hurled down upon the prey world in spore-like drop craft, the Tyranids attack in wave after wave, successively larger and more terrifying monstrosities falling upon the enemy's defences until at last every living defender has been dragged down and devoured. Yet they do not stop there – the Tyranids break down and ingest every shred of organic matter on the planet. Their digestion pools roil and spit as the planet's biomass is broken down in their churning depths before being sucked up by the jostling hive ships. Even the oceans and the atmosphere itself are consumed, until nothing remains but an arid, lifeless rock left drifting in the Tyranids' wake.

Tyranid kill teams are made up of a variety of horrific bioforms, from swarming packs of savage Gaunts to towering Tyranid Warriors and other, more specialised creatures. Each organism is adapted for the sole purpose of slaughtering other living beings so that their biomass

may be absorbed and re-purposed by the Tyranid hive fleets. In place of artificial armour, Tyranids are clad in organic chitinous plates and possess massive blade-like claws, row upon row of armour-puncturing fangs, and projectile weapons wrought of living tissue. Together, the Tyranids within a kill team function like a single predatory beast, stalking their prey across desolate ruinscapes and through darkened underhives before moving in for the kill.

Tyranid kill teams are despatched to prepare a prey world for full-scale invasion. Small groups of Tyranid warrior-organisms are vomited forth by their orbiting hive ship to infiltrate the planet's cities and fortresses, undermine its defences and sow terror throughout its populace. The Tyranids within such kill teams carry out their imperative without question, adapting their tactics with disturbing rapidity to wreak ever more carnage until their hive fleet arrives.

THE SHADOW IN THE WARP

As a Tyranid hive fleet approaches a prey world, it casts a pall of psychic disturbance ahead of it that has become known as the Shadow in the Warp. This effect has been described as akin to the chittering of numberless insects, or the unshakeable feeling of being watched by a monstrously hungry entity. Not only does it smother the psychic abilities of those beings caught within its sphere of influence, it also gnaws at their sanity until they are driven mad or killed outright. So do the hive fleets isolate worlds, choking off their psychic distress cries before they can even begin to ring out across the void…

D10	BACKGROUND: BROOD CLASSIFICATION
1	**Stealth Brood:** This kill team comprises beasts that are highly adapted to slinking unseen through the enemy lines.
2	**Devourer Brood:** These Tyranids excel in rapidly breaking down and devouring the biomass of their enemies.
3	**Swiftkiller Brood:** This kill team is made up of fast, hard-hitting warrior-organisms.
4	**Highcrawler Brood:** This kill team comprises agile, lightweight beasts that stay high and strike from rooftops and gantries.
5	**Bombardment Brood:** These warrior-organisms are specialised for ranged combat, picking their enemies off in ferocious firefights.
6	**Kill-swarm:** This kill team uses numbers to its advantage, flooding the combat zone with expendable organisms.
7	**Living Barricade:** These war beasts are thickly armoured in chitin and bone, able to soak up tremendous punishment as they overwhelm their foes.
8	**Alpha Pack:** This kill team comprises elite organisms, their numbers small but their combat abilities fearsome.
9	**Ambush Brood:** These lethal hunter-killer organisms excel at laying for long periods of time in wait for their prey before bursting forth to slaughter them.
10	**Kingslayer Brood:** This kill team comprises a mix of bioforms designed to work together to eliminate any target no matter how well defended. Some have been spawned to track their prey, some to make the kill, and others to devour its remains.

D10	MISSION: BROOD IMPERATIVE
1	**Devour:** These warrior-organisms must rip the enemy apart at close quarters and consume as much biomass as they can.
2	**Infiltrate:** This kill team seeks to bypass the prey's defences, laying a pheromone trail for subsequent attack waves to follow.
3	**Cull:** The prey's leaders and specialists must be exterminated to facilitate a swift victory for the Hive Mind.
4	**Swarm:** If the prey are able to press their attack in this region, the Hive Mind's efforts will suffer. Their advance must be slowed with ichor and chitin, the mouths of their guns choked with corpses.
5	**Terrify:** The prey are strong here. The kill team must spread panic and confusion to weaken their defences.
6	**Rampage:** The task of this kill team is simple: to cause as much indiscriminate destruction and bloodshed as they can, for as long as they can.
7	**Stalk:** This kill team must hunt the prey carefully, preserving their own biomass while striking only where they are guaranteed to whittle down that of the foe.
8	**Spread:** The hides of these warrior-organisms have been altered to spew Tyranid spores that corrode machinery and inorganic structures. They must spread the entropic touch of these spores as far as they can.
9	**Protect:** The prey are drawing perilously close to a crucial synaptic node. They must be driven back at all costs.
10	**Shroud:** The Shadow in the Warp must be extended by devouring the prey's protective psykers.

D10	SQUAD QUIRK: BROOD STRAIN
1	**Ravenous:** This brood seeks to devour biomass at all costs, and their hunger is never sated.
2	**Cautious:** This brood probes carefully, and will swiftly pull back to try another route of attack if danger threatens.
3	**Slinking:** The beasts of this brood scurry through sewer pipes and crawl through ducts to attack from unexpected quarters.
4	**Bladed Shoal:** These warrior-organisms flock together in perfect synchronicity, moving as one across the battlefield.
5	**Inescapable Hunters:** These beasts stalk their prey relentlessly and will pursue them without rest or mercy.
6	**Shrieker Brood:** These warrior-organisms are adapted to utter horrifying predatory shrieks as they storm into battle.
7	**Sizzling Gore:** These creatures have concentrated bio-acid running through their bodies that bursts out to spray those who wound them.
8	**Heightened Senses:** These beasts have specially honed sensory biomorphs that allow them to react with near-prescient speed to the actions of their prey.
9	**Shorn of Synapse:** This brood has gone beyond the reach of the Hive Mind, and now acts on predatory instinct alone.
10	**Catalysed:** When these bioforms attack, they do so in a violent frenzy that sees them hurl themselves at the enemy with suicidal ferocity.

D10	SPECIALISTS' BIO-ADAPTATIONS
1	**Hive Node:** This beast amplifies the control of the Hive Mind over nearby warrior-organisms.
2	**Sentient Ammunition:** The bio-shot from this creature's weapons is able to actively seek out its targets.
3	**Entangling Tendrils:** Clumps of revolting frond-like pseudopods sprout from this beast's hide, entangling enemies with their clammy touch.
4	**Synaptophage:** This beast can devour the brain matter of its foes to glean some instinctive understanding of their plans and secrets.
5	**Guardian Beast:** This Tyranid's behaviour leads it to viciously pursue those who threaten its broodkin.
6	**Survival Instincts:** This beast possesses something akin to a sixth sense for danger, leaving the prey panicking as their cunning ambushes and booby traps catch nothing but air.
7	**Bloodhunger:** With every victim this beast devours, its metabolism accelerates and its ferocity increases.
8	**Unsettling Presence:** This beast emits a disturbing echo of the Shadow in the Warp, leaving nearby enemies uncomfortable and on edge.
9	**Lurker:** Where possible, this beast sticks to the shadows, slinking towards the enemy through the densest cover it can find.
10	**Mimic:** Through convulsions of bio-resonators in its thoracic cavity, this beast can mimic words and sounds uttered by its prey, luring them into traps or horrifying them.

BROOD NAME GENERATOR TABLE

D66	FIRST TITLE	SECOND TITLE
11	The Omega	Infestation
12	The Creeping	Talon
13	The Crimson	Fang
14	The Kraken's	Claw
15	The Leviathan's	Tendril
16	The Behemoth's	Coil
21	Jormungandr's	Eye
22	The Serpent's	Brood
23	The Hydra's	Shadow
24	The Rising	Dread
25	The Devouring	Swarm
26	The Looming	Barb
31	The Gorgon's	Jaws
32	The Ravening	Assassins
33	The Kolorian	Slayers
34	The Icharian	Executioners
35	The Writhing	Ghosts
36	The Inescapable	Echo
41	The Dark	Terrors
42	Kronos'	Horrors
43	The Nightmare	Lurkers
44	Tiamet's	Heralds
45	The Ominous	Sting
46	Ouroboris'	Bite
51	The Ancient	Doom
52	The Slithering	Butchers
53	The Bladed	Devils
54	The Monstrous	Wraiths
55	The Elder	Menace
56	The Nameless	Shroud
61	The Hunter's	Annihilators
62	The Formless	Scream
63	The Sudden	Pall
64	The Void	Devourers
65	The Lurking	Stalkers
66	The Hungry	Maw

TYRANID KILL TEAMS

If every model in your kill team has the TYRANIDS Faction keyword, you can use Tyranids Tactics.

CAUSTIC BLOOD

Tyranids Tactic

Use this Tactic when a model from your kill team loses a wound in the Fight phase. Roll a D6 for each enemy model within 1" of that model. On a 6 that enemy model suffers 1 mortal wound after all of its attacks have been resolved.

1 COMMAND POINT

SCORCH BUGS

Tyranids Tactic

Use this Tactic when a Termagant with a fleshborer from your kill team is chosen to shoot in the Shooting phase. Add 1 to wound rolls for that model until the end of the phase.

1 COMMAND POINT

LURK

Tyranids Tactic

Use this Tactic in the Movement phase. Pick a model from your kill team that has not yet moved. That model may not move this phase, but for the rest of the battle round, if this model is obscured, shooting attacks that target this model suffer an additional -1 modifier to their hit rolls.

1 COMMAND POINT

FEEDER TENDRILS

Tyranids Tactic

Use this Tactic when a GENESTEALER or LICTOR from your kill team takes an enemy Leader out of action in the Fight phase. Gain D3 Command Points.

1 COMMAND POINT

METABOLIC OVERDRIVE

Tyranids Tactic

Use this Tactic in the Movement phase, after moving a model from your kill team. You can make a second move with that model, but if you do, the model cannot shoot this battle round. In addition, roll a D6; on a 1 the model suffers 1 mortal wound.

2 COMMAND POINTS

HUNTING ROAR

Tyranids Tactic

Use this Tactic when a TYRANID WARRIOR from your kill team finishes a charge move within 1" of any enemy models. You can re-roll failed hit rolls for models from your kill team within 6" of that Tyranid Warrior in the Fight phase in this battle round.

2 COMMAND POINTS

'They came from the darkness, moving faster than the eye could follow. Monsters, with jagged fangs and slashing talons and yellow eyes. We fought as best we could, Emperor knows we did. It wasn't enough. Not nearly enough. Only Jenks and I made it out, and if it takes me the rest of my days I swear we will have vengeance...'

- Veteran Sergeant Rachelyn Culcher, 45th Nachtmor Chargers

TERMAGANT

NAME	M	WS	BS	S	T	W	A	Ld	Sv	Max
Termagant	6"	4+	4+	3	3	1	1	5	6+	–

This model is armed with a fleshborer.

WARGEAR OPTIONS	• This model may replace its fleshborer with a devourer or spinefists. • This model may take toxin sacs and/or adrenal glands.
ABILITIES	**Instinctive Behaviour:** Unless this model is within 24" of a friendly SYNAPSE model, you must subtract 1 from any hit rolls made for it when shooting any target other than the nearest visible enemy model, and subtract 2 from charge rolls made for it if it declares a charge against any model other than the nearest enemy model. **Adrenal Glands:** If a model has adrenal glands, add 1" to the distance it can move when it Advances or charges. **Toxin Sacs:** Any wound rolls of 6+ in the Fight phase for a model with toxin sacs cause 1 additional damage.
SPECIALISTS	Scout, Veteran
FACTION KEYWORD	TYRANIDS
KEYWORDS	INFANTRY, TERMAGANT

HORMAGAUNT

NAME	M	WS	BS	S	T	W	A	Ld	Sv	Max
Hormagaunt	8"	4+	4+	3	3	1	2	5	6+	–

This model is armed with a pair of scything talons.

WARGEAR OPTIONS	• This model may take toxin sacs and/or adrenal glands.
ABILITIES	**Instinctive Behaviour:** Unless this model is within 24" of a friendly SYNAPSE model, you must subtract 1 from any hit rolls made for it when shooting any target other than the nearest visible enemy model, and subtract 2 from charge rolls made for it if it declares a charge against any model other than the nearest enemy model. **Bounding Leap:** Whenever this model piles in or consolidates, it can move up to 6". **Adrenal Glands:** If a model has adrenal glands, add 1" to the distance it can move when it Advances or charges. **Toxin Sacs:** Any wound rolls of 6+ in the Fight phase for a model with toxin sacs cause 1 additional damage.
SPECIALISTS	Combat, Scout, Veteran
FACTION KEYWORD	TYRANIDS
KEYWORDS	INFANTRY, HORMAGAUNT

LICTOR

NAME	M	WS	BS	S	T	W	A	Ld	Sv	Max
Lictor	9"	2+	4+	6	4	4	3	9	5+	–

This model is armed with flesh hooks, grasping talons and rending claws.

ABILITIES	**Chameleonic Skin:** When an enemy player makes a hit roll for a shooting attack that targets this model, and this model is obscured, that hit roll suffers an additional -1 modifier.
SPECIALISTS	Leader, Combat, Comms, Scout, Veteran
FACTION KEYWORD	TYRANIDS
KEYWORDS	INFANTRY, LICTOR

TYRANID WARRIOR

NAME	M	WS	BS	S	T	W	A	Ld	Sv	Max
Tyranid Warrior	6"	3+	4+	4	4	3	3	9	4+	–
Tyranid Warrior Gunner	6"	3+	4+	4	4	3	3	9	4+	1

This model is armed with a pair of scything talons and a devourer.
One Tyranid Warrior in your kill team can be a Tyranid Warrior Gunner.

WARGEAR OPTIONS	• This model may replace its scything talons with rending claws, boneswords or a lash whip and bonesword. • This model may replace its devourer with a deathspitter, spinefists, rending claws, boneswords, a pair of scything talons or a lash whip and bonesword. • A Tyranid Warrior Gunner may instead replace its devourer with a barbed strangler or venom cannon. • This model may take flesh hooks. • This model may take toxin sacs and/or adrenal glands.
ABILITIES	**Synapse:** TYRANIDS models automatically pass Nerve tests while within 12" of any friendly models with this ability. **Shadow in the Warp:** Subtract 1 from any psychic tests made for enemy PSYKERS within 18" of a model with this ability. TYRANIDS PSYKERS are not affected.	**Adrenal Glands:** If a model has adrenal glands, add 1" to the distance it can move when it Advances or charges. **Toxin Sacs:** Any wound rolls of 6+ in the Fight phase for a model with toxin sacs cause 1 additional damage.
SPECIALISTS	Heavy (Gunner only), **Leader**, **Combat**, **Comms**, **Veteran**
FACTION KEYWORD	TYRANIDS
KEYWORDS	INFANTRY, SYNAPSE, TYRANID WARRIOR

GENESTEALER

NAME	M	WS	BS	S	T	W	A	Ld	Sv	Max
Genestealer	8"	3+	4+	4	4	1	3	9	5+	–

This model is armed with rending claws.

WARGEAR OPTIONS	• This model may take a pair of scything talons. • This model may take toxin sacs and/or an extended carapace. • One Genestealer in your kill team may take an acid maw. • One other Genestealer in your kill team may take flesh hooks.
ABILITIES	**Extended Carapace:** A model with an extended carapace has a Save characteristic of 4+ but loses the Swift and Deadly ability. **Lightning Reflexes:** This model has a 5+ invulnerable save.	**Swift and Deadly:** You can re-roll failed charge rolls for this model. **Toxin Sacs:** Any wound rolls of 6+ in the Fight phase for a model with toxin sacs cause 1 additional damage.
SPECIALISTS	**Leader**, **Combat**, **Scout**, **Veteran**
FACTION KEYWORD	TYRANIDS
KEYWORDS	INFANTRY, GENESTEALER

'Lord Governor, allow me to impress upon you the horrific nature of the creatures that I have hunted to your world. There is no defence you can raise that they will not penetrate, no guard you can post that they will not slay. I am your only hope, Governor, for they are already here.'

- Inquisitor Lysette Astromar

RANGED WEAPONS

WEAPON	RANGE	TYPE	S	AP	D	ABILITIES
Barbed strangler	36"	Assault D6	5	-1	1	-
Deathspitter	24"	Assault 3	5	-1	1	-
Devourer	18"	Assault 3	4	0	1	-
Flesh hooks	6"	Assault 2	User	0	1	This weapon can be fired within 1" of an enemy model, and can target enemy models within 1" of friendly models.
Fleshborer	12"	Assault 1	4	0	1	-
Spinefists	12"	Pistol *	3	0	1	When a model fires this weapon, it makes a number of shots equal to its Attacks characteristic.
Venom cannon	36"	Assault D3	8	-2	D3	-

MELEE WEAPONS

WEAPON	RANGE	TYPE	S	AP	D	ABILITIES
Acid maw	Melee	Melee	User	-3	1	-
Boneswords	Melee	Melee	User	-2	1	A model armed with boneswords can make 1 additional attack with them in the Fight phase.
Grasping talons	Melee	Melee	User	-1	2	-
Lash whip and bonesword	Melee	Melee	User	-2	1	If the bearer is taken out of action in the Fight phase before it has made its attacks in that phase, it may immediately fight before being removed from the battlefield.
Rending claws	Melee	Melee	User	-1	1	Each time you make a wound roll of 6+ for this weapon, that hit is resolved with an AP of -4.
Scything talons	Melee	Melee	User	0	1	You can re-roll hit rolls of 1 for this weapon. If the bearer has more than one pair of scything talons, it can make 1 additional attack with this weapon each time it fights.

KILL TEAM

MODEL	POINTS PER MODEL (Does not include wargear)
Genestealer	11
Hormagaunt	4
Lictor	25
Termagant	4
Tyranid Warrior	20
- Tyranid Warrior Gunner	20

RANGED WEAPONS

WEAPON	POINTS PER WEAPON
Barbed strangler	3
Deathspitter	2
Devourer (Termagant)	3
Devourer (Tyranid Warrior)	0
Flesh hooks	0
Fleshborer	0
Spinefists	0
Venom cannon	4

MELEE WEAPONS

WEAPON	POINTS PER WEAPON
Acid maw	0
Boneswords	0
Grasping talons	0
Lash whip and bonesword	1
Rending claws	0
Scything talons	0

OTHER WARGEAR

WARGEAR	POINTS PER ITEM
Adrenal glands	1
Extended carapace	0
Toxin sacs	1

'This brood, that the planetary militia have named the *Writhing Shadow*, they are without a doubt the most ferociously lethal example of their kind I have ever witnessed. Ready yourselves for the fight of your lives...'

- *Inquisitor Lysette Astromar, Ordo Xenos*

GENESTEALER CULTS

From dark depths and shadowy streets emerge the Genestealer Cultists, sinister figures united by a worship of inscrutable star-borne entities. By rolling the appropriate dice on the tables on the following pages, you can generate names and background for your Genestealer Cults kill teams.

Genestealer Cults arise from the heaving masses of Humanity that make up the Imperium. Sprawling clandestine networks of desperate and downtrodden individuals, each cult is bound by a fanatical belief that they will be delivered from oppression by star-borne saviours, a destiny towards which they are guided by the insidious whispers of their monstrous Patriarch.

In truth, the Genestealer Cultists have been lied to in the cruellest and most invasive way imaginable. Their beloved Patriarch is, in fact, a Genestealer, a Tyranid vanguard organism that uses its parasitic Genestealer's Kiss to inject genetic material into unwitting human hosts. These victims, brought into the Genestealer's thrall by its foul touch, pass on that material to successive generations of Acolytes and Neophytes until the cult has proliferated through the underclasses of whatever world is unfortunate enough to harbour it.

Over time, a well-established Genestealer Cult will extend tendrils into the upper reaches of a world's Ecclesiarchy, military and government, working always towards the day when the great uprising can begin and the star gods be welcomed with open arms. When that moment comes, the warriors of the cult fight with fanatical zeal and absolute devotion, compelled by the xenos seed permeating their physiology and indoctrinated into the belief that – when the star gods arrive to validate their selfless quest – all those found worthy will be taken up into paradise, there to enjoy a blessed transcendence. In a terrible way, when the ravenous hive fleets appear in the skies above the cult's world, this belief holds an aspect of truth…

Genestealer Cults kill teams initiate their brutal insurrections armed with the tools supplied by their oppressors, the industrial gear with which they have been forced to toil for generations. Drills, saws, cutting lasers and demolition charges, along with basic firearms that are stolen or cobbled together, are put to violent use against their enemies. Those members of a kill team blessed with more advanced mutations fight with diamond-hard claws and fangs, gutting with savage frenzy those who oppose their cult's uprising.

Wherever a Genestealer Cult exists, kill teams composed of disparate insurrectionists group together to sabotage and slaughter their foes. Such kill teams often emerge from deep within the fabric of planet's society, or they may arrive on a world via freighters and transports, having infiltrated work crews, pilgrimages or colonising expeditions. These kill teams fight with unflinching faith in their eventual deliverance, and will turn their fury upon any foreign invaders who come to take their world from them before their saviours arrive.

LORDS OF THE CULT

As a Genestealer Cult grows, mutant strains appear from amongst its later generations. Some are Aberrants, genetic mishaps useful only as shock troops and line-breakers. Yet there are others whose purpose is far closer to the divine. The Primus, for example, serves as the cult's war leader, a charismatic general with an instinctive knowledge of battlefield tactics. The Magus, meanwhile, acts as the Patriarch's vizier, extending their potent psychic influence to twist the minds of loyal officials and force the cult's enemies to surrender their wills to that of the Patriarch.

D10	BACKGROUND: CELL
1	**Scavenger Cell:** The members of this kill team are looters, stripping priceless ammunition, weapons and supplies for the cult from the bodies of the dead.
2	**The Prophet's Claw:** This kill team is the hand-picked retinue of a Genestealer Magus.
3	**Tunnel Skulkers:** These cultists are close-combat specialists who use demolition charges and mining tools to clear subterranean zones.
4	**Killers in the Fold:** This kill team consists of gene-bonded kin who have long maintained their cover in the midst of the unanointed, and now rise up to turn on their comrades.
5	**Eyes of the Patriarch:** These warriors are forward recon specialists who act as scouts for the cult.
6	**Iconoclast Cell:** This kill team are spreaders of the True Faith, who aim to destroy or deface their enemy's religious iconography in order to better honour the star gods.
7	**Snatcher Cell:** This hand-picked squad is tasked with abducting high-profile enemy leaders so that they may be granted the Genestealer's Kiss.
8	**Shadowstalker Gene-kin:** This kill team is made up of ambush experts who stalk the shadows.
9	**Snare Setters:** These cultists are combat engineers who lay improvised booby traps, mines and razor-wire snares across contested ground.
10	**Veterans of the First Cycle:** These warriors are amongst the few survivors from the cult's first cycle of hybrids – hardened killers who have honed their survival skills over generations.

D10	MISSION: SACRED TASK
1	**Open Their Eyes:** This kill team must drag the unanointed before the court of the Patriarch, so that they may witness the true glory of the star saviours.
2	**Feed the Progeny:** The cult requires fresh meat for its Aberrant gene-kin…
3	**Raid Supply Lines:** With every shipment this kill team steals, the cult grows stronger and their enemies weaker.
4	**Prepare the Killing Field:** These warriors are charged with laying traps and minefields in preparation for the great uprising.
5	**Sabotage Vital Machinery:** This kill team must ensure that critical power, fuel and purification plants are rendered unusable.
6	**Undertunnel Ambush:** As the enemy blunders into cult territory unaware, this kill team prepare to take advantage of their foolishness.
7	**They Know Too Much:** The enemy possesses critical intelligence that might expose the cult's activities – this evidence must be destroyed, along with any who have seen it.
8	**Spread the Cult:** This kill team must ensure that a cargo shipment containing a lurking Genestealer makes its way off-planet, whatever the cost to themselves.
9	**Tear Down False Idols:** This kill team must smash the enemy's symbols of faith, and replace them with the blessed mark of the wyrm-form.
10	**From Below:** These warriors have been tasked with breaching the enemy's holdings from underground, spreading terror and confusion before fading away into the darkness.

D10	SQUAD QUIRK: GENE-DEVIANCE
1	**Deep-dwellers:** These warriors have lived underground for so long that they can sense nearby enemies merely by feeling the tremors of the earth beneath their feet.
2	**Gene-kin Cant:** This team is so firmly bonded by xenos genes that its members converse in a bizarre series of clicks and hisses that only they understand.
3	**Rabid Evangelists:** These warriors are zealous followers of the star gods, and in battle they proclaim their faith with wide-eyed, spittle-flecked intensity.
4	**Anarchists:** These warriors delight in tearing down the old order, and setting fire to the institutions that once sought to dominate them.
5	**Devious Scum:** These warriors will use any method, no matter how cruel or dishonourable, to destroy their foes.
6	**Twisted Physiologies:** Aberrations in the xenos gene have caused these warriors to develop a variety of unsettling mutations.
7	**Fanatics:** These warriors will stand and die rather than fail the cult.
8	**Creeping Killers:** These warriors stalk the shadows, seeking unwary victims to drag into the darkness.
9	**Inhuman Cruelty:** These warriors delight in tormenting those they see as their erstwhile oppressors.
10	**Murderous:** These warriors take any opportunity to spill the blood of their foes.

D10	SPECIALISTS' DEMEANOURS
1	**Acidic Spittle:** This warrior constantly drools trails of caustic slime which scorch metal and flesh.
2	**Strange Twitching:** This warrior's face contorts unnaturally, bones and veins shifting beneath its pallid skin.
3	**Enlightener:** This warrior prefers to capture live prisoners, that they may be given the gift of the Genestealer's Kiss.
4	**Marker of the Dead:** This warrior carves the wyrm-form symbol into the flesh of each of their victims.
5	**Unblinking:** This warrior never closes their eyes, even to sleep.
6	**Proselytiser:** In battle this warrior bellows prayers to the star-spawned gods.
7	**Tunnelspawn:** This warrior has spent so long underground that its eyes are sightless orbs of milk-white. In lieu of sight, it tastes the air with a long, flicking tongue to find its prey.
8	**Destined Ascension:** This cult's Magus has blessed this warrior with a vision of their destiny, their final ascension to join with the blessed Star Children. They fight without fear or hesitation, knowing that this is not their day to die.
9	**Predatory Instincts:** This warrior seeks out lone, vulnerable enemies, falling upon them with vicious glee.
10	**Born Survivor:** This warrior is well used to fleeing from trouble to fight again another day.

NEOPHYTE/ACOLYTE NAME GENERATOR TABLE

D66	FORENAME	SURNAME
11	Gannar	Druchmann
12	Dhraz	Kreel
13	Yohrick	Desh
14	Kol	Cavorla
15	Hastun	Krauss
16	Sayben	Gardlinger
21	Hollan	Zorbech
22	Narek	Stennvar
23	Rauss	Varnway
24	Basc	Starn
25	Davon	Baumgart
26	Zask	Drisso
31	Nasser	Sammer
32	Seimon	Helm
33	Jacobiah	Tarnright
34	Skir	Valka
35	Ghaskin	Kelbrech
36	Foyle	Kheiser
41	Kreen	Madrach
42	Judh	Venner
43	Mordecai	Novek
44	Isaak	Svodnor
45	Michon	Black
46	Jerec	Barchus
51	Aldren	Matterzhek
52	Madrax	Onderghast
53	Vyrion	Thrace
54	Hollun	Lhaska
55	Steen	Rezzekh
56	Pike	Carleon
61	Mallick	Drevender
62	Groust	Seifer
63	Eldric	Vreel
64	Yorl	Xyben
65	Xandus	Gorl
66	Crasker	Arnalt

GENESTEALER CULT KILL TEAMS

If every model in your kill team has the GENESTEALER CULTS Faction keyword, you can use Genestealer Cults Tactics.

Purestrain Genestealers: When you add a Genestealer (pg 179) to your command roster (and create its datacard) you can choose for it to have the GENESTEALER CULTS Faction keyword instead of the TYRANIDS Faction keyword.

INDUSTRIAL BRUTALITY

Genestealer Cults Tactic

Use this Tactic after making attacks with a model armed with a heavy rock drill, heavy rock saw or heavy rock cutter in the Fight phase. Roll a D6. On a 4+ that model may immediately fight again.

1 COMMAND POINT

UNNATURAL SENSES

Genestealer Cults Tactic

Use this Tactic when a model from your kill team is declared as a target of a charge. That model may fire Overwatch at the charging model, even if the charging model is not visible to it. The target is treated as obscured.

1 COMMAND POINT

DENSITY ANALYSIS LENSES

Genestealer Cults Tactic

Use this Tactic when you choose a model in your kill team to shoot in the Shooting phase. Add 1 to hit rolls for that model against targets which are obscured.

2 COMMAND POINTS

INHUMAN REFLEXES

Genestealer Cults Tactic

Use this Tactic when a model from your kill team fails a Falling test. It doesn't suffer falling damage, and won't fall on another model. If it would, instead place this model as close as possible to the point where it would have landed. This can bring it within 1" of an enemy model.

1 COMMAND POINT

FRENZIED HAMMERING

Genestealer Cults Tactic

Use this Tactic when an ABERRANT from your kill team armed with a power hammer attacks in the Fight phase. Increase that model's Attacks characteristic by D3 until the end of the phase, but subtract 1 from hit rolls for that model's attacks until the end of the phase.

2 COMMAND POINTS

STRENGTH OF FAITH

Genestealer Cults Tactic

Use this Tactic when a model from your kill team suffers a mortal wound in the Psychic phase. Roll a D6 for that mortal wound, and each other mortal wound suffered by that model until the end of the phase. On a roll of 5+ that wound is ignored and has no effect.

1 COMMAND POINT

'Now is the time, brothers and sisters! Cast off the shackles of Imperial oppression! Embrace the love of the Four-Armed Emperor. Cry rapturous welcome to the Star Children, for with their coming we shall all be raised up to a higher state of unified glory. Praise be, brothers and sisters, for the Day of Ascension is upon us!'

- Neophyte Leader Mordecai Storn

ACOLYTE HYBRID

NAME	M	WS	BS	S	T	W	A	Ld	Sv	Max
Acolyte Hybrid	6"	3+	4+	4	3	1	2	7	5+	-
Acolyte Fighter	6"	3+	4+	4	3	1	2	7	5+	4
Acolyte Leader	6"	3+	4+	4	3	1	3	8	5+	1

This model is armed with an autopistol, cultist knife, rending claw and blasting charges.
Up to four Acolyte Hybrids in your kill team can be Acolyte Fighters, and one Acolyte Hybrid in your kill team can be an Acolyte Leader.

WARGEAR OPTIONS	• This model may replace its autopistol with a hand flamer. • An Acolyte Leader may instead replace its cultist knife with a bonesword, or its autopistol and cultist knife with a lash whip and bonesword. • An Acolyte Fighter may replace their cultist knife and rending claw with a heavy rock drill, heavy rock saw, heavy rock cutter or demolition charges. • One Acolyte Hybrid in your kill team may take a cult icon.

ABILITIES	**Cult Ambush:** After deployment but before the first battle round, roll a D6 for this model. On a 5+ this model can immediately move up to 6".	**Cult Icon:** You can re-roll hit rolls of 1 for models within 6" of a friendly model with a cult icon in the Fight phase.

SPECIALISTS	**Leader** (Leader only), **Demolitions** (Fighter only), **Combat, Comms, Zealot**
FACTION KEYWORD	**GENESTEALER CULTS**
KEYWORDS	**TYRANIDS, INFANTRY, ACOLYTE HYBRID**

ABERRANT

NAME	M	WS	BS	S	T	W	A	Ld	Sv	Max
Aberrant	6"	3+	6+	5	4	2	2	7	5+	-

This model is armed with a power pick and rending claw.

WARGEAR OPTIONS	• This model may replace its power pick with a power hammer.

ABILITIES	**Cult Ambush:** After deployment but before the first battle round, roll a D6 for this model. On a 5+ this model can immediately move up to 6".	**Bestial Vigour:** When inflicting damage on this model, reduce the damage of the attack by 1 to a minimum of 1.

SPECIALISTS	**Leader, Combat, Demolitions, Zealot**
FACTION KEYWORD	**GENESTEALER CULTS**
KEYWORDS	**TYRANIDS, INFANTRY, ABERRANT**

NEOPHYTE HYBRID

NAME	M	WS	BS	S	T	W	A	Ld	Sv	Max
Neophyte Hybrid	6"	4+	4+	3	3	1	1	7	5+	-
Neophyte Gunner	6"	4+	4+	3	3	1	1	7	5+	4
Neophyte Leader	6"	4+	4+	3	3	1	2	8	5+	1

This model is armed with an autogun, autopistol and blasting charges.
Up to four Neophyte Hybrids in your kill team can be Neophyte Gunners, and one Neophyte Hybrid in your kill team can be a Neophyte Leader.

WARGEAR OPTIONS	• This model may replace its autogun with a shotgun. • A Neophyte Leader may instead replace its autogun and autopistol with one of the following pistols and one of the following melee weapons: autopistol, bolt pistol or web pistol; chainsword, power maul or power pick. • Up to two Neophyte Gunners may replace their autogun with a flamer, grenade launcher or webber. • Up to two Neophyte Gunners may replace their autogun with a heavy stubber, mining laser or seismic cannon. • One Neophyte Hybrid in your kill team may take a cult icon.
ABILITIES	**Cult Ambush:** After deployment but before the first battle round, roll a D6 for this model. On a 5+ this model can immediately move up to 6".	**Cult Icon:** You can re-roll hit rolls of 1 for models within 6" of a friendly model with a cult icon in the Fight phase.
SPECIALISTS	**Leader** (Leader only), **Heavy** (Gunner only), **Demolitions**, **Medic**, **Scout**, **Zealot**	
FACTION KEYWORD	**Genestealer Cults**	
KEYWORDS	**Tyranids, Infantry, Neophyte Hybrid**	

HYBRID METAMORPH

NAME	M	WS	BS	S	T	W	A	Ld	Sv	Max
Hybrid Metamorph	6"	3+	4+	4	3	1	3	7	5+	-
Metamorph Leader	6"	3+	4+	4	3	1	4	8	5+	1

This model is armed with an autopistol, rending claw, Metamorph talon and blasting charges.
One Hybrid Metamorph in your kill team can be a Metamorph Leader.

WARGEAR OPTIONS	• This model may do one of the following: - replace its rending claw with a Metamorph talon - replace its Metamorph talon with a Metamorph whip - replace its Metamorph talon and rending claw with a Metamorph claw • This model may replace its autopistol with a hand flamer. • A Metamorph Leader may take a bonesword. • One Hybrid Metamorph in your kill team may take a cult icon.
ABILITIES	**Cult Ambush:** After deployment but before the first battle round, roll a D6 for this model. On a 5+ this model can immediately move up to 6".	**Cult Icon:** You can re-roll hit rolls of 1 for models within 6" of a friendly model with a cult icon in the Fight phase.
SPECIALISTS	**Leader** (Leader only), **Combat**, **Comms**, **Demolitions**, **Zealot**	
FACTION KEYWORD	**Genestealer Cults**	
KEYWORDS	**Tyranids, Infantry, Hybrid Metamorph**	

'To simply hurl ourselves into their guns would not best serve the Grandsire, my friends. We are a guerrilla army, insurgents and freedom fighters, and thus we must think not in straight lines, but in arcs and angles. Circumnavigate our enemies' strength and strike where they are weakest, for by dictating the shape of the battle shall we find victory.'

- Yorl Krauss, People's Hero of Magnius Delta, favoured son of the Cult of the Pauper Princes

RANGED WEAPONS

WEAPON	RANGE	TYPE	S	AP	D	ABILITIES
Autogun	24"	Rapid Fire 1	3	0	1	-
Autopistol	12"	Pistol 1	3	0	1	-
Blasting charge	6"	Grenade D6	3	0	1	-
Bolt pistol	12"	Pistol 1	4	0	1	-
Demolition charge	6"	Grenade D6	8	-3	D3	Each demolition charge can only be used once per battle.
Flamer	8"	Assault D6	4	0	1	This weapon automatically hits its target.
Grenade launcher	When attacking with this weapon, choose one of the profiles below.					
- Frag grenade	24"	Assault D6	3	0	1	-
- Krak grenade	24"	Assault 1	6	-1	D3	-
Hand flamer	6"	Pistol D3	3	0	1	This weapon automatically hits its target.
Heavy stubber	36"	Heavy 3	4	0	1	-
Mining laser	24"	Heavy 1	9	-3	D3	-
Seismic cannon	When attacking with this weapon, choose one of the profiles below. All wound rolls of 6+ have an AP of -4.					
- Long-wave	24"	Heavy 4	3	0	1	-
- Short-wave	12"	Heavy 2	6	-1	2	-
Shotgun	12"	Assault 2	3	0	1	If the target is within half range, add 1 to this weapon's Strength.
Web pistol	12"	Pistol D3	3	0	1	When making a shooting attack with a web weapon, you can use either the Strength or Toughness characteristic of the target to determine the wound roll – whichever is lowest.
Webber	16"	Assault D3	4	0	1	When making a shooting attack with a web weapon, you can use either the Strength or Toughness characteristic of the target to determine the wound roll – whichever is lowest.

MELEE WEAPONS

WEAPON	RANGE	TYPE	S	AP	D	ABILITIES
Bonesword	Melee	Melee	User	-2	1	-
Chainsword	Melee	Melee	User	0	1	Each time the bearer fights, it can make 1 additional attack with this weapon.
Cultist knife	Melee	Melee	User	0	1	Each time the bearer fights, it can make 1 additional attack with this weapon.
Heavy rock cutter	Melee	Melee	x2	-4	2	Roll a D6 each time a model suffers damage from this weapon; if you roll higher than the model's remaining number of Wounds, it is instantly taken out of action. When attacking with this weapon, you must subtract 1 from the hit roll.
Heavy rock drill	Melee	Melee	x2	-3	1	Roll a D6 each time a model suffers damage from this weapon; on a 2+ the model suffers a mortal wound and you can roll another D6. This time, the model suffers a mortal wound on a 3+. Keep rolling a D6, increasing the score required to cause a mortal wound by 1 each time, until the model is taken out of action or the roll is failed.
Heavy rock saw	Melee	Melee	x2	-4	2	-
Lash whip and bonesword	Melee	Melee	User	-2	1	If the bearer is taken out of action in the Fight phase before it has made its attacks in that phase, it may immediately fight before being removed from the battlefield.
Metamorph claw	Melee	Melee	+2	0	1	-
Metamorph talon	Melee	Melee	User	0	1	Add 1 to all hit rolls for this weapon.
Metamorph whip	Melee	Melee	User	0	1	If the bearer is taken out of action in the Fight phase before it has made its attacks in that phase, it may immediately fight before being removed from the battlefield.
Power hammer	Melee	Melee	x2	-3	3	When attacking with this weapon, you must subtract 1 from the hit roll.
Power maul	Melee	Melee	+2	-1	1	-
Power pick	Melee	Melee	User	-2	D3	-
Rending claw	Melee	Melee	User	-1	1	Each time you make a wound roll of 6+ for this weapon, that hit is resolved with an AP of -4.

KILL TEAM

MODEL	POINTS PER MODEL (Does not include wargear)
Aberrant	15
Acolyte Hybrid	7
- Acolyte Fighter	8
- Acolyte Leader	8
Hybrid Metamorph	8
- Metamorph Leader	9
Neophyte Hybrid	5
- Neophyte Gunner	6
- Neophyte Leader	6

RANGED WEAPONS

WEAPON	POINTS PER WEAPON
Autogun	0
Autopistol	0
Blasting charge	0
Bolt pistol	0
Demolition charge	3
Flamer	3
Grenade launcher	2
Hand flamer	2
Heavy stubber	0
Mining laser	3
Seismic cannon	2
Shotgun	0
Web pistol	0
Webber	1

MELEE WEAPONS

WEAPON	POINTS PER WEAPON
Bonesword	1
Chainsword	0
Cultist knife	0
Heavy rock cutter	4
Heavy rock drill	5
Heavy rock saw	4
Lash whip and bonesword	2
Metamorph claw	1
Metamorph talon	0
Metamorph whip	1
Power hammer	4
Power maul	1
Power pick	3
Rending claw	0

OTHER WARGEAR

WARGEAR	POINTS PER ITEM
Cult icon	5

SQUAD COLOURS

Kill Teams are visually distinct groupings of highly individual operatives. Whether brightly uniformed warriors or mechanical killers, tattered cultists or towering super soldiers, every faction's kill teams have their own distinct look amidst the war-torn battlescapes of the 41st Millennium.

Dorox-0.4343, Vanguard Alpha Kill Team Leader

Actus-1111, Skitarii Vanguard with radium carbine

Sek-XXVII, Vanguard Gunner Zealot Specialist

Tov-66.75/mk98, Ranger Gunner with arc rifle

Kappic-Schoelendt-18.1, Skitarii Ranger Comms Specialist

Xixos-2918, Skitarii Ranger with galvanic rifle

Decima-110, Skitarii Ranger with galvanic rifle

Amidst the ruined streets of the Unguent Sprawl on Vigilus, the Genestealer Cultists of the Devoted Sons face off against the Skitarii of Kill Team Gamma-Zhul-881.

Yorl Krauss, Neophyte Leader Kill Team Leader

Davon Kheiser, Neophyte Hybrid with autogun

Yohrick Cavorla, Neophyte Gunner with grenade launcher

Xandus Rezzekh, Neophyte Hybrid with shotgun

Judh Onderghast, Neophyte Gunner Heavy Specialist

Rival kill teams of Dark Angels and Saim-Hann Asuryani engage amidst the ruins of a hive city.

Raelyn Ranael, Blood Angels Scout Sergeant Kill Team Leader

Leonid Moriar, Blood Angels Scout Gunner with heavy bolter

Faustian Lorenso, Blood Angels Scout with bolter

Rafael Belarius, Blood Angels Scout with shotgun

Erasmus Castevar, Blood Angels Scout Sniper Specialist

Anval Trevan, Grey Knight with Nemesis force halberd and storm bolter

Valdar Kai, Grey Knight Gunner with psycannon

Kaladour Thule, Grey Knight Combat Specialist

Caddon Cromm, Justicar Kill Team Leader

Raelyn Castivar, Deathwatch Veteran Combat Specialist

Vykus Ordaris, Deathwatch Veteran Sniper Specialist

Watch Sergeant Titus Mordelai, Kill Team Leader

Lydus Markov, Deathwatch Veteran Zealot Specialist

Cassius Tarentus, Ultramarines Tactical Sergeant Kill Team Leader

Andrus Acastian, Ultramarines Tactical Marine Heavy Specialist

Marius Cassus, Ultramarines Tactical Marine with boltgun

Titus Aggenon, Ultramarines Tactical Marine Veteran Specialist

Ulfrich Wyrmslayer, Space Wolves Reiver Sergeant Kill Team Leader

Gunnar Greymane, Space Wolves Reiver with bolt carbine

Erik Trollbane, Space Wolves Reiver Demolitions Specialist

Olaf Icefang, Space Wolves Reiver Combat Specialist

Upon the fringes of the Cadian war zone, a lumbering warband of Death Guard Plague Marines advances through a tainted refinery complex. Tasked with halting the foe's progress at all costs, the Blood Angels of Kill Team Donatael launch their counter-attack.

Ollonius Cassus, Ultramarines Intercessor Sergeant Kill Team Leader

Titus Tarentus, Ultramarines Intercessor Combat Specialist

Marcus Acastian, Ultramarines Intercessor Medic Specialist

Gaius Pollandrus, Ultramarines Intercessor with auto bolt rifle

**Scion Eli,
Scion Gunner with
plasma gun**

**Tempestor Ekhter,
Kill Team Leader**

**Scion Tennenbaum,
Veteran Specialist
with meltagun**

**Scion Kyser,
Comms Specialist**

**Scion Lukas,
Medic Specialist**

Amidst the overgrown ruins of an Imperial outpost, Drop Force Imperator clash with the Genestealers of the Writhing Shadow

Hathrak the Cruel, Aspiring Champion Kill Team Leader

Ashkal Korr, Chaos Space Marine Veteran Specialist

Vordian Skullhelm, Chaos Space Marine with boltgun

Drekhlyn Gnar, Chaos Space Marine Heavy Specialist

Gurloch the Reeking, Plague Marine with boltgun

Bubox Urghe, Plague Marine Gunner with blight launcher

Poxwalker

Poxwalker

P'tor, Rubric Marine Gunner with soulreaper cannon

Kalophis, Rubric Marine with inferno boltgun

Ankhu, Rubric Marine Veteran Specialist

Phosis R'han, Aspiring Sorcerer Kill Team Leader

Xela Vexx, Wych with splinter pistol and Hekatarii blade

Vylekh the Untouched, Hekatrix Kill Team Leader

Bithandrel Khaur, Wych Scout Specialist

Nyx Bloodslyk, Wych Combat Specialist

Shexen the Faceless, Wych Zealot Specialist

The warriors of the Astra Militarum face the lethal onslaught of a Drukhari kill team led by a vicious Hekatrix.

Yrilla Iyadolath, Dire Avenger Exarch Kill Team Leader

Tarvaril Bechareth, Storm Guardian Combat Specialist

Ilthryc Farseeker, Ranger Sniper Specialist

Osinell Yn Farwolloch, Guardian Defender with shuriken catapult

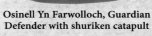

Relentless as the onset of death itself, the Necron kill team known as the Exalted Scythe advance through the conquered hivescape. As if from nowhere, a mysterious band of Harlequins falls upon them, blades flashing.

Kythok the Lifetaker,
Immortal with gauss blaster

Xeoptar the Great,
Immortal Kill Team Leader

Tahar the Gatekeeper,
Immortal Veteran Specialist

Imonekh, Deathmark
Scout Specialist

**Krogskull Drakka,
Spanner Kill Team Leader
with kustom mega-blasta**

**Fragbad Squigbiter,
Demolitions Specialist
with burna**

**Grukk Flame Spitta,
Burna Boy**

**Zogger Stompkrumpa,
Zealot Specialist
with burna**

**Nemesis Enigmus,
Genestealer with
scything talons**

**Nemesis Beta,
Scout Specialist with
flesh hooks**

**Nemesis Alpha,
Kill Team Leader
with acid maw**

**Nemesis Crucius,
Genestealer with
scything talons**

**Shas'la Laserra,
Shas'la with
pulse rifle**

**Shas'ui D'tano, Kill
Team Leader with pulse
blaster and pulse pistol**

**Shas'la E'yaal,
Breacher Shas'la
with pulse blaster**

**Shas'la U'so,
Breacher Shas'la
with pulse blaster**

**MV7 Marker Drone
C-06**

In an impressive display of greenskin kunnin', the Orks of Kill Team Skullrippa ambush a band of Blood Angels Scouts amidst the tangled refinery sprawls of Armageddon.

Whilst scouting through the industrial rust-scapes of an Imperial outpost world, this T'au Empire kill team are set upon by the savage

KILL TEAM CAMPAIGNS

Kill Team campaigns let you collect operatives and fight battles of Kill Team in a series of connected missions. These form a narrative of covert battles fought alongside a greater war, where the skirmishes you fight have an impact far beyond the battlefields you are contesting.

Kill Team can be played and enjoyed in one-off missions – you do not need to use these extra rules in your games. However, playing through a campaign can be a fun and rewarding alternative, giving you and your friends the opportunity to write the story of your own kill teams, charting their successes and failures as they grow in experience. In the end, one of you will be able to claim the glory of total victory!

In order to take part in a Kill Team campaign, you will need two or more players. All players will need a collection of Citadel Miniatures, which they will organise into kill teams. For more detail about choosing your kill team for a mission, see the opposite page.

The players fight missions against each other using the kill teams they create. The combatants in each mission gain experience, and may become more skilled or stronger as the campaign progresses (see page 66). In addition, the outcome of each mission will affect the wider war being fought, as described below. The more success a player has in their missions, the more likely it is that they will be crowned victor of the campaign.

THE WAR EFFORT

The missions that your operatives are fighting are part of a larger war effort, and the mission your kill team undertakes has an impact on this war. If you succeed in your sabotage mission, your opponent's materiel is severely depleted. If you cannot stop enemy assassination missions, your force's morale plunges!

The fluctuating fortunes of the different factions in the war, and your impact on these, are represented by four resources: Intelligence, Materiel, Morale and Territory.

- Intelligence: A faction's spy networks and intelligence gathering assets.

- Materiel: A faction's military resources, whether it be weaponry, armour, transport or more esoteric items.

- Morale: A faction's will to keep fighting, whether through nobility, determination, hatred or spite.

- Territory: A measure of the locations and facilities currently controlled by the faction.

If a faction runs out of any one of these resources, their armies will crumble and they will be reduced to guerrillas in this conflict. You will need to guard your resources while striking at your enemies' weakest points.

Each player begins a campaign with a set number of resource points. We suggest starting the campaign with 8 points in each resource, but you can agree with the other players that you will all start with a different number, or even different numbers in each resource (for example, you might have D6+3 points for each resource, giving each player their own strengths and weaknesses). Note your starting resources on your command roster.

Each mission tells you what impact the mission has on the resources of the players that take part in it. After the mission, record any changes to each player's resources on their roster sheet. Once you have done so, any player who has been reduced to 0 or less in any resource is reduced to a guerrilla faction. This is explained in more detail on page 205.

VICTORY

Unless the players in the campaign agree otherwise at the beginning of the campaign, the last player who hasn't been reduced to a guerrilla faction wins the campaign – theirs is the only force with the cohesion and the means to secure victory over all others!

If the only remaining non-guerrilla factions are reduced to guerrilla factions after the same mission, the campaign will be decided by sudden death. At this point, anyone can win! This is described in more detail on page 205.

You can instead decide at the beginning of the campaign to set your own victory condition – this might be when one player has won a certain numbers of victories, or the player with the highest combined total of resources after a certain number of games have been played. It's up to you!

MISSION CRITICAL

Following the orders of their commanders, kill teams battle in the darkness of a nightmarish and war-torn landscape. The leaders of these teams play games of cat and mouse with their foes amidst monolithic refineries and tangled hab-complexes, leading their squads in daring strikes against their enemies.

Choosing a Mission

You can arrange to fight missions as and when you wish, and can use any Kill Team mission that is available to you. Either choose a mission that you and your opponent(s) want to play, or roll off, and the winner rolls 2D6 and consults the following table. Where a mission has an attacker and a defender, whichever player has more Territory than the other is the defender. If there is a tie, the players roll off – whoever wins is the attacker:

2D6	RESULT
2	The player with the highest total resources decides which mission will be played. If there is a tie, the tied players roll off and the winner decides.
3-4	Play the Disrupt Supply Lines mission (pg 52) (or Take Prisoners matched play mission (pg 57) if you have more than two players).
5	Play the Ambush mission (pg 53) (or Recover Intelligence matched play mission (pg 58) if you have more than two players).
6	Play the Feint mission (pg 54) (or Terror Tactics matched play mission (pg 59) if you have more than two players).
7	Choose the Assassinate mission (pg 55) or Sweep and Clear matched play mission (pg 56).
8	Play the Take Prisoners matched play mission (pg 57).
9	Play the Recover Intelligence matched play mission (pg 58).
10-11	Play the Terror Tactics matched play mission (pg 59).
12	The player with the lowest total resources decides which mission is played. If there is a tie, the tied players roll off and the winner decides.

Choosing a Kill Team

Once you have chosen a mission, the players choose kill teams using the rules for choosing a Battle-forged kill team (see page 62) subject to the mission you are playing, with the following exception: they must each choose their kill team from their campaign command roster (see below). Players choose their kill teams in secret – they will be revealed together once the battlefield has been set up. We suggest that each player keeps the Faction keyword they chose for the length of the campaign.

Campaign Command Roster

Each player in a campaign has a campaign command roster, from which they choose their kill team for each mission. This roster is created in the same way as for a matched play command roster (see page 62), with the following difference: it starts with up to twelve models, rather than up to twenty, and can grow beyond twenty models as the campaign progresses.

If a player has already played a mission in the campaign, they can choose their kill team from any of the models on their campaign command roster but they can also choose to add new models with new datacards to their kill team (though see Adding Members to a Fire Team on page 205), or even use a kill team chosen entirely from new models. Each time a player completes a datacard for a model that they add to their kill team, they should also record that model's details on their roster. Adding new models to their kill team for a mission in this way is the only way for players in a campaign to increase the number of models on their roster.

The campaign command roster therefore becomes a record of all of the models that you have used in the campaign, and comes to represent the 'pool' of Kill Team models available for you to choose kill teams from. A player might, on their command roster, have models from every specialism, and a number of Leaders. However, they need to choose a kill team from their campaign command roster (and any new models) that matches the restrictions for each mission. This means that kill teams will often be made up of a mix of experienced and new models, and players will need to balance the flexibility of using their whole collection against the reliability of using certain stalwarts.

Play the Mission

Once you have decided on a mission and the players have chosen their kill teams, play the mission!

Strategic Withdrawal

At the end of the third battle round, and at the end of each subsequent battle round, before any dice roll to determine whether or not the battle ends, a player can make a strategic withdrawal. Players make the decision about whether or not to do so in the order determined in the Initiative phase. If a player makes a strategic withdrawal, they lose the mission – if there is only one other player remaining, that player wins the mission. When a player makes a strategic withdrawal, all of their models are removed from the battlefield. They must roll a dice for each model with one or more flesh wounds when they do so to determine whether or not they go out of action, as described in Casualties (see overleaf).

CONSEQUENCES OF BATTLE

As the dust settles after a battle, each side retreats to count the cost. Territory may be won or lost, and morale may suffer a devastating blow. Whatever happens, the fighters in each kill team come away with new experience and scars, gaining in value even as they prepare for their next death-or-glory mission.

After each mission, each player who took part in the mission should play through the following steps.

1. Resources

2. Casualties

3. Experience

Once the players have all completed this sequence, it's time to start planning the next mission!

RESOURCES

Each player should update the resources listed on their command roster as described in the mission. Players may find themselves reduced to guerrillas at this point, as described opposite, and if there is only one non-guerrilla faction left, that player wins (unless you agreed on a different way to end your campaign).

CASUALTIES

Each player should roll a D6 for each model from their kill team on the battlefield that has one or more flesh wounds. On a roll of 1-3, that model recovers. On a roll of 4-6, that model goes out of action.

Each player then makes a Casualty roll for each of their models that is out of action at the end of a mission by rolling a D10 and consulting the following table:

CASUALTY ROLL	
D10	**RESULT**
1	**Dead:** The model is dead! It can no longer be included in your kill team – discard or erase its datacard and delete it from your command roster.
2	**Convalescence:** The model cannot be used in your next mission. Check the Convalescence box on its datacard.
3-8	**Full Recovery:** The model makes a full recovery and can be used in your next mission.
9-10	**Hard Knocks:** The model makes a full recovery as described above, and if it is a specialist it gains an additional experience point (see right).

After making any casualty rolls, each player removes all flesh wounds from their models.

EXPERIENCE

Then, the members of your kill team progress as described below, becoming even more formidable as they gain experience.

Specialists

Each specialist in your kill team gains an experience point – check one of the experience boxes on their datacard. They also gain an experience point at the end of the mission if you used at least one Tactic from their specialism. Check the boxes left to right; when you check a box with an orange outline, your specialist has reached the next level – a Level 1 specialist becomes Level 2, and so on. You can then choose a new ability for them as described on page 66, and you may also gain access to new Tactics for that fighter. Once you have checked all the boxes on the model's datacard, it cannot progress any further – every fighter has their limits!

Fire Teams

The other models in your kill team may not be specialists, but they are all learning a thing or two during these covert operations, and their bonds of camaraderie are growing!

The non-specialist models in your collection are organised into fire teams, where each fire team consists of all of the non-specialist models chosen from a single datasheet. For example, if you had 6 Rangers on your command roster (not counting specialists), those 6 Rangers would be a fire team.

As long as two or more models from a single fire team were in your kill team and are not dead as a result of Casualty rolls, all models in that fire team (even those who did not take part in the mission) gain an experience point. In addition, all models in a fire team gain an experience point at the end of the mission if at least one enemy model was taken out of action by an attack made or psychic power manifested by a member of that fire team. Check these points of experience on your models' datacards in the same way as described above. When you check a box with an orange outline, all models in that fire team have reached the next level – Level 1 models become Level 2, and so on. At each level, roll a D6 and consult the table on the opposite page to see what advance your fire team gains. All members of the fire team gain this advance. Each fire team can only gain each advance once – if you roll a result you have already rolled, re-roll until you roll a new result.

D6	RESULT
1	**Fleet:** Add 1" to this model's Move characteristic.
2	**Lucky:** You can re-roll save rolls of 1 for this model.
3	**Courageous:** You can re-roll failed Nerve tests for this model.
4	**Skilled:** Choose one: - You can re-roll hit rolls of 1 for this model when it makes shooting attacks. - You can re-roll hit rolls of 1 for this model in the Fight phase.
5	**Lethal:** Choose one: - You can re-roll wound rolls of 1 for this model when it makes shooting attacks. - You can re-roll wound rolls of 1 for this model in the Fight phase.
6	**Die-hard:** You can subtract 1 from Injury rolls for this model.

Once you have checked all the boxes on a fire team's datacards, it cannot progress any further.

Crack Troops

As your fire teams grow in experience, so their worth increases. In a Battle-forged kill team, this greater value is accompanied by an increased cost for each member of that fire team, as shown in this table:

Fire Team	Cost per model
Level 1	+0 points
Level 2	+1 point
Level 3	+2 points
Level 4	+3 points

ADDING MEMBERS TO A FIRE TEAM

Even as your fire teams grow in experience, you can recruit new members to replace losses or to expand their presence in your kill team. However, your green recruits will take some breaking in!

When choosing your kill team for a mission as described on the previous page, you can add a new member to a fire team: take the appropriate model and fill in a datacard for it. You must include it in your kill team in this mission. You can even do this with multiple new members if you like. For each new member you include in your kill team you must include at least one experienced member of the fire team (to 'show them the ropes'). This means if you only have one member of a fire team remaining, you can only include a single new member alongside them in a mission.

In their first mission, new members of a fire team cannot use the advances that the fire team has earned – check the New Recruit box on their datacard to show this. At the end of the mission, you can erase the check and fill in their experience points so that they have the same number as the other members in their fire team. They also gain the fire team's advances at this point.

Note that, if all members of a fire team are dead as a result of your Casualty rolls, their experience is lost! You cannot add new members to a fire team that has been wiped out in this way.

A player can choose to disband a fire team after a mission. When they do so, they discard or erase all datacards for that fire team and delete them from their command roster. They can then add a new fire team chosen from the same datasheet to their kill team in the next mission.

GUERRILLA FACTIONS

When a player has had one or more of their resources reduced to 0 or less, they are reduced to a guerrilla faction. A guerrilla faction has had their strength broken, and fights without central leadership or territory they can call their own. A guerrilla faction cannot normally win a campaign, with the exception of a campaign that is decided by sudden death (see below).

A guerrilla faction has no resources and cannot gain resources, but otherwise they take part in missions like any other player. In this way they can still take part in the campaign, and have an impact on who wins in the end. If a guerrilla faction is very successful, they may even manage to manipulate events so that they have a shot at victory!

A guerrilla faction cannot add new members to a fire team. They can, however, disband a fire team in the same way as described above.

SUDDEN DEATH

If all non-guerrilla players are reduced to guerrillas after the same mission, the campaign enters sudden death! At this point, any player can win, as there is no faction in the lead. Play a game of Kill Team using any mission that allows all players in the campaign to play at once. If you cannot agree on a mission, determine one randomly. Whoever wins the mission wins the campaign! If there is no victor, resolve the steps after the mission as normal, and then play another game as described above. Repeat this until a victor is decided.

ESCALATION

If all players agree, after a set point in the campaign (it could be after a certain number of battles have been played, or after a certain number of weeks – it's up to you) you can increase the size of the kill teams to represent the increasing resources being poured into this escalating conflict. If you do so, your Battle-forged kill teams can cost up to 150 points (though you should still apply any adjustments to this total as described in the mission you are playing).

COMMAND ROSTER

PLAYER NAME			RESOURCES		CURRENT KILL TEAM'S FORCE		POINTS
FACTION			INTELLIGENCE		CURRENT KILL TEAM'S NAME		
MISSION			MATERIEL				
BACKGROUND			MORALE				
SQUAD QUIRK			TERRITORY				

NAME	MODEL TYPE	WARGEAR	EXP	SPECIALISM/ABILITIES	DEMEANOUR	PTS